Huddle

It's a word about drawing together; not only with other humans but the ecosystems that hold us. The huddle of words in this book take their cues from the Pallanganmiddang people. I have a sit spot, a place I return to again and again in pursuit of understanding. Pre-colonisation, the Pallanganmiddang people knew this entire region intimately; its water catchments, weather patterns, places of celebration and ceremony, where to find protection, how to locate healing plants, and places to feed and nourish their people. They connected to this earth through the soles of their dancing feet. And with that came mutual reciprocity and respect. This knowledge was impacted by the rapid onslaught of colonisation, which forced Traditional Owners to be dislocated from this country.

They held a knowledge of this landscape we can now only imagine, and while the piece of paper claiming ownership of the place I now refer to as Black Barn Farm has my name typed on the title, *owning* Country is about as problematic as trying to own another person.

This land is unceded and despite my love for it, I can only stand in awe at the unfathomable intimacy the First Nations People who walk this land understood beyond words. It will require many more generations before us whitefellas can truly understand what it means to connect with Country, but while we relearn this art, we can continue to honour those who made it their home for 60,000 years.

To huddle was to know yourself, your people and your place within them; a cosy nest of concentric understanding. Democracy held no place, rather decisions were made through complex frameworks of elderhood, where the huddle looked to the knowledge holders for guidance and direction, and they in turn looked to the natural world.

Their culture still echoes in the landscape, and while our conscious memory may not recall the details, our bones know the way home. Our task is to stop talking and deeply listen as we are guided by the earth back to our huddles, both human and ecological.

We cannot heal the damage of the past, but we can commit to a lifetime of less extraction and greater harmony, moving together from 'what's in it for me?' to 'what's holding me?'. **And it's always, always Country.**

For all who are yearning to return

And
For Charlie, Harry, Bertie and Minnie –
my primary reason to build huddles of
hope to hold us.

JADE MILES

Huddle

Wisdom, skills and recipes
for building a tomorrow
of togetherness

Hardie Grant

BOOKS

Preface

We all have profound moments that inspire action. My first book, *Futuresteading*, was spurred during the depths of the 2020 fire season while on top of our hill with my skirt over my head to keep me from choking on the suffocating smoke. While Charlie was away fighting fires, I was bleary-eyed and exhausted on the farm, managing children and animals, irrigation and endless worry. All the while a rising population of galvanising humans was declaring their desire to see change – significant change! This newly emerging narrative (from both country and city cousins alike) gave me the confidence to write a book that encouraged everyday folk to take agency for the way they lived their own lives. Its objective was to build people's individual skills in creating new rhythms that honoured the seasons, celebrated local, harnessed simple rituals and fostered connection to one another.

Having these fundamental skills is a great place to begin but ultimately, if we all still walk alone it's not enough to change our culture or our ability to exist in perpetuity on this finite planet. We each need to bring our skills into the messy, complicated, compromised place of community where together as the sum of the parts we can rebuild a new way of being.

This book was spurred by a less collective crisis and one that took me by surprise in an entirely impractical and unexpected way.

Inside the confines of a conference, I existed in a whiplashing state of perpetual paradox for three days. Keynotes and panellists repeatedly outlined the frighteningly dire ecological reality of the globe, making me nauseated with every new angle the story presented. Yet I was in a room full of regenerative farmers. These were my people, and the idea of collapse inevitability didn't scare them. In fact, as a unified huddle of like-mindedness they harnessed a can-do sense of camaraderie, possibility and open-hearted affection that somehow made it all okay. You'll see, we've got this!

I was in a part of the world I'd never been before and on the back of many weeks of work-related travel. I was exhausted, physically and emotionally. The conference was illuminating, gut-wrenching and cup-filling, all in one. At the end of it I hopped into my hire car and made the long trip back to the city alone, with nothing but my thoughts wondering where and how the fuck this was all going to end.

Despite my kinfolk-full cup, the sense of being alone sat heavily in my gut. With little sleep, lack of nourishment for multiple days on end (as is the case when you're travelling for work) and no sense of consistency, order or rhythm for altogether too long, I was low on resilience.

I contemplated what it feels like to belong – really belong: where people know your name, mutual trust abounds, where we can confidently dive deeply into conversation without the need for mindless small talk and have an understanding of the ecosystem you stand in. How the water flows, where the sunshine falls, the length of the shadows, the sounds of the night-time animals, the light in the sky. Belonging!

You belong when you share something: a common language, a purpose, a fear or vulnerability and you hold hope in the same tools of earthly regeneration.

As I drove that unfamiliar road, I longed for my huddle who made me feel as though I belonged. In a moment of tired self-pity, I did a mental roll call of those I was missing, only to be greeted by an involuntary surge of salty water welling. There's no more powerful feeling of belonging except perhaps the exact opposite ... of being alone. In a city far from home, having had my fill of 'diredom', I climbed into bed with a heavy heart and a deep sense of loneliness, set my alarm for an early flight and went to sleep.

The alarm didn't work. My phone had gone flat. My body must have known, for I was up and out in seconds. In a flurry I dropped my bag, spilling everything. I scurried to collect myself in the dark, throwing it all in the car and just driving, without a map or the ability to call anyone. I drove following nothing but intuition. I was against the clock to catch my flight so had little choice but to trust my instincts. I suspected I was driving too fast and likely to get a speeding fine, but that would be tomorrow Jade's problem. Through the unfamiliar streets, I felt my way to the airport while watching the minutes tick closer to my departure time. Who knows how, but at some point I spotted an airport sign and blindly followed. I was at the wrong terminal. I dumped the hire car and paid a gouging price of forty dollars for a three-minute cab ride because I didn't have my credit cards – they were still in the gutter where I'd dropped them. Of course, I didn't realise this until the cabbie refused to drive me unless I paid cash, charging twice the price for the honour. Thankfully Mum had given me a birthday present the week before and I had the cash stuffed in the zipped pocket of my handbag.

My name was called while in the queue for security screening with hundreds of others, but without my phone to show my boarding pass, the security guy wasn't convinced. I got to the gate too late, and without a phone or licence to prove my identity, my pleas fell on deaf ears. It wasn't until a change of staff that I connected with someone who was happy to put me on the next flight home. An hour of airport chaos later, I was boarded onto my original flight, and I fell into my seat just in time for fat salty tears to roll down my cheeks.

I cried for the entire four-hour flight. I cried because I was safe and heading home. I cried because I was exhausted. I cried because the girl sitting next to me had plastic nails five centimetres long. I cried because the magazine in the back of the seat was advertising plastic balls from a multinational chain store for three dollars.

I cried because, despite the relief at being back on track, I was wedged into an aluminium tube heading to my home state with four hundred other people who I was so utterly disconnected from. I cried because I was flying away from a huddle of humans who could hold me and everything I knew to be true without explanation. I cried because my grief for the state of our world was so enormous I could no longer swim against it, especially while I was alone.

My body was broken and desperately gasping for air. As I snivelled my way through the minutes, I mentally hand-picked a select group of women and took myself onto Country where I sat on the earth – fireside and silent – dwarfed by a night sky that reminded me of my insignificance, in the company of those who told me I was loved without words.

It's intriguing to recall who I chose; women of all ages from different places and times in my life. Women mostly unknown to each other but linked by their joint yearning for a new way of existence. One where they know their bodies, know their place and know their huddle, a profound harmony in their daily rhythm.

While surrounded by clouds, further from Earth than humans should ever be, I finally stopped sobbing, my heart stopped racing and I actively slowed my breathing. I found paper and asked the question, 'What does regenerative leadership mean?'

Braving a transitionary state between two worlds. Grieving a departure from the old world – where everything feels familiar but no longer stable and congruent – and tentatively stepping into the unknown of a new world where there are no maps, no signposts and no obvious systems except a deep knowing that it's where we need to go.

It requires bravery I don't feel equipped for; a vulnerability I don't feel strong enough to be in; and a community I don't have in my physical proximity right now.

As I looked out of the plane window, I saw the coastline leave us and be replaced with the ocean. The open unknown of a great expanse of water. The timing of this view was not lost on me and only reinforced a sense that my time had come to leap. Leap into the unknown of that deep blue abyss. A new world for my terra firma. I saw the archipelago island chains that my brother had paddled twenty years earlier. In my emotional state I symbolically imagined that they resembled earthside sprinkles of hope that I'd been clinging to for the past few years. Some were large enough to cling to and some were too small to even step onto. Even if I did, my feet would get wet. Eventually even this smattering of islands was gone and the deep blue ocean stretched out in front of me yelling, 'Jump! It's all you can do.'

I'd finally cracked the facade and could no longer maintain the performance of it all being okay. The grief I was experiencing was surely that of multiple generations. A knowing that had long been painted over in a pretence of fortune and opportunity. Something very deep within me knew that this was unstoppable, and I needed to let it happen. The eruption was coming and an attempt to stop it was futile. I frantically began to write:

The cracks are deeply etching into our collective psyche and no amount of refurbing will solve the scale of our impending global collapse. With the help of human greed and a commitment to endless growth, we've created an unstoppable storm that's culminated in an ecosystem with all but two of its nine planetary boundaries surpassed.

Collectively we've stopped being human. Distracted by the abstractions of a system that breaks our bond to ourselves, our place and each other. We move at a pace not intended for human bodies in a world we can't feel and without a community of people we can thrive with. Our culture revels in consumerism rather than ritual; celebrates celebrities rather than the cycles; and functions in silos and to the drum of KPIs rather than weather patterns and seasons.

The call back to the earth with our people is so strong it's beating in my body so loudly and can no longer be ignored, and I know that the time is now, but I can't do it alone. I need my huddle around me because together is the only way to create a new tomorrow.

The tail end of the flight was turbulent and we circled for an hour. I had my head in the vomit bag until we landed and on entering the terminal I rushed to a bin just in time to throw up in front of a large audience of impatient travellers. I sat on the ground and resumed crying until a generous woman offered me her phone. I called Charlie, who booked me a train ticket. I called the local bank manager in my little town, who cancelled my cards without proof of identity, which made me cry again. I was brought to tears for the final time that day when I was offered a free seat on the airport bus into the city because the service didn't take cash. Apparently without cards and a phone, humanity is lost.

It was a distressing end to a big few weeks, but I was going home. Home to my huddle, in a landscape I was connected to and a rhythm that held me tight.

I was going home to write a book!

The speeding fine arrived two weeks later in the mail.

Introduction

Hello fine human.

We may not have met in person, but something has drawn us together. I love thinking about how we come to find each other, how ideas call us in and how kindred spirits coalesce. Thank you for joining me in this challenging, but deeply rewarding, pursuit of recreating a world where we seek our kinfolk and learn ways to build community – big and small, near and far. I call these clusters of kindred spirits 'huddles'.

Before I dive right in, let me introduce myself. I am a lover of wild places, big sky, small birds, long days and the smell of the earth across the seasons. Although my reputation for being exhaustively busy precedes me, if the day is mine, the hands of the clock point not to hours but cups of tea, usually from fresh herbs picked from the garden and sipped on the grass, perhaps in the paddock with Sunday, my milking goat, or down by the hoop house with chickens and geese underfoot. And my feet? Bare and typically the colour of a strong English Breakfast.

While gregarious on request, I'm actually quite introverted and my happy place is outside following a seasonal rhythm that connects me to the land through my senses and ever-growing gardening to-do list.

I'm lucky to be muddling through life with my husband Charlie and three kiddos. Together we run Black Barn Farm on the beautiful, if frosty, Stanley Plateau in North-East Victoria. We have planted, and now nurture, a biodiverse orchard with over eighty varieties of apples (did you know there are thousands of registered varieties?), and run a nursery and workshop space for school groups and those eager to build their Futuresteading skills.

From January until June you'll find us all at the Black Barn Farm Gate. It's been a long-held, calloused-hands vision that we've been bringing to life for the past decade, all in the name of reconnecting people to nature, food, a simpler existence and most importantly, each other.

With the bush in my bones and business in my head, I'm a poly-jobist right down to my muddy toes. I've been a local food advocate and educator across the country for a decade. A few years ago I co-launched the *Futuresteading* podcast and still chat to folks doing bloody amazing things at every chance I get to press the recording button. Those chances can be hard to snaffle as I funnel all my remaining pep into Sustainable Table, an organisation helping regenerative agriculture and local food systems get the funding they're hungry for – and deserve. Building bridges between worlds, and people who seem to exist in different galaxies, is a big job!

Hopefully you'll stick with me as I join the dots through the power of storytelling ... though I'm not here to mince words. The time for that has passed. So lean in, listen up and let's call a spade a spade. While our current civilisation might be breaking apart, it's community – in all its gluey glory – that'll stick us back together.

Huddle will show you our immense capability to exist this way. We human folk were there not so long ago, living pretty darn frugally in the village. If it weren't for the atomising effects of industrialisation, the 'want more/need more' fever of consumerism, we might still be. Did you know that 'buying stuff' just because it's new or trendy wasn't even a thing before advertising and psychology teamed up in the twentieth century and started appealing to our fears, inadequacies and desires? Before that, people mainly owned or shared things that were durable and functional.

Now more than ever, it's time to huddle. Returning to a more grounded and connected existence shatters the illusions driving our own demise. It's calling a spade a spade while reawakening what really matters.

As you turn these pages, I invite you to open your head, heart and soul to the idea of creating a tomorrow of togetherness. It's an invitation to challenge the paradigm; to reflect, refute, rebuild and reboot. More ritual, less rubbish. More culture, less consumption. Building a tribe, connecting to place, shadowing the seasons and drawing insight from our disillusionment. Told through the broad stories of many and threaded with practical experiences from our Futuresteading life at Black Barn Farm, *Huddle* is about building a bold, shared life that values tomorrow. We're only as strong

Every decision we make has an impact on other humans, creatures, ecosystems and culture. How you make your decisions will result in a degenerative, sustainable or regenerative outcome. Decide wisely!

as the community we live in and we can only move at the speed of our people, so in the face of a rapidly changing world, now is the time to find solidarity and weave an existence that values *all* other beings – not just humans.

Standing shoulder to shoulder in this time of great transition is a comforting stance – who wants to go it alone? It doesn't take many to start paving pathways forward: experimenting, unpacking, unlearning, making mistakes, reskilling, reconnecting and getting comfortable with what it really means to be human. Fall back in love with the natural world and all the things money can't buy.

Join me in shrugging off our constructed cloaks and stepping boldly over the edge. It's the huddle that will catch us. Through reshaping our patterns, language, rituals and fundamental way of being together, we start to find harmony with our local lands and reciprocity

with everything living. In these pages I'll offer ideas to set us all on the path to tell new stories, embrace emergence, build ritual, redefine enough, really learn to talk, accept our complicated humanness and share food.

We have a duty of care to this land and every human and non-human thing that springs from it. We are cared for in turn. The time to start exercising our custodial responsibility is now. So, the ideas in this book are for you, wherever and however you live, so we can get on with the show!

It's time to huddle.

I'm so glad we are doing this together.

Jade x

10

Why huddle?

This world we call home requires regeneration on an urgent and massive scale. As individuals working alone, we simply cannot bring the necessary change in the time we have available to us. We are in a Gaian emergency!

Tim Hollo's book *Living Democracy* framed it like this: 'Yes, the world looks bleak. Across our society there's a mounting sense of desperation in the face of the climate crisis, gaping economic inequality and racial injustice, increasing threat of war and a post-truth politics divorced from reality. Extinction is in the air.'

But take heart. As we see in so many natural disasters and crises, humans – for all our folly – also have epic fortitude.

I remind myself of the goodwill, problem solving, courage and immense care that kicks in when communities experience a shock. Now to channel that chutzpah on a global scale, bringing much-needed restoration to our planet, culture and ecosystem.

It starts with finding your niche. Everything in the natural world has a very specific contribution, one that can't be subtracted without consequence.

Find your role, lead with your strengths and step up, make your voice, money, vote, time and energy count IF. YOU. CAN. This is important. Not all things are designed and doled out equally, and our personal capacity differs based on (but not limited to) age, sex, financial capability, country of birth, colour of skin, level of education, health and physical capability. But IF you have the ability – and let's be honest, we are alive and well in one of the wealthiest nations on the planet – we have a duty to STEP UP.

Stepping up looks different to each of us and how excellent is that? It means we can come at this complex global issue with forks on all sides. But there are some fundamental principles that we need to lean on.

Endless extraction = extinction: Let's accept we are part of the natural living world, that can only give so much. 'Endless progress' and 'limitless growth' are illusions based on our unprecedented access to fossil fuels, but as they dwindle, let's swap extraction for deep connection and avert extinction while we're at it.

Silos suck: This calamity cannot be solved with siloed solutions, where information or ideas are held hostage rather than freely shared, unable to mingle or iterate. This results in a shrivelled existence, entirely separate from the truths of the natural world. We're wired for co-creation, conversation, cooperation and conviviality. We are beings who are at our best when huddled.

We can't keep stacking: Are we complicating our current mess by introducing tech solutions, thinking it'll solve the calamity? Instead, let's compost the complication, close the loop and get back to foundational thinking. Technology absolutely has a role to play in our collective transition, but in most instances the shiny new ideas purported to save us simply maintain the energy-hungry, growth-oriented, extractive paradigm. To the compost pile!

Ownership of change: The person who plants a seed tends to be the one who waters and nurtures it. In the same way, when communities dream up and grow their own solutions, they take ownership and drive the outcomes themselves. It might seem as though governments tell us what to do, but in reality, they're led by us. If we take action at a grassroots level and raise our voices together, governments will meet us with top-down initiatives.

Uncertainty is the new normal: Uncertainty is a call to wake up! Accepting that life is uncertain taps you into all kinds of enlivening states: openness, clarity, adaptability, humility. Sure, it's an acquired taste, but in that truthful discomfort we find deep motivation to develop skills, connect with our kin, question the status quo and consider the generations to come.

We are not a nuclear species: No, not radioactive apes. I mean the kind of separate, individualist, closed-door humans we've come to see as normal. A nuclear life may avoid complications and messy human relationships, but it goes against the grain of our entire 100,000+ year evolution. Village life may not feature in our living memory, but it's one millimetre behind us on the broader scale of time – and is where we thrive.

Change isn't just possible, it's inevitable: Enough said. It's coming whether we're ready or not, so let's start practising adaptability, which will be our #1 superpower.

Humanity is a custodial species

'Us two-leggeds are designed to live in tribes, villages and communities that caretake and live in deep reciprocity with our ancestral lands. Across the centuries of empire building and colonisation, many have strayed far from our motherlands and from our important, custodial role in the web of life.

'The symptoms of disconnect are everywhere. We all long for reconnection to life. We have a deep sense of knowing that we need to live differently and together, but we don't seem to know how to get there.'

Billa Lauiti-kolkr, founder of The Wild School

The global garden was entrusted to us and our response has fallen short. For humanity to meet this multi-generational challenge, large numbers of willing, capable, skilled and empowered individuals need to work collectively to undertake the restoration of our earth and repair our human culture.

Huddles form through adversity, experience, need and pure simple desire to keep certain humans in your inner world. They ebb and flow with the seasons of the annum. Mostly, they're relational; geographically close enough to hug and hold, but sometimes they're at the end of a letter, phone or screen.

Sometimes they're intentional, carefully accumulated and nurtured, but sometimes they form organically and eclectically, catching us by surprise when we realise their strength.

Huddles come in all shapes and forms. They make us who we are and reassure us of our place in the world.

Let the feelings out

Our deepest sense tells us to feel our way free, not just think our way out, of complex problems. To listen to our bodies and feel love, hope and fear; to be led by our heart as well as our head; to reinstate agency to our intuition.

Despite the inordinate capability of our 'gut-led' feelings and emotions, our modern approach continues to ignore half our skills when formulating policy, assessing risk and creating scientific solutions.

The results of having made decisions using rationality rather than feelings are plain to see all around us and it's not working, so let's allow our feelings to flow and once they're unlocked, let's imagine the impact of adding love to technology, empathy to institutions, human belief to policies, grief and joy to our daily lives and heart-led decision-making to our very way of being.

I hope you fall in love with being alive.

Do not disassociate

Rationalist disassociation is perhaps what our culture has enabled for far too long. This disconnection has enabled unbridled progress, but to the detriment of what?

When we're disassociated from the webbed reality of our ecological existence, the outcome can only land in one place. A disassociated culture cannot care for, or be careful with, the things we are not connected to. We sidestep our mutual obligation to nurture and consider the needs of other things, human or otherwise. Our long supply food system exemplifies this well and food waste is the result. So too does endless urban sprawl, which concretes over our agricultural food bowls, resulting in urban food deserts. While the short-term vision of progress reaches its goal, the legacy impact generates problems far greater than the solutions offered.
For us to do the work we need to do, our collective knowledge needs to form huddles, be whole and far more capable as the sum of the parts than as a series of siloed individuals.

Our reality

This book won't provide every piece of solace and in many ways, this is the point. There will be no escaping the hardship we are facing, but the most hopeful way through this modern-day quandary will be in huddles. Our desire to huddle is a response to a culture that isn't working. Before we make a mad dash towards a better one, it helps to understand the problems and connect the dots to our current reality.

>>>

14

DWINDLING BIODIVERSITY

Biodiversity = resilience, but only ten per cent of food varieties from 100 years ago still exist. One-third of all insects are now endangered.

RAMPANT FOOD WASTE

Due to long supply chains, fifty per cent of the world's food is wasted – never picked on farms, sold cheap by wholesalers, only prime cuts used by restaurants.

GLOBAL HUNGER

805 million people are undernourished.

FEWER FORESTS

Of the 10 million hectares of forest cleared every year, twenty-seven per cent is 'commodity-driven deforestation' – that's 2.7 million hectares.

DECLINING FOOD LITERACY

Less homegrown and more eating out = decreased knowledge of where food comes from, how to cook it, when it's in season and nutritional value.

TOPSOIL LOSS

24 billion tonnes annually = 3.4 tonnes lost every year for every person on the planet. Soils store more than 4000 billion tonnes of carbon.

DISCONNECTED EATERS

Sixty per cent of the global population is predicted to be urban dwellers by 2030, living in food deserts without an ability to grow the majority of their own food.

GROSS INEQUALITY

There's an ever-widening wealth gap. Since 2020, the five wealthiest individuals on earth have doubled their profits, while close to 5 billion people around the world have got poorer. There's decreased access to fair and equitable income, education, healthcare and employment.

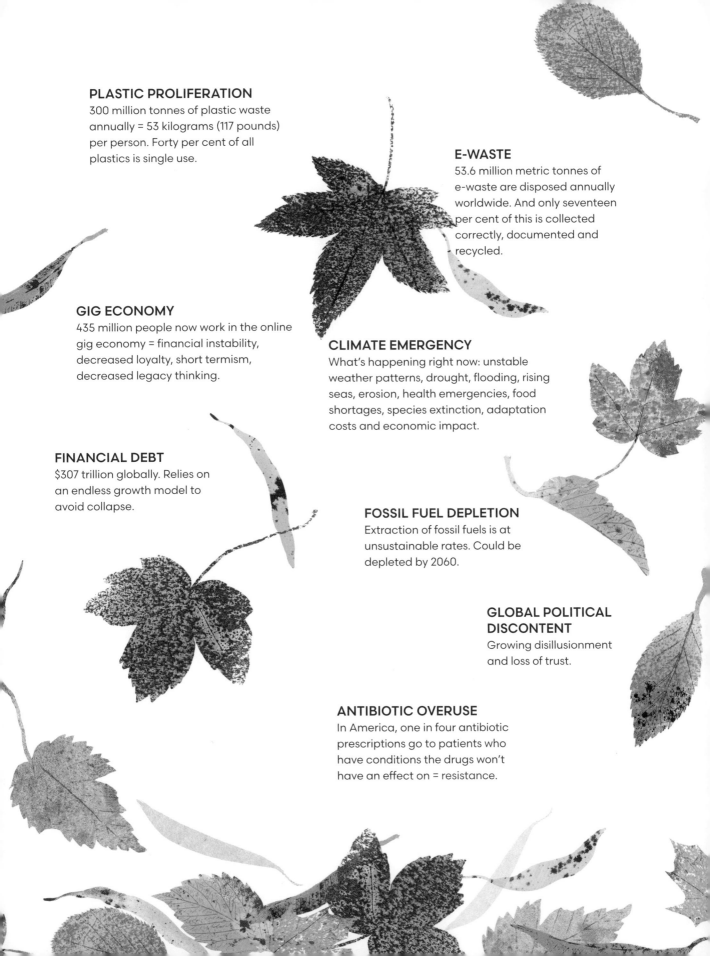

PLASTIC PROLIFERATION
300 million tonnes of plastic waste annually = 53 kilograms (117 pounds) per person. Forty per cent of all plastics is single use.

E-WASTE
53.6 million metric tonnes of e-waste are disposed annually worldwide. And only seventeen per cent of this is collected correctly, documented and recycled.

GIG ECONOMY
435 million people now work in the online gig economy = financial instability, decreased loyalty, short termism, decreased legacy thinking.

CLIMATE EMERGENCY
What's happening right now: unstable weather patterns, drought, flooding, rising seas, erosion, health emergencies, food shortages, species extinction, adaptation costs and economic impact.

FINANCIAL DEBT
$307 trillion globally. Relies on an endless growth model to avoid collapse.

FOSSIL FUEL DEPLETION
Extraction of fossil fuels is at unsustainable rates. Could be depleted by 2060.

GLOBAL POLITICAL DISCONTENT
Growing disillusionment and loss of trust.

ANTIBIOTIC OVERUSE
In America, one in four antibiotic prescriptions go to patients who have conditions the drugs won't have an effect on = resistance.

HUDDLE _____ *HOW?*

Where to begin?

Right here, right now, where you are with what you've got ...
and a friend or even three.

What is it that gives you a physiological quickening and allows you to become the subtle encourager of good things done by good people?

Self-audit: With a cup of tea and some quiet time, ask yourself these questions and be brave enough to be honest.
• How do you define 'enough'?
• Where are you actively collaborating?
• What do you do alone that could be created with others?
• Who would rely on you in an emergency?
• Can you secure food if our shelves run empty again?
• Can you medicate yourself if pharmaceutical supplies are impacted?
• Do you know where the moon cycle is at?
• Do you know where your water comes from?
• How many food miles does your average meal travel to feed you?
• How often do you sit on the earth?
• How often do you do a body scan; checking in with your mental and
  emotional wellbeing?
• When asked to describe or introduce yourself, what defines your
  self-identity?
• What's your annual carbon footprint?
• How much waste do you generate?

Create a huddle vision: What do you imagine a life of reciprocity and mutual aid to look and feel like? Write this down or draw a picture of the vision.

Find a friend: You're not in this alone. As a custodial species we thrive when well supported – even by just one other, so huddle up!

Set goals: Nothing like a goal to enable a plan.

Let it go: This paradigm changing stuff is hard, slow and full of paradox. Even more reason to keep at it, BUT being earnest about it will suck you dry. Do the work but be okay to take a break.

Smile: I'm told that six-year-olds laugh more than 300 times a day. Adults only laugh 15–20 times a day. Be six again!

18

What does it mean to huddle?

What does the word *huddle* evoke for you? I love that it rhymes with *cuddle*, bringing a sense of safety, comfort and holding. But really, huddle has many associations. It can be intimate: huddling around a fire with friends and family and a battered old guitar. It can be formalised: a facilitated group, a regular meet-up, a gathering of activists. You can huddle under a blackwood tree, blue robins and mozzies as your compatriots. You can huddle in a meeting room, nutting out a wicked problem and scribbling insights on a whiteboard. At its heart, huddle signifies a moment of closeness and coordination among individuals. How structured or organic it is remains entirely up to you.

Together we ...

Let's contemplate for a moment how the question of 'what if?' changes if we add 'together'. 'What if we did X together?' That's fertile ground.

What if TOGETHER we:

Ensured that everyone had enough.

Prioritised mental health and soil health over wealth.

Replaced new things with new skills.

Turned education into an experience rather than a striving towards excellence.

Rewrote the rules of success as happiness not status.

Valued the food on our plate and the farmer who grew it, and acknowledged it was the foundation of our existence.

Mapped the miles on everything we purchased and made a commitment to reach new localised goals.

Contributed equally to building our communities to be the most incredible places they can be.

Created love projects as often as we created industrial projects.

Could spend time weekly learning skills from our elders and teaching skills to our children.

Acknowledged that you feel as good when helping others as when you earn money.

Celebrated growing food instead of growing dollars.

Honoured our individual gifts by using them rather than sidelining them as mere hobbies.

Normalised repairing rather than replacing.

Considered the lives of generations still to come.

Took care of the fruiting trees on the common land in our neighbourhood.

Got to know our local bird families and protected them.

Let go of the riverbank and floated away from stability and financial return to a place that followed our hearts.

Hosted gatherings where we invited perfect strangers to tea because they had a friendly face.

Committed to carry our waste on our backs for the rest of our lives.

Committed to only buying second-hand.

Agreed to never buy another present that we didn't know the maker of.

Together let's imagine a life where some of these contemplations became reality in cohesion with other co-creators.

21

A vision for a new tomorrow!

What's your vision for tomorrow? How will you bring this vision to life and offer it to the collective for codesign and contribution?

Could it be that as a people, we have become so accustomed to such an abundance of readily available, inexpensive, single-use consumables and choice that the reality of it ever becoming a scarcity is so far removed from our expectations? Not only have we clean-slated historical memories of poverty and starvation, we have imagined ourselves into a false reality of endless abundance; enough to lure us into thinking we will never need survival skills again.

I don't suppose a new way of being can be created overnight. Let's imagine we won't experience a dramatic systemic collapse. Let's imagine we have just a moment to collect our thoughts, pause and imagine a different way of being. How will you begin?

What gift will you offer to the collaborative creation of a patchwork of regenerative existence? Together we can build a very different tomorrow, but we all have a role to play.

It's okay for us to have slightly different visions, but it will only become reality if we have the gumption to share them; our willingness to share for the sake of a better world. We need to get past fear and the reasons not to share – even if we suspect the gap between our hope and our reality will be painful.

It's time to be practical, nourishing and connected during this process of creating a world of regeneration.

Don't let it overwhelm. Let it add to the foundation of knowledge that will spur us on collectively in our actions to create a better future, because we CAN create a tomorrow of togetherness. **We just have to begin.**

22

23

Emergence___

It's time to let go of destructive paradigms, stoking the old ways and kindling the new. It's time to reclaim our ancestral skills and remember what it feels like to belong. Let's keep all those great and revolutionary advancements, so long as they lead us towards one another and into the 'Symbiocene'. It's time to get comfortable on shifting ground while also putting down roots, learning to deftly adapt and tapping into deep comradeship.

These might just be the secrets to becoming an emergent culture.

24

To ensure humanity has a place to call home into the future, the time has come to turn towards the sun, with eyes and hearts wide open, to face our problems with courage. Face their truth, brutality and complexity, and find a new path, a different way. It's a request made all the harder while the current paradigm – only a facade at this point – is still luring us with solutions that feel easier and more convenient. No longer can be stand by and surrender our values to an economic system that does not value what we love.

26

EMERGENCE

Patterns of humanity

For more than six million years, humanity has embarked on a remarkable journey of evolution, guided by the intricate nuance of instincts woven into our very being. Across diverse cultures and civilisations, patterns have emerged, shaping the course of our collective existence and laying the foundation for the modern world we inhabit today. Our core, primal urges have driven us to seek sustenance, shelter and safety. From the earliest hunter-gatherer communities to the complex societies of today, the pursuit of survival has been a central force propelling human progress. These instinctual drives have spurred the development of tools, ingenious farming techniques and sophisticated systems of governance.

Yet, it is not merely survival that has moulded our path. The yearning for connection, companionship and love has given rise to intricate social structures and the formation of communities. Our human need to belong has forged bonds that transcend time and place, uniting us in families, tribes and nations. These social patterns have laid the groundwork for cooperation, collective decision-making and the creation of cultural norms that shape our interactions.

As Jeremy Lent outlines in his book, *The Web of Meaning*, our earliest experience of collectivism began with the changing landscape that took us from a life protected by trees to Savannah grasslands six million years ago. At this time, our ancestors became more vulnerable to predators with less access to food. However, we could protect and feed ourselves if we cooperated. This process enlarged our prefrontal cortex as we developed new emotions that fostered deep collaboration and feelings, such as guilt, embarrassment, shame and gratitude.

  All these emotions assisted us with group dynamics. This is ultimately the modern-day theory of mind, social intelligence and the initial separation of self in our consciousness. With the development of such emotional capability, our world expanded exponentially and our innate curiosity propelled us towards exploration and discovery. The thirst for knowledge – driven by an insatiable desire to comprehend the mysteries of the universe – has led to profound scientific advancements, philosophical insights and artistic expressions. From the ancient wisdom of indigenous cultures to the cutting-edge discoveries of modern science, our quest for understanding has propelled us forward ... and now here we are, right where we were always headed.

This evolutionary journey matched patterns in the natural world for the vast majority of our existence. Only in the last few thousand years – a poofteenth

28

of our long winding time on earth – have we had the ability to slowly extricate ourselves from our instinctive and animus ways of being, thanks largely to the discovery of fossil fuels. The interplay of our instincts, shaped by diverse cultural influences, has birthed languages, customs, rituals and belief systems that reflect the rich tapestry of our shared humanity.

At some point in more recent history, we transitioned from LORE (legend, origin, respect and elders) over to LAW (legal, administration, Westminster). A missed opportunity to not adopt elements of First Nations culture, instead imposing an existing culture or way of life in a completely different geographical place.

The Industrial Age saw the growth paradigm spring up like a pumpkin from the compost pile of western countries, with flow-on effects for the 'developing' world. This endless need for expansion and growth has been nurtured (to put it politely) by mainstream media and corporate boardroom KPIs. Our society, transfixed by exponential growth framed as progress, is nothing short of suicidal. It's sustained by unsustainable food systems and rife with loneliness and isolation, seeding its own demise.

The hippies or 'earth connected' among us have pushed against being dragged into the industrial machine defined merely as resources used to increase the wealth of just a few. And because those hippies cannot be found in the halls of government or the boardrooms of media agencies, they have had a limited voice and influence over mainstream narrative. When we do stop and listen, they tell us that the earth is our home; it touches us, nourishes our souls, feeds our bellies, warms our limbs and guides us with whispers and teachings. To be in harmony with earth is to defy the reductionist industrialists.

The choice is ours. It has always been ours, but the lure of grandeur, growth and human exceptionalism has been a short-lived but mesmerising fault of the modern world. To be in harmony with earth is to quietly opt out and defy the machine. Coming into harmony with the earth means one less cog in the churn.

While our modern lives resemble something quite different to our long ago ancestors, we find ourselves at the crossroads of a life that is existing beyond its resources and in defiance of its evolutionary patterns and instincts. Now it's important that we take a moment to reflect on those who have gone before us, and the connection we share to them.

Could it be time to sit still, dig deep and relearn the wisdom inherited from countless prior generations? Respect the diverse cultural expressions that enrich our global tapestry? Forge a future that honours our instinctual roots while fostering unity, understanding and harmonious coexistence? *Sounds great to me!*

A slow but necessary shift

We need to find the cause of our pain. It will at some point inevitably require solo journeys for each of us to unpack who we are and what we need to become. Ultimately, these individual quests will lead us back to each other in huddles of human and non-human beings. It's time to embark on an ecological reconnection of great magnitude.

Philosopher Aldo Leopold said one of the penalties of an ecological education is that one lives in a world of wounds. Patterns of enduring destruction can feel impossible to bear. The answers do not lie in the halls of politicians but in the hearts and actions of each and every one of us. We all have agency to build symbiotic alignment with our broken ecological world.

This is by no means an easy task. It requires us to manage an unspoken grief that is sometimes understood and voiced, sometimes not. Regardless, we all hold this grief, because ultimately since birth our expectation of being loved and held in a community, in deep connection, empowered to be our individual self, ensconced in a huddle that we are bound to by reciprocity, is never met in an industrial world. This grief is rarely articulated, so it lays nascent in our culture, misunderstood and festering into wounds so deep we can't find the end to begin the untangle.

After completing the Permaculture Design Certificate, I resonated with Leopold's sentiments; no longer anchored to my sentinels of friendships or way of being. My ecological education had illuminated our disconnected, short-term approach to existence, and I couldn't unknow what I'd spent seven months absorbing in my head and heart. However, my paradigm no longer had a toolbox of tricks to help with the daily easing. I floated – figuratively lost at sea and unsettled – for quite some time. Fortunately, I was married to a man who had walked this path before me. Together we clawed our way out and created a passage towards healing. The 'doing' was our salve. With calloused hands and muscles sore, we spent a decade creating the flagstones of our long envisaged community barn and farm.

Slowly the cast-adrift grief we had both felt abated. Via the contribution of so many, we participated in mutual aid, reciprocity and celebration of the simple. Reconnecting to ourselves, our place, our community. No longer were we wandering without hope. Rather we were filled with joy and purpose. We beat to a very seasonal drum and spent a lot of time on the earth.

Our grief had been acknowledged and addressed every single day. But rather than feeling sombre, it seeded a sense of purpose and potential. While it could be considered a rebirthing, it was really a new way of seeing and being in the world.

While the pathway to our modern-day patterning has taken hundreds of years, we now require a rather urgent shift, with the need for immediate and collective response stamping its feet impatiently.

30

From the Anthropocene and into the Symbiocene

For the past 300 or so years we have been in the geological epoch known as the Anthropocene. Its primary trait has been its stamping of responsibility for our reality on human activities that have become the dominant force shaping the earth's ecosystems and climate. While the level of this influence has been a distracting debate over the past two decades, finally we seem to have reached a consensus: we are responsible for taking corrective action.

Australian environmentalist Glenn Albrecht stated in *Earth Emotions* that during the Anthropocene we have 'socially evolved ... under the influence of a fundamentally flawed set of dominant themes and ideas. Our economic, scientific and technological evolution has taken most of humanity onto a path that reduces the diversity of life, both biological and cultural, into one globalised, homogeneous and interconnected economic and technological system. It is this ecocidal system that is putting life at risk.'

He offers an invitation: 'To avoid such a fate, a new meme for the future is needed to guide our thinking and provide inspiration to all generations, but especially the young. I suggest that systematic symbiotic thinking leads to the Symbiocene, a new era that nurtures all aspects of being human in a world of other beings.'

How we go about this significant change is really up to us, and when life in western culture has become so greatly accustomed to such high degrees of comfort and convenience, it's a difficult paradigm to step away from.

But step away we must, for the earth is in a state of grief. **Can you feel it?**

Earth – we promised to nurture it

Australia's Post Carbon Institute refers to this time as 'The Great Unravelling'. For more than fifty years, we've been warned that the costs of exponential growth of population and consumption, and the exploitation of people and planet, would eventually come for us all. No longer looming, this time is here. Ouch. And over the coming months, years and decades our primary challenge – individually and collectively – will be to navigate this 'Great Unravelling' of environmental and social crises in ways that ensure the most collective wellbeing. All while putting humanity on a path of resilience, justice and sustainability.

It's not the world that needs saving, it's us. There's capability in the collective but to see it sprout we have to give up commodities and replace it with communication, swapping the notion that it's our human right to manage, control and dominate. We must replace it with an attitude of adaptability and collaboration, working with and for all living things. This is emerging as some kind of a returning. Returning to what we know to be true. A journey into interdependence where we resign ourselves to the influence of the earth that exists in seasons and ever-evolving lifetimes to maintain balance.

We need to get real about our own importance by getting wise about time. We are but a flash in deep time, dwarfed by the stars, the cosmos, even cockroaches. Seeing our species in context is critical to tapping into humility; those humbler states will help us accept the need to change.

My brother once made a hefty, oversized serving board from the branch of an oak for me. Simply looking at the rings sitting under my quince paste and cheese serves as a reminder that I'm but a short-lived passer-by on this earth. I'll come and go as merely a few rings in this oak's total existence. Humbling indeed. If the rings in an oak tree don't prompt a reminder, consider the aspen, a species that has been spawning from the same single root mass for as long as humans have been on earth. As we come and go in twenty-five-year generations, the aspen mass continues to be one of the largest living organisms on earth. It continues to spawn new suckers from the foundation root mass, unperturbed by our short-term tenancy as a species.

Have you heard the term 'polycrisis'? It refers to the unravelling of multiple crises simultaneously. Right now we are seeing ecological, cultural and political turbulence that, when all happening at once, sees our systems wince and struggle.

So, it's time for action.

As we recognise our planet's fragility and the importance of equitable resource distribution, a cultural awakening awaits. As we exit the Anthropocene and enter the Symbiocene, expect a renewed focus on wellbeing, resilience and the pursuit of long-term benefits over short-term gains. Our day-to-day existence will thrive on sustainable living, social justice and a zest for creating a brighter future for all.

STORY

Ancestral knowledge keepers

Since the beginning of human existence, there have been revered custodians; let's call them ancestral knowledge keepers. These wise souls bear the torch of ancestral heritage, carrying within them the treasury of traditional wisdom of the land, and age-old customs. They embody the living connection to their forebears; the guardians of stories that intertwine with the very fabric of our culture. They share the teachings, rituals and ancestral narratives, keeping alive the essence of their people's identity.

These incredible humans are the luminous bridges between generations, the torchbearers of a timeless legacy, nurturing the bonds between the past, present and future. Their presence reminds us of the richness of our collective heritage and invites us to honour and embrace the wisdom woven within the tapestry of our ancestry.

When seeking our modern-day knowledge keepers, I was referred to many friends' grandparents and met with cynical quips: 'our society values the knowledge passing through YouTube and from the mouths of ill-equipped celebrities more than the wisdom from our elders' or 'we have to find direction in the endlessly shared memes that circulate' or simply 'we don't have any'.

One particular friend responded with immediate tears in her eyes. She recounted her well of sadness from having searched for years in the hope of surrounding herself with an eldership blanket of wisdom to no avail. She said, 'Our society shuts these voices out through an insidious cultural reform that values knowledge in fifteen-second time slots, delivered via tech platforms by voices and faces we will likely never meet, much less have the opportunity to be in proximity and relationship with.'

Her grief at this lack of guidance was weighty and, in a scramble to offer solace, I suggested she step up to the mantle. 'I will, but only when I feel the time is right and I have the knowledge to share. In the meantime, I seek the company of those just a little older than I am so I at least know what to expect in the chapter I face immediately.'

She and I are the same age, so of course it led to discussion about perimenopause and ageing parents, teenage children and transitioning aspirations. We banged around in the dark building solidarity in our experiences, and it felt good to share our vagueness. While her desire to build relationship with elders has not been diluted, we concluded that perhaps we are simply the generation that does not have ready access to this. Our role is to ensure the next generation doesn't suffer the same void.

Having introduced me to the idea of taking an ancestral journey, we revisited the idea and felt building excitement at the prospect of digging deeply into our heritage, visiting the lands of our people's past and bringing that knowledge to the generations still to come.

Her parting words that evening were, 'I may not be ready to be a knowledge keeper yet, but I can only hope to become one if I actively pursue the knowledge of both landscape and humanity.

The beauty will be in the way I build confidence to share it, and I imagine that at some point, I'll realise what I've become.'

Making tomorrow's foundations today

This is multigenerational work, beyond our own lifetimes. Unrequited love stuff. Make peace with that!

Plenty of traditional cultures show us what it means to think seven generations hence. Let's be straight up in saying it's uncomfortable to accept that we may not taste the fruits of our labour. In all honesty, the work that needs doing begins with you and your acceptance that you may only be the foundation, the fertility, the seed, before stepping aside to make way for the next generation. These changemakers will fill your shoes (and appreciate you wearing them in), taking your vision further than you ever thought possible.

   Don't underestimate the impact of gifting your children, grandchildren or people in your life a love of the earth and framework for tending it. This is the patient and plodding work of intergenerational transformation, and we have the privilege of being some of the western world's pioneers in this complex process of unlearning.

Fire keepers – are you one?

The licking light and warmth of fire has kept us fed, warm and safe in our communities since almost the very beginning of time. We have revered and ritualised fireside and our very existence is inextricably tied to our ability to generate a spark. In the modern world it's as easy as lighting a match, but not so long ago the skill of lighting a fire meant survive and thrive. The lesson was taught early and the role of fire keeper was greatly honoured. From the edges of the glow we've birthed our babies, grieved the dead, cooked our sustenance and ceremoniously marked occasions of reverence. If you've ever sat by its warmth you'll know the hypnotic lull of its crackling speech, the pensive state you find yourself in and the blanket of completeness it wraps you in just by keeping its company.

My rewilding women's circles are always held fireside – even in the rain. We boil ceremonial tea or cacao in silence; we warm our bodies if we've dipped in the dam; and when stories are shared, it offers kinship without judgement, holding the pain and the joy with ease.

   There's no wonder this ancient tool still holds us all. It's in our cellular memories. How often do you sit fireside now? Can you light one from scratch with no match?

The discomfort of losing control

I live very close to the mountains, where the shades of blue and grey layer into each other like an impressionist artwork. When I walk in the mornings with the mountains on the horizon, I see the past of all those who've been before me and all those yet to come, both human and otherwise. Not far from where we live is a redwood forest plot and the sound of silence while standing under these sentinels is humbling. Their sobering height forces humility, and a solid reminder of our insignificance is close to the surface.

Could it be time to reassess the human story from one of towering over to instead being tethered to the fates of other creatures? We cannot tell the human story without including the detail of the surrounding neighbourhood of nature.

Tyson Yunkaporta, author of *Sand Talk* and *Right Story, Wrong Story*, tells us that all yarns need messy parts and chaos without control. In fact, by always trying to 'straighten things out' we disengage with our animas, our creaturely self and fall into step with the industrial system, with its straight lines and machinery. We lose the skill – and yes, it is a skill – of holding messiness and multiplicity. To rewrite the patterns that dictate the way we navigate our days we need to reintroduce messy chaos and get comfortable being in the uncontrolled for just long enough to rewire our relationships.

When I asked Tyson in a *Futuresteading* podcast interview if we needed to reindigenise, his response was fast and harsh. 'What are you? A fucking dickhead?' A long, awkward pause followed ... just long enough to destabilise me – even in my seat of podcasting-host security. But as I was gulping hard and contemplating the truth of his assessment, he finished his sentence with, 'Of course you are, but we all are and we all have to be because we don't know how to do this with ease. It's in our unlived memories, but it's going to take some awkward practice to build it into our lived memories.' Then he said, 'We all have to get uncomfortable and be happy to be dickheads

together while we relearn a way of existing without the systemic abstractions in the way of what it means to be truly human. With the abstractions removed we can return to our connection with nature. To be fully alive we need to feel connection to our surrounds and each other. Not just the human species but all other species that make our wild and complex world.'

Nature has been othered. We don't want weeds on the path or bugs in the house; we want manicured parks for our pleasure, wholly separate and controlled. Despite the success we've had in scientific research, combined with our ancestral capability to intuitively understand the ecosystem, we can't begin to know the depths of what is needed to live in cohesion.

What we can do is change our aperture. We are part of life and for life to thrive we need to live differently. This will require adaptation and mitigation.

Time to take risks

It has been mused that the more risks you allow children to take, the better they learn to take care of themselves. I suspect his wisdom might be relevant to the grown-up children in our world too. With risk-taking comes experience, learning opportunities, calculation of capabilities, interaction with those outside our usual realm and confidence building, with successes and inevitable failures. Anyone who has ever tried their hand at an entrepreneurial startup knows how much of a challenge it can be. It's risky for so many reasons, but even those start-ups that don't end up as Fortune 500 companies and close their doors – like forty-one per cent of small businesses in the first four years – the lessons learned from the risk-taking are invaluable and should be seen as courageous. Entering into daily life is risky and the more we take the chance, the better we become at it, so keep going!

My twin pregnancy was high risk as they shared a placenta and were growing disparately. Hyperemesis gravidarum hospitalised me regularly and I lost loads of weight. Despite this, we made a six-hour round trip to Melbourne every other week for scans to assess whether they had moved into a state of 'Twin-to-Twin Transfusion', where one of the twins ceases to grow due to a lack of nutrients.

All in all, it was one hellish pregnancy that we had been fighting for from the very first day, navigating past one doctor's advice to terminate, Charlie sleeping in a swag because I couldn't bear his smell or movement in the bed and every single thing I consumed being thrown up for six solid months.

At the twenty-four-week scan our fears came to fruition with the news that the smaller twin had stopped growing, meaning experimental micro laser surgery to my placenta. The saving grace was that it was Christmas and I had two weeks to prepare for the risky procedure. Having fought the debilitating

nausea with every possible tool I could muster, I changed tack and let everything go. Instead of fighting, I lay on the beach daily and meditated. On returning to the specialist's office in anticipation of surgery, I was greeted with a shocked doctor and healthy babies. 'I'm not sure what you've done over the past two weeks, but what I'm looking at is an entirely different scenario.'

The experience gave me immense confidence in my body's knowing. I'd been using my head to apply rational, controlled solutions to little effect, but the minute I let go and listened to my body, something far more clever than my mind took over: my evolutionary knowing. While the boys arrived eight weeks premature and the work of modern medicine proved its immense value, I marvelled at the ability for ancestral knowledge to meet modern technology. I realised the immense power in being comfortable to let go and be out of control. From there change can begin. When life is at its hardest, our tendency is to grit our teeth and fight. When we stop fighting and skid into the difficulty, we let life show us the way. It knows how, but we need to be willing to hand over the reins.

The fraudulence
of a nuclear life

Tribal life predominantly saw men with men and women with women. Rarely did man, woman and child spend a full and isolated twenty-four hours together and be reliant on each other for ALL things.

Women relied on women and men relied on men. We had lore and ritual to guide us through our days that were repetitive, intuitive and harmonised with each other and the ecological systems that held us.

There was no opportunity to head inside our private gate, shutting the hard things out, and there was no way to make things black and white by paying for something. Instead we had little choice but to sit in the discomfort of compromise, conversation, interaction and all degrees of greyness while we negotiated an outcome that benefitted all. The decision-making process considered the whole before the sole and in return the community carried joint responsibility to meet the needs of all.

37

Open hearts and minds

The Industrial Age has indeed transformed our way of life, placing emphasis on efficiency and productivity at the expense of our wellbeing and innate human nature. However, a growing movement is emerging. A pushback against this mechanised way of existence. People are yearning to untangle themselves from the suffocating grip of a social fabric that feels disconnected from the true human essence. We have become accustomed to behaving like machines, adhering to rigid schedules and norms that stifle our individuality and suppress our natural instincts.

Together, let's rediscover and relearn our human capabilities, embracing a way of life that is centred around our hearts and minds. It is a call to listen to the wisdom of our bodies and reconnect with our instincts, which have guided us for countless generations.

Before science emerged as the dominant authority, we relied on our bodies and instincts to navigate the world. We trusted our gut feelings, intuition and deep-rooted knowledge of our animus state. There was an inherent understanding that our bodies held valuable wisdom and insights. Our DNA passed on more than just our eye colour or height.

In this age of information overload and external validation, there is a yearning to return to that primal trust in ourselves. We are beginning to recognise the importance of listening to our bodies, honouring our emotions and nurturing our wellbeing. By reawakening our human-centric approach to life, we can reclaim our authenticity, find balance and cultivate a deeper connection with ourselves and others.

Trusting our gut, while innate, is perhaps long buried in many and we've become accustomed to listening to the voice in our head rather than the feeling in our heart.

When we say YOU, what springs to mind? Do you visualise your own body looking back at you in the mirror, a lone individual? Is this a cultural illusion? When we allow true kinship, the question of you becomes more permeable. We can identify across species, and our own destinies are dependent on one another. Together we begin to contain one another and become larger for it.

38

HUDDLE _____ *HOW?*

Building collective emergence

While the patterns of modern-day humanity may not be the result of our own individual choices, they are the result of 60 million years of emerging evolution. We are still emerging and need to rekindle a friendship with many parts of our previous selves and the earth mama that holds us. While next steps are not mapped in a nifty little guide, now is the time to be directing attention to the cry of life and given the ecological calamity, we'll need to hurry slowly in the reimagining and repatterning of a modern-day emergent world.

Tackling this requires the hands and hearts of many – all moving at the speed of trust – easy to say, perhaps harder to do. Where to begin?

Be honest: Honest with yourself and everyone around you. Speak your truth with clarity. Engage in conversations, unafraid to dive deeply. When honesty becomes your compass, emergence will flow.

Know your place in the world: I don't mean know your 'station'. I mean geographically. Where does your water come from? Where does the sun rise in winter and set in summer? At what altitude do you live? Which direction is your prevailing weather? What's your annual rainfall? What can you forage locally? What type of dirt is under your feet and is it good for growing food?

Cultivate trust: Trust begins within. Take a moment to tune in and listen to your heart. Nurture the seed of self-trust by knowing and owning your values, honouring your strengths and setting healthy boundaries. Journalling helps to unpack this. Give trust freely; it's a gift, a treasure to be shared. Be generous, albeit discerning, by extending yours.

Practise active listening: Dust off those attentive ears and engage with intention, be fully present and set aside the distractions of a buzzing world. Seek to understand without interrupting or imposing your own story.

Embrace vulnerability: Get real! By removing the protective armour we make room for two-way sharing of fears, hopes, dreams, challenges and relational connection. Drop the performance and seek those who are also tired of the show.

Go barefoot: Kick off your shoes and listen to the earth. Ask it, what's next, where to, who with? Learn to listen closely.

Plant things that grow: Got a spare windowsill? Plant a pot of herbs. Perhaps you have an empty backyard – thought about a veggie garden? If you have a bare paddock, plant a tree or three. It'll connect you to the seasons and be a marker of time. Dish out a dose of patience and heighten your sense of stewardship for things non-human. Watching plants grow never gets old.

Be consistent and reliable: Stay true to your word. Let your actions be a picture of dependability. By showing up reliably, with unwavering commitment, we build a base that will allow us to emerge together.

Learn your Country: Whose Country do you live on? What's it called? How do you spell it, say it, honour it?

Actively grow: Relationships take time to grow and deepen their roots. Be patient with yourself and others through the ebb and flow, making sure to sidestep division. It's prevalent in our culture, but can be shunned in your own day-to-day by seeking the things we have in common rather than the things we don't.

With these waypoints as our guiding stars, we'll build a foundation that enables transitionary emergence and softens us. Heck, I know that's daunting because we won't all soften at once, so the fear of being crushed is real. But I also know that we can take agency for our attitude. If we'd rather operate from a heart-led place, we find our people, our language and our way of being so we can continue to emerge together.

In the words of the late Dan Palmer, 'Only when you have confidence in an emergent approach to the creation of new things can you truly allow collaboration to happen.'

41

HUDDLE ACTIVITY

INTENTIONAL MEANDER

An intentionally slow, purposeless walk to nowhere with no reason at all is easier said than done, but there are plenty of reasons to do it!

You can complete this activity alone or with others, but do it in silence and without a set timeframe, if possible.

Build these into your week and allow your wanders to unfurl in any direction. With bare feet, no kids and a pot of tea, set off aimlessly and let your senses become curiously heightened, leading you towards sounds, smells and textures that appeal. You might bend or sit, close your eyes and just feel. Perhaps you'll find things and pick them up along the way.

Return to a journal to capture your insights and rambling thoughts, not for any sort of monitoring but to consolidate your experience and to embed your comfort with the unplanned emergence.

42

HUDDLE

STORY

Cathy McGowan's road from the kitchen table to Parliament

Trusting the process of emergence doesn't come easily to many. Even with a leap of faith it can still be a pathway marred with challenges. For Cathy McGowan, she was able to combine her experience as a strong female leader in agriculture with the support offered at magnitude from her twelve siblings and an army of nieces and nephews to achieve the unimaginable by throwing away the book and letting the process unfold as it was meant to. Unfazed by the stronghold major political parties had on her community, she envisioned and actioned a different path to represent her people in the Australian Parliament!

McGowan, a seasoned community activist, was well connected to the Victorian Women's Trust and together they hatched an unconventional plan to bring politics back to its roots, to the very heart of the community. Inspired by the warmth and authenticity of family gatherings, McGowan introduced the concept of 'kitchen table conversations' to politics. With an open mind and deep listening capability, she traipsed across the vast electorate of Indi and was welcomed into the homes of constituents to share stories and break bread. These intimate gatherings weren't about political rhetoric; they were about listening, understanding and finding common ground.

As word spread, the kitchen table conversations became a movement of their own. People from all walks of life gathered to discuss the issues close to their hearts. McGowan's approach broke down barriers, and the aroma of homemade meals became a symbol of community unity.

Social media caught wind of this grassroots revolution, amplifying the tales of kitchen tables that transformed into platforms for genuine conversation. McGowan's message resonated far beyond Indi, capturing the imagination of those yearning for a politics rooted in authenticity.

Come election day in 2013, the unconventional became the triumphant. McGowan emerged victorious, securing Indi's seat against the odds stacked by traditional political structures. Her journey proved that, sometimes, all it takes is a humble kitchen table and genuine conversation to redefine the course of politics.

McGowan went on to serve two terms and her successor, Dr Helen Haines, became the first independent in Australian history to succeed another independent in a federal seat.

Her story became a beacon of hope, reminding the world that the power to shape the future often lies not in grand speeches but in the warmth of shared moments around a kitchen table.

Creating a _____

Humans are hardwired storytelling animals who've yarned around fires since primitive times. The stories we tell ourselves and each other inform our interactions with the world around us. These stories weave into our collective consciousness and serve as a manual for 'how to be', shaping our behaviour in subtle and profound ways. But some of these stories are pretty rusty. No longer can we believe that humans are separate from nature, can exist in nuclear households and that we must grow endlessly in order to 'succeed'. These are like rumours repeated so often they seem true, but we know better. We know it's time for a new story; not one in which the hand of man hounds order into Mother Nature, but one that considers us as revered guests who always leave a place better than we found it. Our survival depends on healthier stories, so let's start dreaming and yarning.

_ new story

CREATING A NEW STORY

Since the beginning of time, we've told stories to make sense of the world. Factual, fictional, practical, inspirational, it doesn't really matter – we're lured by the tale regardless and it's these stories that have shaped the way we see ourselves, interact with each other and integrate with the non-human world around us.

With storytelling – written, spoken, crafted or performed – comes self-doubt and bravado in equal measure. If told well, we believe the unbelievable, and if told enough we begin to live the unbelievable.

These stories build our dreams so now it's time to change the dream, plant a different seed, teach your children to dream new dreams.

46

CREATING A NEW STORY

According to Kurt Vonnegut, author of *Slaughterhouse-Five* and storyline researcher, there are only eight different story shapes. The most common of these he coined 'man in a hole', which more or less follows along the lines of character leading an okay life, finds misfortune, overcomes it and is happier afterwards. Another similar theme is 'boy meets girl'. Person finds something they like, loses it, then gets it back just in time for the happiest of endings. Given these storylines have been playing out since the beginning of written communication, it's little wonder we've built cultural expectations around them. Even without actually knowing the ending, we think we've got a handle on it, it feels familiar. So, when things don't play according to the script, we are incredulous and seek answers.

This inclination to build a belief based on repeated patterns could well be the reason we continue to hurtle towards a place of degeneration. The familiar story on repeat is, ultimately, one of a happy ending. The interesting point to note here is that there is always a moment of realisation, and post epiphany there's simply no way of unlearning or unfeeling it, and their actions need to change in order to reach a happy ending.

It begs the question, how will our modern-day eco calamity play out? Humanity has something it loves (earth), and it can't actually live without it. What will be our moment of realisation and what then will be our actions to salvage the thing we love and ensure a happy ending?

A new story may very well not actually be a new one at all, instead one that is unique to this country, with respect and deep listening required to understand it. Has the time come to return to the storylines of First Nations Peoples whose stories always begin with Country? Healthy Country means healthy people. Healthy people perpetuate healthy culture. Respect for Country means honouring the past, present and future, and taking responsibility. So, rather than reinventing the wheel, re-storying ourselves is more about deep and respectful listening.

Are we brave and humble enough to consider Indigenous wisdom as our compass and guidance system towards new ways of being, thinking, learning and sitting with discomfort? This is the story-within-a-story that we need to consider; distinctly different to the one of nature as a commodified resource to rape and pillage, which we've been swallowing and living by for centuries.

As Australian film director Damon Gameau said, 'We are being guided by a collective story that tells us human beings are separate from the natural world, and although many of us know this to be false, the facts don't matter if they don't match the story.'

In between the concrete of our cities and towns, there are 65,000 years of Indigenous cultural stories. These are stories of an integrated existence where Mother Nature and humankind operate united.

Slowly throughout millennia, in tandem with the elegance of evolution and survival, this culture has been replaced with an indifference to our mother.

How did this happen? We were enabled by a low-cost, readily available energy source called fossil fuels that, despite the cognitive dissonance, we forged into the industrialised modes of convenience we see as 'normal'. But are they?

There's no doubt that a life supported by the unprecedented power of ancient plants and animals is cushy and convenient (for some). Fossil fuels and mechanisation certainly make us efficient and productive, allowing progress and growth to be pursued endlessly – or so it seems. But this is an anomaly, a departure from nature's limits and lore. And I wonder if you too ask yourself, to what end? Am I any happier for all these efficiencies?

It is beyond time to return to an Indigenous way of being in connection with our natural world, and not simply for reasons of responsibility and activism. The complexity of First Nations cultures is only now being understood by non-Indigenous peoples. The sustainability and careful balance maintained over millennia required a deep understanding of Country and place, and this is something that should be revisited to ensure the longevity of our race. So many of us feel a yearning towards a more grounded existence, and I think this is the new/old story tugging at our hem.

Connection leads to protection

Reflecting on my education, it strikes me that a lot of what I was taught was totally lacking in context. Rather than maths being presented as a key to unlocking the universe (and perhaps, our place in it – how thrilling!), it was a series of rules and equations, which seemed wholly disconnected from real life.

We are creatures of context. A deep part of us knows that information in isolation is about as useful as a flyscreen on a submarine. It's only when we get intimate with the hows and whys of things – when we connect ideas and action – that we tap into our intrinsic motivation.

When we understand how stuff works – whether that's the life cycle of a carrot or the relationship of our menses to the moon – we are far more inclined to care for it.

The spanner in the works was inheriting a grand dowry of petrochemicals – a legacy of 400 million years of plant life and decomposition – which has afforded us a short-lived period of hyper-abundance. This fortune has given us the illusion of autonomy where we think we can opt out of the natural cycles of energy, squandering this windfall for the sake of future generations.

One of the ramifications of this energy surplus is transcending our 'natural' limits and rising above the laws and lore of the land to become 'accidental gods', as author Manda Scott puts it. In outsourcing our needs via fossil fuels, we've lost touch with the hows and whys of existence because we're busy working at our screens. Is it any wonder we've forgotten our intrinsic motivation to care for Mother Earth?

This story has defined the modern western world and diligently, we've all bought in. Who are we to challenge progress? But who's the author and why can't we challenge them? Because we've temporarily cut away from those old, earthwise stories, our comfort in seeking them out is diminished too. Unless we are familiar with something – which comes from seeing it, feeling it and experiencing it – we find it harder to sit in the nuance. While our individual tolerance for leaping across chasms of uncertainty varies, even the most courageous of us find it challenging to run headlong towards something we've never come across before.

This is a call to start spinning those new/old stories around your campfire and living the lessons too, because many of us 'gotta see it to believe it'. This starts with a mind's eye view of how things can be different and a glimpse of what our wacky neighbour is up to over the fence with their vagabonding pumpkins and street-front seed library.

When we see things for ourselves, we suddenly believe they're possible and from there we can grow towards a new story. Words and wisdom create change – so will you be one of the lone heroes and early adopters singing us in a different direction?

We've been colonised into believing the idea that the human story is self-generating and self-justifying. It places human beings at the top of the ecosystem and lulls us into a false sense of control. But the world is a living organism, with wills and ways of her own. Once we surrender to that truth and topple human exceptionalism, we make room for collective ways of thinking.

'The bleaker and emptier life becomes under capitalism, the more intense is the yearning after beauty.'

Georg Lukács

Life as a tree

A tree is a tree no matter what. It evolves within its ecosystem, as true to itself as it could ever be. It might twist towards light or hunker down and become a little gnarlier than its usual form. Regardless, it stays true to its DNA because it doesn't have to morph to appeal to all birds.

The creation of this book coincided with an intensely busy time of my life. Our three kiddos were in the guts of their to-be-expected self-oriented phase as teenagers. We had opened our you-pick orchard at the farm and were open six months of the year. We were still not quite at the top of our decade-long start-up phase, so it had been eight years of working seven days a week both on and off the farm. It was a time of physical, emotional and mental intensity that was held by early starts, late finishes and brave, if confronting and nonlinear, conversations every day.

We know our head, heart and health are inextricably linked. To make this point, my body – which had been threatened from time to time with various viruses and lethargy – finally pulled me up. A frozen shoulder gripped my left side and disturbed my daily flow.

The unpacking of the healing process was painfully slow, but the pathway turned repeatedly to the analogy of our bodies as trees. A special friend was training to become a Craniosacral therapist, and after I'd spent a few hours on her therapy bed she shared a message with me. 'While treating you, I kept seeing an incredible majestic eucalypt with gnarly hollowed trunk and canopy, and light shining through. It was alive in itself, but also shimmering with the lives of hundreds or thousands of creatures supported by and living in relation with this tree. It felt like you and all the webs of connection you weave and the lives intertwined with and held by yours. So, the question I kept wondering was, how this tree holds this responsibility in a way that nourishes its own life? I kept feeling into the roots somehow. Just something about that big tree holding centre for so many lives, somehow felt like you and the gifts you bring.'

Her words felt like the wayfinding direction I'd been seeking and, as the healing path for my shoulder continued, I found myself 'being a tree' almost daily. I closed my eyes, found a seat on the earth and with hand on heart I imagined my feet as the roots, legs as the trunk, body as the canopy and fingers as the leaves. I knew there was potential for life in this tree – not just mine, but all the creatures I offered a safe place to call home. I also knew I had to focus on the way my roots dug deeply into the earth, sharing a symbiotic relationship with the mycelium network that connected me to the broader, albeit unseen, ability to become intertwined with the mother. This connection to Country is minimised through the use of words, but I felt it powerfully. I was offered reassurance that I was rooted deeply in place, and I would be held through each of the seasons across each of the passing years.

Depending on the lives we've lived and our varied personalities, we grow as different trees. Those that grow alone are deep rooted, strong, wide and sturdy, capable of withstanding high winds and unpredictable weather. Trees that grow close are tall and whippy, reaching for the sky, giving each other strength in times of turbulence. If we are all different trees in the forest of life, what kind of tree are you?

Have you ever noticed how you feel when surrounded by different species of trees? As our protectors, healers and landscape markers, we are deeply derived from our relationship with trees, despite the possibility that this contemplation has never consciously been considered, specifically those from the bioregion of our heritage. Regardless of how far back we venture into myth and legend, trees always sit central to the stories. They challenge our modern-day beliefs that we sit removed from the natural ecosystem. These stories draw us back to kinship and remind us that our existence is intertwined with the natural world.

After her sister took her own life, Australian author and journalist Indira Naidoo centred her emotional journey back to good health around the roots of a Moreton Bay fig, which wrapped its branches and coiled its roots around her fragile state until she was able to breathe again.

Terry McCosker, who could be considered one of Australia's grandfathers of regenerative agriculture, finished presenting at a gathering by asking us all to 'listen to the trees'. What an intriguing idea, I thought, but how? A further conversation with him explained it quite simply: with our bodies. Knock on the trunk with your hand and feel the density of it; listen to the wind move through the leaves; hold a branch and feel the vibrations; observe the insect and bird life moving through the bark; kick fallen leaves on the ground and ponder their lifetime and the gift they are returning to the earth; breathe deeply under its canopy and be humbled by its size; and listen to its creaking movement and move with it.

Even without being consciously aware of it, Australians are connected to eucalypts while those from North-East USA are calmed by the sight of sugar maples, and Eastern Europeans are reassured by pines. These trees are visible markers that remind us of who we are and where we belong.

To plant a tree is to believe in tomorrow. My little brother challenged himself to plant as many trees as there are minutes in a day. When he created an update video for his YouTube followers, he said he 'planted them as real estate for anything but humans and as shade for people he will likely never meet'. It takes real foresight to plant a forest you will never see.

'It takes a wise man a lifetime to grow a tree and five minutes for a foolish man to cut it down.'

Unknown

Composting life

At the foot of a tree is well-composted earth. Unsexy and not much mentioned in everyday life (unless you're a market gardener), but what sits in the roots at the foot of this tree is a world so potent with life that despite our inability to see it with the naked eye, it forms the foundation of our existence.

To continue the analogy, different stages of our life can be like compost; a time where we take no longer used resources and actively discard them, letting them become part of the earth and allowing us to move into a time of grief for what we say goodbye to. The melding of the discarded has the chance to then become the fertiliser for the next phase of life we embark on. Which parts of ourselves, our system and relationships can be composted? Without the natural life and death cycle, there simply would not be balance. Mother Nature does not tolerate an imbalance; always rebalancing with acts such as fire, flood or drought.

52

Community conversations

'We each have two lives and the second life begins when we realise
we only have one.'

Confucius

When travelling through towns and villages in Australia and the US with my first book, *Futuresteading*, I was wrapped in community conversations that felt intimate, vulnerable and of that place.

Every conversation, while threaded with similar themes, moved within its own familiar language and localised culture. While my speaking style ensured no event was ever the same, the general flow had me talking through my backstory, my reason for wanting to Futurestead in the first place and some macro themes spreading across the western world that we can influence. Questions came from the audience then eventually, we'd all settle with each other, and I would return the questions back to the group. This is when the magic really happened. How could the individuals and the collective actions of this little village create a community that lived like tomorrow matters?

On following up these conversations I've been tickled to discover that many of the complex localised issues raised by individuals have been held by the group, who've worked together to find solutions.

One of the best ideas that has come to fruition is the yellow ribbon abundance share initiative. It goes a little like this. A little shop in town has placed timber boxes on the footpath for locals with an abundance of food to donate, allowing others easy access. On any given day these boxes offer lemons, quinces, walnuts, silverbeet, zucchini (always zuc), olives, grapes, seeds, oranges … the list goes on. For those who don't have the time or ability to pick and deliver, they simply take a yellow ribbon from the basket and tie it to their front gate with a little sign that says 'lemon tree backyard' or 'quince tree behind the shed'. The yellow ribbon is an open invitation for anyone who's eager to help themselves to an abundant tree or veggie patch. It spreads the love and vanquishes waste.

I'm told that since this kicked off, the town has become kinder, closer and better fed, with less waste and more sharing of jams, chutneys, pies and cakes.

Finding a new language

Ever wondered about the genesis of words and their relationship to each other? Words such as human, humane, humanity, humble and humility or socio, socialism and society. What about community and communication?

The linear way in which spoken and written communication influences us has had a profound impact on the way we've slowly but surely moved out of our bodies and stopped referencing our feelings, intuition and emotions. Instead, we've moved into a pattern of disassociated intellectualising. The trouble is, when we speak about our responses to things in this way, we can't help but act in the same way. As a result, we've moved away from our heart, gut and hands, and instead we're dominated by our head, where words are associated with progress, efficiency and outcomes.

If we examine the evolution of language while under the influence of the modern progress paradigm for just a tick, the way we explained our mentally fragile soldiers comes to mind. Before the turn of the century, we referred to them as having a 'soldier's heart' – it spoke to the visceral emotional state he was in. By the time World War I arrived, we described them as having 'shell shock' or 'battle fatigue'. This at least still referenced the reason for their mental state and still evoked a collective and emotional understanding. By World War II they had 'operational exhaustion' – no longer referencing their feelings or the state of their heartfelt way of being. At least it was still taking collective responsibility for their state. For the Vietnam War it became PTSD – removing emotion entirely, as well as removing collective responsibility and transferring the 'weakness' to the ownership of the individual, who is now labelled with a disorder.

With each battle, the terminology increased in syllables and slowly removed heart and emotion. Ultimately it loses all feeling and becomes clinical, easily assessed efficiently without emotion and not in the community but resting with the individual. The body slowly gets removed from it and it becomes non-human. It's a powerful example of how language has removed us from our ability to communicate anything that feels.

Where did the heart go? What happened to our feelings? Is this the fault of language or a more complex cultural reality that merely plays out publicly via the written and spoken word?

Moving beyond heroes

To create a new language in our modern world will require bravery to push against the prevalent hero narrative, which reduces our influences to so few.

We don't have time for heroes and none of us can create the necessary momentum on our own. We never have and we never will. Not even social media can perpetuate the message of one voice enough to negate the need of others in their movement. In many ways it's reassuring that no one person needs to carry the burden of the pickle we've landed in. We got here collectively, so collectivism is the way forward. Telling the stories of many is a powerful way to inspire, collectively action change and ensure those voices are heard. To dilute the single voices of those being endlessly perpetuated (mostly celebrities and high-profile politicians) we need to seek the stories of the unsung heroes in small, unknown places, without cameras and personal brands. When did 'personal brand' become a thing? We need to go looking in the crevices and crinkles of unexpected places and listen to the story of the people, not the hero.

Creating a non-written story

Given the limitation of words and our desire to reintroduce feelings back into our way of being, let's consider ways to build a story without using words alone.

We can create art, music, food, gatherings, rituals. All of these are profoundly important in the creation of a new story with relevance to all.

Performers can sing a song to 100 different people humble in the knowledge that it will speak to each of them in 100 different ways. Depending on the language and tone used, your words might evoke sadness or happiness at exactly the same point for whoever your audience is. Their reaction will be dependent on the sum of their lived experiences to date. We bring the entirety of our complexity to the table as we navigate each new experience every day. Using alternative mediums, which are open to interpretation and are not reductionist or minimising, gives us the opportunity to get comfortable with the idea of grey, rather than black and white. These new grey stories can be created collectively – publicly as equally as privately – and they can emerge as we need them to. They can adapt to hold and encourage a new narrative that is filled with emotion and feeling – even if it's not spoken or written.

Patterns influence the story

Everything is a construct – yep, we made it all up. How then do we make sense of it all and how do we find the storylines that resonate with us to urge continuation of our days with purpose? Patterns learned in infancy dictate the way we navigate life and continue to impact the way we interact, build relationships and tell stories. These stories began before any of us were even alive. They have been stitched into our very being AND they will be threaded through the lives of our children, children's children and however many generations are yet to come.

Just because our story plays into our daily patterns, internal monologue and ability to interact with others doesn't mean we can't change it. While doing this collectively is a greater challenge, the potency of rewriting language, narrative and expected outcomes might be one of the most profound things we can do for future generations.

I'm going to generalise a little here but stay with me ... When you're a kid, the common questions sound like: What do you want to be when you grow up? What subjects did you study? What was your year 12 mark?

As life continues it becomes: Which university are you going to? Which school did you attend? Which suburb do you live in? How much money will you earn if you train for that job?

Later again it sounds like: Where are you taking your holiday this year? When will you make partner? Where are your investments?

While there are threads of other storylines, collectively the general western world story we tell ourselves is focused on two things: status and wealth. Both are geared around growth and neither consider our deep need for belonging or connection to our ecological foundation. There's little room for the collective and a complete focus on 'progress'.

The investigation of separate stories started in post-war industrialised times and it was focused on manipulating and seducing us into thinking we could go it alone and no longer be part of each other's interdependent needs.

Stepping away from our colonised beliefs and actively building decolonised ways of being are going to take conscious effort to battle the pull back to what at first appears more convenient and less complicated. In reality the opposite is true.

There is little consideration given for the messages from our body and even if we offer a moment of contemplation, are we listening? It takes active listening to hear ourselves and we need to be careful to hear it truthfully without amplification of untruths or exaggerations. This can be a hard task given the white noise of modern media messaging. Did you know we can encounter up to 10,000 advertising messages in an average day? Replace that with a shot of self-assessment. No, really. Instead of absorbing another person's desire for you to consume something else, consider finding a quiet place and doing a body scan instead.

Reinstating AWE and WONDER

A solid dose of awe and wonder for the natural world brings our ecological reality front and centre. Packing a picnic, pitching a tent and stargazing begins this process, but creating an interdependent relationship really drives this home – growing food, caring for animals, building relationships through sit spots and intentional observation.

Awe as an emotion is close to other uncomfortable emotions, such as fear, and avoidance of our own mortality and humility, and the realisation that there is no separate mode of existence – our very lives are dependent on the lives of others whom we can have no control over. It's not enough to be delighted, amazed and intrigued by the beauty and function of the natural world. You need to be aware of your own transience and cognisant of our own insignificance in this huge and complex community of human and non-human beings. To go from being master of our domain to just another member of the big community is a very tough reality to reckon with, but reckon we must.

We need to relearn the art of walking together side-by-side, truth telling, honesty and vulnerability meshing to make the whole. Ancestral knowledge is in our DNA and the future of our children is on the line.

If we wish for this, the only way forward is to bravely face the regenerative relationships with our past. What if the work we're doing isn't about fixing? It's about dissolving what's been the norm, tells the truth, speaks from our hearts openly, is alive with vulnerability and has judgement checked at the door.

We can do all that is needed at scale on our land mass to return ecological vibrancy. We can do it simultaneously. We need to mirror our natural systems.

Ask the question: What makes it worth me being here for Mother Earth?

In this country we don't need to be poised for war, where we tussle between fight or flight. We don't need to be ready to kill. Yet this is the language pervasively pushing into mainstream narrative: war on waste, fight for a win, they were warriors. What if we changed our narrative to be collective, symbiotic, non-divisive and inclusive of nature.

HUDDLE —————— HOW?

Rewriting our story

Acknowledge your privilege and put it to use:
Everyone's reality is different, but most of us are
in positions of greater privilege than others in one
aspect or another. This privilege is the result of many
things. Regardless of how you came upon your
fortune, call it, look it squarely in the eye, thank it for
being bestowed on you, then seek a way to put it to
good use:

• Discuss it openly with your networks and encourage
  others to acknowledge their privileges.
• Identify where disadvantages exist in your world and
  use your voice to call them out.
• If your network is strong, seek their support for things
  that make a difference.
• If you can write, publicly speak or have a platform,
  use it with regularity for purpose and to create
  opportunities for those who are not so privileged.
• Be honest enough to check your biases and
  discomfort with things that don't 'sit right'. Check
  your internal monologue and be kind to yourself
  as you reframe your perspective.

Rewrite your language: Find forms other than spoken
and written words to create a new story. Consider art,
gardening, cooking, ritual or acts of nourishment as
part of your toolkit to build new storylines.

Realise your inter-relationships: Push beyond the
personal synthetic-invested world and move into a
living world with agency and awareness of the needs
of non-human beings. Only then can we realise our
position of privilege and experience a deep reckoning
with our lives being contingent on the health of other
systems, such as water, soil and air.

Pay attention to your context: Sometimes it's simply a
matter of context, time and place – right story/wrong
place or wrong story/right place.

Become tree/plant literate: Challenge yourself to
learn the names of the different trees/plants
around you.

Be in service to the collective: Ask, 'How am I in
service to the way we collectively rewrite our cultural
story?' and set yourself some goals to reiterate your
commitment and connectedness to the climate
action voice. Write to your local member; express
your opinions on social media platforms and be
proud to have your opinion – even if you get pushback
from followers; participate in local action groups;
and support local initiatives and businesses over
multinational ones.

Celebrate slow and simple: Use language and tell
stories about having less, shopping second-hand,
making gifts, holidaying locally. Normalise a slower,
gentler existence – rest is resistance.

**Tap into multigenerational knowledge of those
who came before us:** It's a potent way to garner
insight into how we can live in the world – unpacking
their story while simultaneously rewriting your own.
Perhaps you could ask your parents, grandparents or
great-grandparents these questions before they die:

• What was your first year of being a parent like?
• Are there any family secrets?
• What's your happiest memory of us as a family?
• How do you want to be remembered?
• What have been the best and worst parts of
  getting older?
• What would you do differently if you could?
• When have you changed your position on something
  and for what reason?

**May you find contentment when happiness isn't
an option.**

CREATING A NEW STORY

HUDDLE ACTIVITY

COLLECTIVE STORYBOOK CREATION

The only thing more powerful than story creation is doing it with others, and if you keep it lighthearted, it's really bloody fun!

Set the table, make a cake or two and invite your crew to a fireside or cosy lounge gathering for morning/afternoon tea or an early dessert. Provide small booklets for each guest and to kick off you'll need some butcher's paper for a little brainstorming.

To write a collective storybook with others is easier than it might seem, but you'll need a few foundations to get you started. This initial set-up will take 20–30 minutes.

Together, answer these questions:
• What is the genre?
• How long is each chapter? A good guide is to expect approximately 1000 words per person per hour of writing.
• Who are the main characters, what are their personalities and what are their relationships with each other? Aim for two to three primary characters and four to eight secondary characters.
• Where is it set?
• What happens to the characters and in what order? Divide these events into chapters – aim for one chapter per person. Give each chapter a name and allocate one to each guest.

Off you go! Each in your own little patch, creating your own chapter, adding as much or as little detail as you like, taking the characters in new directions and experiencing new things. Not too much sharing makes it more fun at the end, but just enough sharing makes for a boisterous afternoon.

Break up the process with cups of tea, glasses of wine, chocolate or cake and let the creation come to life from different hearts and minds.

The idea is not to take too long but to give people adequate time. If you are aiming for a frivolous and fun outcome, stick with an hour all up. If you have some genuine creatives who are eager to bring a beautiful masterpiece to life, allow at least two to three hours and really sink into each other's company and the task at hand.

At the end of the creative writing time, come back together to share each of your chapters. This part is exciting and always filled with anticipation as you hear the story unfold.

Getting the book printed with a copy for each of the authors is a beautiful way to cherish your joint story-writing efforts. Making it an annual affair will give you a beautiful range of books that tell more than just the story on the pages for your story writing huddle.

You might create a series!

HUDDLE

STORY

New narrative from Sweden to outback Australia

A desire for a new story is emerging in all corners of the globe – sometimes in unlikely places. We've all watched the Greta Thunberg climate crusade. It's more than just the story of a girl who cared. It's the saga of a new narrative, a call to action that transcended borders, generations and political ideologies. Greta ignited a flame that refused to be extinguished – a beacon reminding humanity that the power to change the world often rests in the hands of those who dare to speak, to act and to create a new story for a planet in need.

Her tale began with a solitary strike outside the Swedish Parliament, armed with nothing but a sign declaring, 'School strike for climate'. Her protest echoed through social media, capturing the hearts of a generation seeking a voice in an adult-dominated world. The simplicity of her storytelling – driven by raw honesty and a deep sense of responsibility – resonated across continents.

Her rallying cry, 'Fridays for Future', inspired a youth-led movement that was heard from the cobblestone streets of Stockholm to the bustling cities of Asia. It wasn't just about skipping school; it was a rebellion against the inertia that threatened the very future of the planet. Greta's narrative ignited a spark, empowering the youth to believe that their voices mattered and could shape the world.

Greta's storytelling extended beyond picket lines. Her speeches, delivered with a maturity beyond her years, reverberated through the halls of power. In the chambers of the United Nations, she addressed world leaders with a fervour that left no room for indifference. The impact was undeniable.

Greta became more than an activist; she evolved into a symbol of hope. Documentaries chronicled her journey and interviews dissected her message. Through her storytelling, she not only influenced policies but also seeped into the cultural fabric, challenging societal norms and encouraging a collective shift towards regeneration.

On a somewhat less public and global scale, another example of creating new stories played out in the heart of outback Australia. A community embarked on a unique journey to reclaim their narrative to ensure their stories weren't lost in the winds of change.

Embracing a mission to bridge cultural divides, this mostly First Nations community engaged a white artist to paint places of significance in a way that could resonate with the broader world – the 'white man's way'. These paintings weren't just strokes on canvas, they were conduits for storytelling, waiting to be translated into the 'black man's way' by local Elders.

This artistic endeavour held a profound purpose: to reconnect local Elders with the youth, who had their language banned during a 1990s education reform. It's a story of resilience against cultural erosion, of a community striving to preserve its identity, its culture and its lore.

Four murals of scale representing four different places of significance were created, enabling the local children to gather around, listen and learn. The Elders, armed with the narratives of their ancestors, spoke of the 'black man's way' – in their language, which had survived despite the attempts to silence it.

The children now found solace in the stories of their Elders. The paintings, born from a collaboration of cultures, became a testament to the resilience of narratives.

Against the backdrop of vast Australian landscapes and the urgency of global climate action, Greta's story and the humble yet significant efforts in the red dirt provide beautiful examples of how a narrative of interconnectedness has the power to shape not just local landscapes but the very essence of a global conversation.

Being human

The good news is that we are living, breathing, adaptive creatures who are immensely clever. The great news is that we can still rekindle our capabilities as custodial beings, creating harmonious pathways through story, art, health, challenge, head, heart, hands and gut. We need to trust that life knows what to do. Deep in our bones lies timeless ancestral knowledge, just waiting to be stirred. It's time to wake up so we can make the dash between the dates that matter while we're here and leave a legacy once we're not.

BEING HUMAN

Our political, financial and ecological polycrisis is no longer news, but the trouble is the tools we've used to maintain a semblance of order no longer cut the mustard. While we dream up increasingly complicated tech solutions, it's easy to overlook that the issues we face are fundamentally human issues. Within us, we possess the remarkable capacity for generosity, compassion and innovation, offering us the means to address these challenges. The limitations are not in our capabilities, but in our capacity to envision new possibilities.

Perhaps the real challenge is building a sense of communal agreement, creating an atmosphere where we can envision attainable goals, imagine optimal outcomes and instigate the beliefs, behaviours, strategies and actions required to actualise them. This shift in thinking fosters trustworthy relationships and authentic connections that provide fertile ground for transformation. Advancements in one area initiate restoration in another, healing individuals, systems and the collective. The feeling of confinement transitions into expansiveness, and scarcity transforms into abundance.

It's time to reorient towards uncharted territory. This idea of 'new ground' allows for the emergence of novel solutions that go beyond individuals and towards the collective. As complex but capable humans, we can do this.

'People travel to wonder
at the height of the mountains,
at the huge waves of the seas,
at the long course of the rivers,
at the vast compass of the ocean,
at the circular motion of the stars,
and yet they pass by themselves
without wondering.'

Saint Augustine

This was written in 399 AD. Even back then, Saint Augustine had a sense that humanity was in search of something more. Intriguing isn't it, given the wonder we are as mere humans? Even when we do nothing beyond simply being, we are indeed mysterious, multitudinous things. Complex, whole, interrelated, full of paradox, capable, fragile ... I'm going to make time to simply wonder a little more often. Will you join me? Because while my world is safe, filled with opportunity and full of privilege, the greatest privilege of being human is that we thrive when functioning as an interrelated organism. Individual humans, on the other hand, didn't survive. We survived as a collective. If banned by the tribe, we inevitably died. While we are currently functioning in a post-industrial reality, where individuals are enabled by excessive energy consumption, being autonomous is not aligned with the type of social animal we have evolved to be.

Our evolutionary roots are deeply intertwined with smaller, tight-knit groups. Communities were as small as thirty in the Stone Age, growing to around 100 during medieval times. This was only the 1400s, so relatively speaking, not so long ago. It wasn't until the early modern period that scaled agriculture and technological innovation enabled our villages to grow into the thousands, eventually resulting in cities once mineral wealth became easily accessible. The rise of mega populations and the capacity to flock together is a very recent way of being; post World War II when,

as comedian Barry Humphries quipped, we created 'the age of Laminex. Everything was covered in it, including our minds'. His statement can be stretched to mean significantly more than a mere coating of plastic on things; it is referencing our inability to think critically and in cohesion with one another without becoming homogenised. It's a lesson we should ponder more.

Anonymity is a modern phenomenon. Prior to this our evolution kept each of us held to account through the binds of mutual aid and reciprocity for the community that kept us safe, fed and unified. The potential for authentic connections, effective communication and a shared sense of purpose flourished.

In centralised communities, the sheer scale of population can lead to a sense of disconnection from fellow human beings. The anonymity and fast-paced nature of city life can create feelings of isolation,

disengagement and a lack of communal support, not to mention the role this centralisation has on resources and infrastructure.

Megapopulations require extensive systems for housing, medical support, education, transportation and resource distribution, often leading to environmental degradation and social inequalities. The demands placed on centralised systems can result in inefficiencies, increased pollution and disconnection from the natural world.

By contrast, when we intentionally nurture smaller-scale communities, we rekindle the power of authentic connection, effective communication and shared purpose – akin to the way we functioned evolutionarily. Human potential thrives within close-knit communities that value individual contributions and cherish the interconnectedness of all.

Rollo May, author of *Man's Search for Himself*, wrote, 'Many people suffer from the fear of finding oneself alone, so they don't find themselves at all.' This is really where it begins.

Humans are a custodial species

What does this mean? We were given the breathtaking ability to use our heads, hearts and hands all at once for a reason. We're here, in all our plate-spinning, idea-juggling, complexity-holding glory, to *serve life* – kind of like wizened park rangers who keep an eye on things and intervene only when necessary.

The ultimate value in using not one, but all three of these 'tools' (head, heart, hands) lies in the holistic and balanced development of humankind. When we engage our intellect (head), empathy and compassion (heart) and active involvement (hands), we unlock immense potential for personal growth, societal progress and the betterment of our collective culture.

66

Our head isn't just a pretty face, it's the seat of cognitive awareness, critical thinking and problem-solving. Our bulging craniums/intellectual capacity enables us to innovate, invent and dream up solutions to complex challenges. We're able to understand and analyse the world around us, fostering scientific advancements, technological breakthroughs and intellectual pursuits, which enhance our quality of life.

Simultaneously, our hearts connect us to emotional intelligence and empathy. We can understand and share the experiences, feelings and perspectives of others. Through empathy and compassion, we build bridges of connection, promote social harmony and nurture inclusive communities. Hearts drive us to care for one another, advocate for justice and equality, and work towards a more compassionate and interconnected society.

Lastly, our hands take action, actively participating and creating tangible impact. They love plunging into the earth and playing in the garden, sculpting clay and comforting people. They represent the practical application of our skills, talents and efforts to effect positive change – even if we're left with dirty fingernails. Through hands-on action, we contribute to our communities, protect the fragile and shape the world around us.

Custodial humans exist in reciprocity, engaging in a dynamic and interconnected web of give/give relationships, where individuals – both human and ecological – contribute to and receive mutual benefits. Tyson Yunkaporta, author of *Sand Talk* and *Right Story, Wrong Story*, outlined why this is much richer than a give/take relationship. He said that what's yours is ours and what's mine is ours; there's no point scoring, no returning of favours, no keeping track of whose turn it is – just an overarching sense that in this community, what is needed will be provided by the entire community to ensure everyone has enough, including the MOTHER, who holds the lot. A life of reciprocity recognises that actions have ripple effects and that each contribution plays a role in sustaining the overall system. Those old-fashioned give/take relationships? Let's go with Tyson's reimagining: it's all about give/give.

In an ecosystem of reciprocity, every entity – whether it's you and me or an organisation – actively seeks opportunities to contribute and share their skills, knowledge and resources. They understand that by doing so, they not only support others but also create an environment where their own needs are more likely to be met. This goes beyond the transactional and embraces a broader perspective of interconnectedness and interdependence. Nature gives us a fine example in the symbiotic relationships that exist between mycorrhizal fungi and tree roots. The fungi help the tree forage nutrients that it could not otherwise get for itself, and the tree provides carbohydrates to the fungus that it can't produce through the process of photosynthesis. Together they coexist for mutual benefit. Not limited to immediate exchanges or linear relationships, this extends to a network of connections, where the benefits flow in multiple directions and can even amplify over time. Each contribution becomes a building block for the growth and resilience of the entire ecosystem.

Perhaps you can glean examples from your own life of indirect reciprocity and an unexpected flow of gifts. Maybe you give in one way – say, volunteering at an animal shelter – and rather than 'gifts' flowing equally and directly back to you from that source, you find meals on your doorstep when you're sick, word-of-mouth work opportunities or a surprise windfall of second-hand clothes from a posh mate. Existing in reciprocity or a gift-style economy takes a bit of practice and trust because it's rarely the tit-for-tat we're used to in our transactional world.

I know this all sounds idealistic, and our modern culture requires a mindset of abundance rather than scarcity. It encourages cooperation, collaboration and the sharing of knowledge and resources for the greater good. It fosters a sense of community and collective responsibility, where individuals actively seek to uplift and support one another, because we're all part of the whole organism that benefits. It's a recognition that we are all interconnected and that by working together, we can achieve more than we could individually.

Go on, hug it up!

A legend, who goes by the name Pauly, is a jack-of-all-trades lover of living who taught me that while the average hug lasts three seconds, we have a superpower in our hands and arms that can be activated simply by taking a little longer with the squeeze. When a real-deal hug lasts at least twenty seconds there's a therapeutic effect on the body and mind. Our body releases the hormone oxytocin, also known as the love hormone. With this surging in our system, we are calmer, feel safer and are more relaxed. This free-to-give dosage is available every time we have someone in our arms. When I held my newborn niece for hours on end at my dad's exhibition, rather than feeling lactic in my arms, I genuinely felt full in my heart.

Us humans can't hug enough – research tells us that we need four hugs a day for survival, eight for maintenance and twelve for growth. Good advice to onboard and do our best to reinstate physical tactility into our daily lives. As my gran says, 'You can hardly imagine when you are in the throes of raising your children and grandchildren, when you have children attached to your skirt more often than you don't, that a time will come in your life that days and days will pass without being touched in any way at all. Cherish the busy and affectionate times. They don't last forever.'

Co-regulation

One of my first jobs out of uni was an intense, seasonal job in a remote location. We worked long hours, seven days a week and rarely left the village. I was out of my depth and I was as lonely as heck.

The intensity of the place was amplified by a boss who was renowned for their unpredictable moodiness. I tiptoed on eggshells and despite building an arsenal to sidestep or placate, I spent a lot of time in tears following regular growling. I'd leave the main office and traipse to the machinery shed. Filled with lads smelling of grease and diesel, it was where I'd curl up on the grubby couch and listen uninterrupted to the shed shenanigans. Their boss knew without explanation that I needed a place to be without answering questions. Despite the camaraderie and antics, the energy of the place was calming. A place to take a figurative deep breath and build strength before returning.

I learned much from this experience of finding an unlikely bolthole with humans who perhaps didn't even realise their part in my salvation. I learned the potential of co-regulation.

Co-regulation is fundamental for human connection and emotional wellbeing. It plays on the reciprocal, interactive process in which individuals regulate each other's emotions and create a sense of safety, trust and understanding in relationships. It recognises that we are not meant to navigate our emotions and experiences alone, but rather, in the company of others who can provide support and empathy. When we engage in co-regulation, we attune to the emotional states of those around us, offering comfort, validation and empathy.

Not only to be used during times of distress, it can reflect a way of being, just like the villages in Guatemala renowned for making rugs or in the highlands of Vietnam where they weave fabric, or indeed indigenous villages that still function mostly untouched by the modern world. They enjoy co-regulation through artistic production and co-creation. They collectively create beautiful pieces of art, silver or basketry using skills passed between generations, with the masters gently guiding the learning generation to one day take their place. These skills have been learned painstakingly over time with patience and persistence, side-by-side in a state of co-regulation.

You don't need a machinery shed or a village of skilled craftsmen to access the rewards of co-regulation. Now I walk in the morning, often in the dark, with a different mate most days. We voice our internal monologue, knowing the walking space is sacred and safe. A seven-second hug with someone you love can impact your heart rate. The simple act of placing your hand on each other's heart before synchronising your breath can settle even the most heightened state of anxiety.

Co-regulation helps us feel seen, heard and understood, reducing feelings of isolation and promoting a sense of belonging. It's especially vital during times of stress, trauma or uncertainty as it allows us to share our burdens and co-create resilience. By fostering co-regulation, we build stronger connections, enhance our emotional wellbeing and create an environment where everyone feels valued and supported.

69

Moving at human speed

Have you ever sat on the side of a road and marvelled at the speed of the humans whipping past in cars or woken up after a flight in a different country to the one you were in the day before? Discombobulating, isn't it? I had this thought when I was foraging for peaches by a road one midsummer day. I was so struck by the unnatural speed that the humans were travelling at that I vowed to intentionally slow at every opportunity to counteract the rest of the western world.

We were never designed to move at such speeds and in acknowledging our evolution, it's worth questioning whether this pace of existence is contributing to our heightened states of anxiety, poor mental health and cultural demise. The faster the pace, the more we desire, like a rat moving faster and faster on a wheel with every new invention – designed to make life easier.

The simple act of slowing down and embracing the rhythm of our own footsteps holds a unique allure. Moving at human speed allows us to reconnect with our surroundings and savour the subtle nuances of our environment, which would otherwise go unnoticed. It grants us the opportunity to observe the intricate beauty of a circling bird, a waft on the wind, patterns in bark, birdsong or swelling buds. By deliberately choosing to move at a pace dictated by our own bodies, we become more attuned to our own thoughts and emotions, fostering a deeper sense of self-awareness. This deliberate deceleration invites us to engage with the world in a more meaningful way, enabling us to engage in conversations, appreciate the company of loved ones and savour the flavours of a carefully prepared meal. In an age when efficiency and productivity are often prioritised, moving at human speed becomes an act of rebellion, a deliberate step towards reclaiming our humanity and reconnecting with the essence of our existence.

Re-rooting where we belong

Imagine we created localised and unified efforts where we are rooted. Replanting native flora species, protecting fauna, minimising travel, adventuring in our own backyards and supporting local businesses.

Being human is filled with paradox. Just because we can, doesn't mean we should IF it's to the detriment of our immediate sphere. If we all operate in such a way then the swirls of hope, reciprocity and mutual aid will keep our energy harnessed in the way it was since time immemorial.

If our roots are deep – entwined with the mycelium of mutual obligation, multigenerational memory, connection to country, intuitive understanding of local flora and fauna – we can be boldened as a species to be our strongest selves. With deep foundations, our branches can reach high into the sky to support others, feed many, seek sunlight, provide shade and build culture within its canopy. However, in a world where western hedonists operate with entitlement to travel far, free of obligation and with little care for the true cost of their actions, being forced to contemplate another reality is hardly palatable.

HUDDLE _____ HOW?

Go slow

Try intentional walking. Deliberately wind your movements right back to a pace that is the slowest you can manage – in line with your breath and moving without a destination in mind. Feel your senses heighten with each step.

Building relationships

In light of all of this, one fundamental truth emerges: the need to build deep and meaningful relationships.

Easy! Actually, it's possibly the most complex challenge we face. Its realisation requires a profound transformation that demands immense patience, collaboration and non-linear approaches to integration. Above all, it calls for a seismic shift in the western mindset, which has grown accustomed to an existence that expects an uncompromised life, feels entitled and seeks relentless convenience.

It demands a commitment to nurturing connections that transcend the superficial and delves deeply into our humanness. As David Fleming beautifully wrote in *Surviving the Future*, 'At present, culture is decorative rather than structural; although it may lift the spirits.'

Like any commitment, it takes time and focus. It requires setting aside the distractions and busyness of modern life to truly engage with others, actively listen and seek understanding beyond surface-level interactions. It calls for empathy, compassion and a willingness to be vulnerable and receptive to the experiences and perspectives of others.

Collaboration is the cornerstone of relationship building when huddling. It invites individuals to come together, transcending traditional hierarchies, to embrace diverse skill sets, knowledge and experiences. It recognises that the collective wisdom of a group is far greater than the sum of its parts. It fosters synergy, innovation and the co-creation of solutions that address the complex challenges we face as a global community. It requires setting aside the distractions and busyness of modern life to truly engage with others, to actively listen and to seek understanding beyond surface-level interactions. It calls for empathy, compassion and a willingness to be vulnerable and receptive to the experiences and perspectives of others.

Building meaningful relationships will require us to embrace non-linear approaches to integration. The path is a labyrinth of twists, turns and unexpected encounters, which require open-mindedness, adaptability and a willingness to step outside our comfort zones. Non-linear integration challenges the notion of rigid structures and linear progress. It encourages exploration, experimentation and the integration of diverse ideas and practices to create new pathways forward.

Yet, at the core of relationship building lies the urgent need to address the western mindset that has become entrenched in a culture of uncompromising entitlement and convenience. This mindset, while providing certain comforts, has led to disconnection, isolation and a lack of empathy. The time to challenge it has arrived – to advocate for a return to our innate interconnectedness, a reverence for the natural world and a deep understanding of the interdependence between all living beings.

'Because these wings are no longer wings to fly
But merely vans to beat the air'
T.S. Eliot, 'Ash Wednesday'

Evolving storylines for different stages of life

Author Erskine Caldwell believed that slowing, respect and diversity are the greatest challenges being faced by humanity. Renowned climate scientist Gus Speth has been quoted saying, 'I used to think the top environmental problems were biodiversity loss, ecosystem collapse and climate change. I thought that with thirty years of good science we could address those problems, but I was wrong. The top environmental problems are selfishness, greed and apathy ... To deal with those issues we need a spiritual and cultural transformation – and we scientists do not know how to do that.'

In an early *Futuresteading* interview with Tricia Hogbin, we addressed these challenges and unpacked where to begin for this cultural transformation. She shared the four seasons theory as a way to rewire our collective and individual responsibilities. In short, the four seasons theory is an acceptance that each of us is an individual who forms a small part of the whole, and that as our life passes, we need to evolve and so too will the contribution we make. Women experience their lifetimes as the Maiden, Mother, Maghre and Krohn.

Spring as a maiden until her mid-twenties, embodying renewal and growth, symbolises the beauty of new beginnings. She carries the essence of rejuvenation, bringing warmth and positivity. Just as spring breathes life into the world after winter's dormancy, the Spring Maiden inspires change, embraces transformation and fosters a sense of hope and vitality.

Summer as a mother until her mid-forties – regardless of whether she bears children – is a time for embodying the warmth and nurturing energy of the sun-kissed season. The Summer Mother radiates love and provides comfort. She creates a familial atmosphere filled with joy, like the carefree days of summer. Leading with kindness, she cultivates a sense of belonging and security. The Summer Mother is a beacon of strength, offering shade in times of adversity and fostering an environment where love, like the summer sun, shines brightly.

Autumn as a maghre until her mid-sixties, embraces the rich change with grace and wisdom. Like the falling leaves, an Autumn Maghre understands the beauty in letting go, allowing space for transformation and renewal. This persona symbolises resilience and the ability to navigate life's transitions. Just as autumn leaves create a mosaic of colours, she weaves experiences into a rich narrative of lessons, celebrating the bittersweet beauty of life's cycles. She finds strength in acceptance and inspires others to appreciate their own evolving chapters.

Winter as a khron stands resilient amid stillness and introspection. She brings the beauty of solitude and a calming hush. She recognises this as a time to turn inward and let go. Symbolising endurance, she finds strength in the quiet moments, mirroring the stoic presence of snow-covered landscapes. A Winter khron navigates the cold with grace, understanding that beneath the surface of stillness, there exists a profound depth of wisdom and potential for rebirth. She acknowledges that the natural end of a lifetime is near, inspiring others to find peace in the acceptance of life's cyclical nature and the gentle release that comes with winter's embrace.

While these descriptions might not resonate with everyone, part of being human is to face the reality of being on a shared trajectory from the moment we are born. Some paths are longer, some shorter, but we are never the same, decade to decade. We grow older, our minds mature and our bodies change. Our contribution to others evolves and with each year we move past the bell curve that takes us from looking up and out, with influences from outside, to seeing and accepting our own mortality, and having enough lived experience to seek guidance from within.

HUDDLE ACTIVITY

COME TO YOUR SENSES

Ever received this piece of advice? I recall something similar coming from my mother's and grandmother's mouths frequently.

In modern days it was used to snap us into a state of efficient practicality. But its origins were steeped in faith that our innate human capability will look after us. It takes us back to the five tools in our arsenal, no matter what the situation. Our sight, smell, touch, taste and hearing. These senses orient us in our surroundings and let us decide what to do next. If we listen to our bodies, there are whisperings of advice well suited to our needs as humans. Are we in danger? Do we need company? Are we underdressed? Are we witnessing something of magnitude? Will that food nourish or poison?

The uttering of this worldly advice now prompts me to close my eyes, take a deep breath and feel what it is my body is telling me. I spread the fingers of one hand and I run the pointer finger on my other hand along one finger at a time, simultaneously taking a deep breath as I tune into each sense.

Breathe in. Can you hear what's in your immediate surrounds? What's out on the edges? Is there a repeating sound? What's become white noise and what's still sharp and cutting through? Breathe out.

With the tracing of each finger, move to a new sense.

It only takes a few minutes. At the end, bring your hands together and check in with how your body feels as a result of tapping into an awareness of the world around you. Do you feel settled and relaxed or anxious and uptight? Is your heart still or racing? Is your breath deep or short?

While writing this book I attended the Purpose Conference in Sydney. Feeling somewhat overstimulated, I found a quiet corner to 'come to my senses'. When I opened my eyes, they were met by a young woman and we struck up a conversation. She, of course, asked what I had been doing and understood immediately by detailing her sense of captivity.

'I often wonder if we are much like zoo animals existing in captivity,' she said. 'I've been living in the city for the majority of my life, but more and more it feels like I need to get out. I'm currently living under a flight path and as a result, I often have a burgeoning headache, my sleep is disturbed and I'm beginning to behave in a way that doesn't feel true to who I am.'

She went on to tell me that researchers observing animal behaviour in zoos reported traits that are categorically never seen in the wild. It made us both ponder whether that was in fact, what our urbanised existence was doing to us – existing under flight paths, near train lines or noisy roads, surrounded by wi-fi, with neon lights and moving billboards screaming at us relentlessly. Our bodies respond to this in ways that are a long way from our evolutionary path and the way we would if we were in nature.

The result of an existence in captivity is a slow and steady erosion of our humanness. It begs the question of what superpowers we each have when we're in nature that make us vulnerable when in captivity and how we might combat this.

74

Escaping captivity?

Ideologically, we can all imagine life in smaller rural villages away from the churn of the big smoke. In reality, we are increasingly urbanised, with more than half the world's population living in cities and a predicted seven out of ten of us expected to be city dwelling by 2050.

So, we need to find ways to escape and reconnect with our animus states. We need to find a way to do this from the places we call home. How?

• **Go out:** 'When in doubt, go out' is advice that never fails. With bare feet and a clear calendar – even fifteen minutes – you can recalibrate with sun on your skin, dirt underfoot – bare feet essential (even a grass nature strip will work).

• **The power of sound and movement:** Sing and move like no-one's listening or watching. Hum if you're too self-conscious. Play music that takes your head and heart to other places and makes your body want to move. Allow the vibrations and rhythms to awaken your emotions, elevate your mood and really get into your own skin.

• **Moon watch:** Sync your body with the phases of the moon and observe how you behave and feel.

• **Morning sunrise salute:** Build a daily ritual of watching the sun creep into its new day.

Making the dash between the dots matter

That innocuous dash between two very important dates in every human's life says nothing but everything all at the same time. Without using a single letter, it represents our entire lifetime and serves as a reminder that our existence is not merely defined by the moments of birth and death, but by the experiences, contributions and impact we make during that dash.

We are mortal beings and in order to embrace the living, we need to get comfortable with the inevitability of death. There has been a shift towards an existence that defies the reality of death – not only for humans but for all living beings and the natural world. We are so busy in the churn of the present that we have limited capability to create a worthwhile, connected future. The idea of facing our own mortality has long been shoved into the dark corners of places we are unwilling to go. Facing this grief and embracing the reality that life must come to an end is a cycle that has been evolving since the beginning of time. It will continue to be, irrespective of whether we use face cream and drink water with lemon in it. This phenomenon is evident in various aspects of our lives and society, leading to a disconnect from the inherent cycles of life and the fragility of existence.

One of the key manifestations of this defiance of death is the cultural emphasis on youth and the fear of ageing. We glorify youthfulness, perpetuating the idea that staying young and avoiding the natural process of ageing is the ultimate goal. The result is an aversion to acknowledging and accepting the inevitability of ageing and the natural progression towards the end of life.

An endless obsession with youthfulness is not only fraught with unattainable hope, but it undermines the value of growing old and it removes the value placed on our elders.

In this modern western world we distance individuals from the cycles of the natural world. These cycles have long been the tool to repeatedly remind us that there is always a beginning, a middle and an end for all things, seasons, years, stories, lifetimes of anything living, including humans.

The dominant paradigm of industrialisation and urbanisation has created an environment where many people are disconnected from the rhythms of nature. With the rise of urban living, concrete jungles replace literal ones, and many people find themselves disconnected from the processes of birth, growth, decay and death – intrinsic to our existence.

This defiance of death can be witnessed in the aversion towards discussions and rituals surrounding death and dying. Death is often viewed as a taboo subject, pushed aside and shielded from daily conversations. The focus on preserving life at all costs and a general avoidance of confronting mortality contribute to a collective discomfort and fear surrounding the subject of death. Avoidance of normalising an inevitable outcome has slowly eroded our ability to navigate grief, cope with loss and engage in meaningful conversations about the end of life.

By denying and avoiding the realities of death and the cycles of life, western culture breeds a sense of anti-fragility, an illusion of invincibility and a detachment from the profound interconnectedness of all living beings. This denial prevents us from fully embracing the beauty, richness and transformative power of the life cycle.

To counteract this, it is crucial to reframe our relationship with death and the cycles of life. Embracing the reality of death can lead to a greater appreciation for the present moment, a sense of gratitude for the time we have and a celebration of the interconnectedness of all life forms. Ultimately, this shift can lead to a more compassionate, mindful and ecologically conscious way of living.

In recent years I've had two friends lose their battle with mortality. Both before their time, with the unanswered question of why? Both happened quickly, leaving little time to reach acceptance and process their own grief, let alone that of their kinfolk. Their deaths were similar in so many ways but so vastly different in others.

One was shrouded in secrecy and shame, without opportunity to ask questions, hold her in person and say goodbye with open grief. The doors were closed and those who loved her didn't have access. It was heart wrenching, confusing and the loyalties of those who were close were tested because we couldn't share in our grieving, as privacy was so closely guarded.

The other openly shared her day-to-day experience of dying. She engaged a death doula and together they hosted a 'living wake' to celebrate her life with those she loved. While still living, she participated in her own goodbye.

These two incredible women managed their final weeks earthside in a way that only they knew how. Neither approach could be deemed better or worse, right or wrong. As a sideline participant however, the goodbye that was more easily accepted was the one that allowed her people to openly share their grief and hold her at this time of immense vulnerability. It was confronting, yes. Filled with plenty of rawness not often shared so publicly, but it allowed time for acceptance, celebration and ultimately, a togetherness that, once she was gone, continued to hold each of us. The huddle holds us through death. While still alive we can consciously live with intention, purpose and a commitment to making a positive difference. We can ensure that the dash between our start date and end date carries significance. It becomes a testament to a life well lived, marked by personal growth, meaningful connections and a lasting impact on the world we'll inevitably leave behind.

Homogeneity

Despite mainstream narrative leading us to believe we are morphing into a species of same-same, we actually wouldn't survive by becoming homogenous. Without doubt we are attracted to like-mindedness. However, much of this familiarity sits within our values and beliefs, as much as the way we look and our lived/shared experiences.

While at a conference about reconnection, I got to chatting with Rob, a wizened mentor I rarely spent time with. We skipped through a conversation about the need to avoid homogeneity, and he shared a very modern-world analogy about how we are all different by design. 'We cannot be the same as there are too many variations to the necessities that need doing,' he said. 'Based on this alone, it stands to reason that we each have different skills, interest areas and an ability to offer something unique to the community we are operating in. Some of us are trains, some are buses, others are planes and even still some of us are sails.'

Trains are those of us who are linear thinkers. We aim for the destination in mind and stay on track until we reach the end. We get on and get off. We have no chance of taking an unexpected turn.

Of buses he said, 'They can go anywhere, but the decision as to where the bus will turn is made by everyone as a team. These folk don't like autocratic leadership and they feel most comfortable when they have other like-minded folk by their side, deciding on the direction together.'

Planes are the easiest to explain. They are the visionaries who need a good view from above to get their ideas flowing and the big picture bolting together in a sensible way. They don't seek the details as these are small features, but they do like to see how all the pieces will come together in order to deliver something worthwhile.

'What about the sails?' I asked.

'These are interesting because they go as a crew when the wind is blowing. Working side-by-side, they make great progress in fits and spurts. When the wind stops, they need to work together to tack to the next breeze.' I immediately thought of many friends who have set up themselves as project contractors, going in, rising to the challenge with a crew of others just like them, getting to the end of the project, then taking big blocks of time away.

Having managed bustling seasons of farm volunteers from our kitchen table for years, I recalled exactly how our different ways of approaching everything – from irrigation to preserving fruit, sowing seeds and mulching trees – was navigated depending on who we had living with us at the time. We've observed over the years that when new volunteers arrive, it takes us about ten days to settle into a rhythm as a cohesive work crew. Much of this time is spent figuring out how we operate cohesively as trains, buses, planes and sails in a group dynamic and finding ways for all our skills to be harnessed.

When the dynamic is in flow, each person brings a specific energy, and it fits like Lego with all the other pieces. When a singular person is missing – even when the group is large – you can really feel the dynamic change.

Thankfully, all of us are different; not just our gender, but the way we think, behave, make decisions and interact with others around us. Our differences, while grating at times, have always kept us safe in equal measure with our similarities. Collective action is powerful. Avoidance of homogenising into the churn of capitalism is an important step in reframing our collective capability to retain the commons within a community that has room for diversity.

Simply put, huddles create a space where others are enabled to be the strongest version of themselves.

HUDDLE ACTIVITY

EPHEMERAL CREATIVITY
CATCH-UPS

The point of this activity is to remind your huddle that in fact all of us are creative. It's part of being human, but the way in which it's expressed by each of us differs. Thankfully.

Invite your huddle to a day of purposeless creativity. Encourage them to bring paper, paints, knitting needles, wool, clay, fabric, card, stamps, scissors, shapes, leaves, bark, pinecones, wax ... and get creative with your comrades.

Encourage expression to flourish and the senses to come alive by having little reason to partake in the activity itself. No-one will sell or gift their creation and the activity isn't a one-size-fits-all, so no-one is comparing. It's amazing how much more creative you can be when there's no pressure to deliver something. Enjoy the tactile textures, colours and materials; ask each other for ideas and help if experience exists in the group with particular skills.

To kick you off, try paper mandala colouring, natural material 'nests', knitted wool or a group mural. The only rule is that everyone will make something. There's no expectation for the outcome but some may decide they want to hold onto their creation. Others may decide the process was lovely and they're happy to burn it, float it, unpick it. The pleasure is in the doing, co-regulation and time for unbridled thought!

CREATIVE REAWAKENING MANDALA

'Creative? Who, me?' How many of us have uttered these words, protesting against the idea that we are in any way creative, because we can't draw like Leonardo da Vinci or paint like Frida Kahlo?

Wherever you are on the scale of creative comfort, the truth is we're all creative beings and embracing this is a boon for both you and your community. Creativity helps us return to the senses, reconnect with play, rekindle lateral thinking and remember that we are creatures who can make (good) shit happen.

Bring your huddle together and set aside a few hours to create a nature mandala!

This non-permanent piece of art is usually circular or oval, made from found materials like leaves, petals, flowers, rocks, sticks, shells or other wild debris.

Start with everyone wandering with a bag or basket to collect things from the natural world.

Create the mandala on the earth or the floor; wherever works for you. Start from the centre and move outwards, adding objects in patterns.

You don't need to discuss what to put where or how it's going to look – simply add intuitively, working in and around the others in your huddle.

Eventually you'll get a sense that the mandala is finished; everyone stepping back to admire their beautiful, organic and collective creation that's entirely compostable.

Nature mandalas offer so many lessons, especially when they're co-created. These unplanned works of art teach emergence; how something wonderful can arise seemingly out of thin air. There's an intelligence with the huddle that doesn't need words to work. We all have an eye for patterns, relationships (between the materials and between each other) and design. The impermanence of this is something to be celebrated.

Easy is hard!

I read a quote by James Clear, author of *Atomic Habits*: 'Strangely, life gets harder when you try to make it easy. Exercising is hard, but never moving makes life harder. Uncomfortable conversations are hard, but avoiding every conflict is harder. Mastering your craft is hard, but having no skills is harder. Easy has a cost.'

This feels intuitively relatable, and it turns out there's a region of the brain called the anterior mid-cingulate cortex, located in the frontal lobe, which plays a crucial role in various cognitive and emotional functions. It contributes to the integration of information related to pain, emotions and decision-making. It helps regulate and adjust behaviour. It takes care of physiological responses, such as heart rate, and manages stress. It's also responsible for processing physical and emotional pain. It plays a role in the perception and evaluation of pain, conflict resolution, attention and focus. This part of the brain processes the things that are hard. Not surprisingly, if we don't use it, it shrivels up and loses its capability to function. Understanding the functions of the anterior mid-cingulate cortex is an active area of research. It feels timely to bring science to the table where it can meet our intuition.

The DIS-age

We have entered the dis-age. Dis-ease, dis-illusionment, dis-satisfaction, dis-content, dis-claimers, dis-information ...

The prefix 'dis' comes from Latin and originally meant 'apart'. Now, we use it to mean 'the opposite or reverse of'. We have the discombobulating honour of being alive at a time of unfathomable connection thanks to technology. Yet these same platforms have systematically deleted the relational threads and replaced them with commoditised attention-sucking tentacles – screens, apps and 'smart' everything.

Artificial intelligence (AI) tools are gaining momentum with millions of users globally – and how many more by the time this paragraph is published? There's not a game nor device that doesn't claim to 'connect and improve your existence'. But do they really?

In reality, we're experiencing a global pandemic of loneliness. You can have twenty active chats in your pocket and no true friends. Despite its techy-cleverness, online friendships lack the depth, tactility and shared purpose your old village soul yearns for.

Even if we identify as 'introverted', humans aren't designed to fly solo – that's simply not how you survive in the tribe.

In the same way, we're maladapted for ease and convenience – the very things our modern world reaches for. To truly thrive, we need regular and healthy doses of challenge, purpose, ceremony and shared bonding. Does this ring true for you?

I was pleased to find a silver lining to this story. 'Dis' in Scandinavian mythology refers to female deities associated with fertility. Time to water those Scandi language seeds and grow something positive from all this dis-stress.

HUDDLE _____ *HOW?*

Partake in the non-monetary economy: Make a list of all the things in your life that are not part of the financial system but which make up a valued part of your life. Having a friend pick up your kids from school, tool-sharing, abundance-swapping, a shared newspaper subscription, a gate between houses.

The wonder of being human
Shove the abstractions of an industrial world aside and tap back into your most uncompromised animus state.

Immerse yourself back into the natural world: Put down that screen and go outside. Reignite awe and wonder at the simplest of things: inspiring landscapes, patterns made by the wind in the grass, early morning birdsong, drifting scents from new blooms, dew on the grass. Remember you're not in control or superior to any of it. Our relationship is interconnected and symbiotic.

Create an end-of-life plan: Normalising the reality that we all die is a big step. Create a will openly with those in your life, discuss your post-death wishes and even consider planning your own funeral.

Accept grey: If you think life is black and white then you are not looking closely enough. Check yourself when making statements or internal chatter that forms definitive and divisive judgements.

Feast, mindfully: When eating, take your time and relish each morsel deliberately, as if time were suspended. Explore different flavours, use different foods, cook in different ways. Let the act of mindful eating become a sacred ritual.

Face your mortality: As with all living things, it's inevitable that you too will come to an end. Make peace with this as a true and necessary reality for all of us.

Let REST be okay: Despite what the modern world tells us, the point of rest is NOT to get ready for work. Work exists so we get to luxuriate in rest.

82

Drop the act: We don't need to be limited by the idea of being 'professional'. We can and should be human first and foremost.

Let go: Actively let go of the things that hold you in hard, heavy, preoccupied places. Name it to tame it! At the end of the week, say out loud the things that are gripping you.

Listen deeply: Authentic listening is perhaps the most significant gift we can offer one another. A group where members truly listen to each other becomes a genuine community. Knowing one's voice will be heard liberates people to be creative and genuine.

Prioritise trust: Engendering trust through reliability, deep listening, collaboration and compromise builds a foundation that allows for clarity and calmness. In turn this fosters productive group dynamics.

Embrace uncertainty: While uncertainty can be easy to shun – favouring situations that seem to have all the answers – uncertainty creates the ideal conditions for learning to work with others and unlocking ideas from new paradigms.

Take your time: Assign time to thinking and take a think week. Be somewhere quiet and have minimal plans, eat good food, drink plenty of water and move your body. Limit screens and be happy to let your mind wander in all the directions it fancies.

Learn your love language: You might have a different preference to those in your huddle, but that's not to say you can't make it work.

Experiential learning: True understanding is most profound when individuals arrive at their own 'knowing' through firsthand experience. This form of learning is also a precursor to meaningful change.

Egalitarianism: A level playing field aims to balance power dynamics, preventing disenfranchisement for those at the bottom and reducing isolation for those at the top. By equalising power, it empowers individuals who are usually marginalised, eases the burden on leaders and encourages innovative solutions beyond current structures.

Ikigai: This is a Japanese approach to creating a life of balance so you can live authentically to yourself. It's a beautiful and simple way of defining parameters in your life.

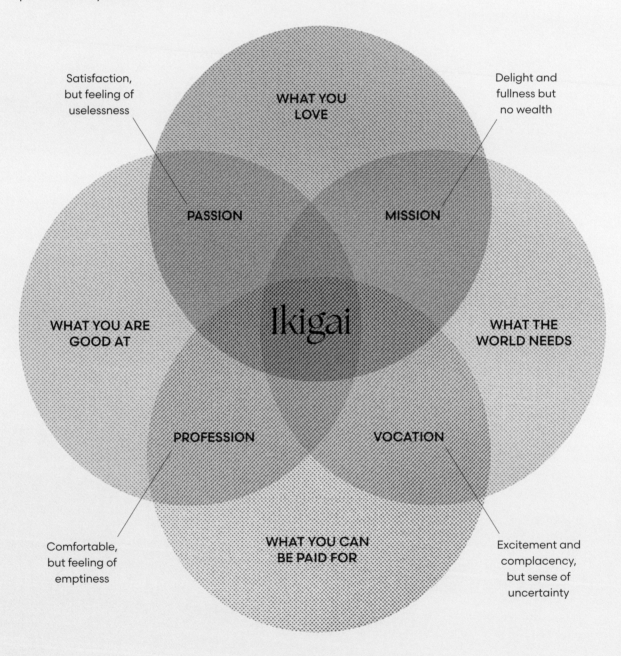

Satisfaction, but feeling of uselessness

Delight and fullness but no wealth

WHAT YOU LOVE

PASSION

MISSION

WHAT YOU ARE GOOD AT

Ikigai

WHAT THE WORLD NEEDS

PROFESSION

VOCATION

Comfortable, but feeling of emptiness

WHAT YOU CAN BE PAID FOR

Excitement and complacency, but sense of uncertainty

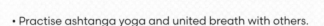

Small actions to reignite being human

- Practise ashtanga yoga and united breath with others.
- In the words of Banksy, 'If you get tired, learn to rest not to quit.'
- Bring together 'women of the village'.
- Co-regulation with a partner or close friend. Seven-second hugs or place your hand on the heart of your loved one standing opposite you until your breathing is in unison. Hold it for seven seconds to reap the rewards of lowered heart rate and calmer breathing.
- Go fly a kite. Let the wind and sense of anticipation blow out the cobwebs and fill your sails.
- Hand-feed animals. Be still with a horse and replicate its movements and motions, breathing out when it does, sighing when it does.
- Play card games in the evenings instead of screens. I have a memory of playing cards in every imaginable location in Guatemala. Broke but in a beautiful place with incredible people. A pack of cards filled in hours and hours, and even now two decades later, I can still evoke the feeling of many of those locations.
- Create your own sit spot.
- Practise creating a 'caim' sanctuary: an invisible circle of protection, drawn around the body with the hand to remind one of being safe and loved, even in times of darkness.

86

HUDDLE

STORY

The bigness and smallness of Sadie

It's okay to feel small in the vastness of it all. As is a common rite of passage, a friend's eighteen-year-old daughter, Sadie, left the bush and moved to the big smoke for uni. On a trip home I asked her how she was going. Her response was altogether human in the best possible way.

She said, 'Well, I've been humbled. I don't know anyone when I walk down the street. There's no chance that people of all ages will ask me how my mum or dad are going. I won't get spotted when I'm up to no good and have the story make it home before I do. I'm anonymous.

'It's daunting but humbling and good to realise the limits to our humanness. This feeling, I know is partly because I am so young and have so much to learn, and partly it's because I am in a new landscape with different boundaries. But with time, I know I won't feel so anonymous. I'll build a mind map of my new world. I'll become familiar with the sounds and what was huge will begin to shrink.'

I asked, 'So, where will you begin?'

She replied, 'By finding some comrades to walk with. That way we can get lost, and then found together.' She finished by saying, 'It's okay for me to have limited answers and to be filled with awe and hope. I am young and forming my identity. It's the phase of life I'm revelling in. With age I know I will become wise and capable of offering guidance, but right now I have to go experience the ups and the downs that will provide the foundation for my years of being an elder.'

Her comfort with her humanity was mature beyond her years and her head was on her shoulders.

Ritual

Be led by the outside world. It was here before you and will be around long after you leave, so let it be your cherished mentor and guide. Within this rhythmic and seasonal framework, acknowledge your own daily rhythms, the pace of your broader community and the opportunities for celebration; a full moon, a dark night, a bumper harvest. Not only do these seasonal signposts point us in the direction of deeper connection, they rebuild our community scaffolding to become something safe and certain. Large or small, it's intention that creates the ritual.

89

'A lot can be solved if you ponder
the world with your hands in the
daily sink.'

Adventurer and author Beau Miles

What's in a ritual?

We exist in a world that would make our ancestors dizzy, such is its pace. This suffocating consumerism has replaced cultural wisdom. Our political and corporate leaders are driven by elections and annual returns. We think short term, rather than collective- and legacy-led. As a result, under a blanket of industrialised, reductionist options, our culture has been smothered in its ability to find deep connection to people; our desire to stop, take time and ritualise our lives is hiding under the duvet.

Is it any wonder we ended up here after so many decades of postwar growth, no one generation or ideology standing against the slow and steady erosion of our ability to think past ourselves in what has become a narcissistic, impatient and relentless way of life?

Some suggest it's now time to 'learn', but I prefer 'remember'. We all have cellular knowledge of what an existence of connectedness feels like. We need each other to help us remember.

By considering those before us and those yet to come, we shift our cultural heartbeat from instantaneous satisfaction to one of slow respect. We make different decisions and value attributes that differ from productivity, yield and margins. We ask, 'What will the spiritual infrastructure of the future look like, and will it hold us in the way we need to be contained and connected?' Hear each other's stories, learn and remember together.

How do we connect more deeply with our neighbourhood? How do I connect to my ancestry? How do we build spiritual friendships? Invite folks into our spheres and build a sense of belonging. How do we push past superficial connectivity and genuinely build bonds with others? Ritual holds the keys to unlock many of these modern-day quandaries.

Rituals are a way of making our values VISIBLE. They take abstract emotional values and turn them into embodied practices to connect each other. More than a habit that simply fulfils a practical task, such as hair-brushing or water-drinking, rituals add a layer of symbolic meaning and the communication of our values.

Rituals can be demarcated as religious or not. They can be secular but importantly, they need to be sacred. They have intention, attention and repetition.

In our modern world, where efficiency has obliterated the role of deep connection, our familiarity with slow, intentional actions comes with a healthy dose of scepticism and our pace leaves little room for ritualised activities.

Something as simple as cleaning your teeth before work in the morning is an opportunity to look yourself in the eye and say out loud, 'Life is bloody great. It's filled with both joy and grief. Today will be no different, but whatever I face today I'm ready for it.' Something so basic and repetitive becomes a ritual simply by overlaying intention.

Ritual allows us to accelerate embodied practices – simple things like singing, cooking and camping together. When you feel part of a rhythm, there's something in our bodies that knows we are no longer alone. We move in unison to the beat of a drum, literally or figuratively.

HUDDLE ———— *HOW?*

Let's start at the very beginning: A touch of paganism

Before Christianity, pagans walked the earth. Their existence was steeped in ritualistic customs and earth-based traditions, which fostered connection and belonging, not only within communities but to the land and seasons. These revered practices from the past hold valuable lessons for us today as we strive to build meaningful huddles in the modern world. By reclaiming and reimagining these rituals, we can start to tether ourselves to place and thicken the ropes of connection between each other and the mother.

If shells hold the whisper of the sea, our bones know the beat of an old pagan drum. Despite our modern sensibilities and with a little adaptation to suit you and yours in the place you call home, we can hark to our pagan ancestry. Try these simple ideas:

Full moon circle: Create a regular practice of gathering under the full moon with your crew to celebrate lunar cycles. Make it a time to share stories, dreams, worries and aspirations, while harnessing the moon's energy to manifest intentions as a collective.

92

Nature retreat: No overthinking or over-planning this one – just go. Go out there and breathe the fresh air. Lie beneath gum trees and marvel at the skyward branches. Find patterns in clouds and let the white noise of the river drown out your busy brain. Take friends, sit on the grass, walk barefoot and read to each other. If time is tight, find a local park on a school night and make it happen in an hour; it'll still have more impact than if you don't go at all.

Celebrate a milestone: Weddings, birthdays and anniversaries all feel a little hallmarked these days, but if you strip back the consumption culture surrounding such events, they are the perfect opportunity to collect your crew and intentionally mark the occasion; turning today's stories into tomorrow's nostalgia. Being a celebration initiator for occasions – big and small – is a beautiful gift to offer those who are close to you. Inevitably your kin will return the hosting favour. Make a point of calling friends for their anniversaries, send seeds as gifts on birthdays, pack picnics to feast in newly purchased homes and pick wild flowers for those who've achieved something big or small.

Ancestor acknowledgement: Create rituals by paying homage to our ancestors via collectively shared stories If your knowledge is limited, this is your chance to ask questions of those still alive. While fireside recently, I was asked to acknowledge my female ancestors. 'I, Jade, daughter of Cherry and granddaughter of Margaret and Alice, great granddaughter of Annabel and ...' At that moment, I realised I wasn't able to go further back than two generations. I felt shame in this and have since hung images of both my grandparents next to my bed. Now, I top and tail every day by considering my lineage.

It can be so easy to let the simple fade into the shadows of the bright, shiny and big, but these simple, seasonal pagan-inspired practices have an immense and positive impact when they are ritualised.

93

Get ritual rich

It can feel a little strange to recreate a ritual – forced, full of pretence, lacking in agency – especially when it's not a ritual that speaks to your own heritage.

With this awareness of discomfort, I was keen to learn from someone who has unpacked these fears. I asked the writer and founder of Nature's Apprentice, Claire Dunn, what it looked like to thicken the layer of ritual in your life. She reflected on her year living alone outside in the bush, relying solely on herself, leaning into ecological literacy. She really noticed the changing patterns of the seasons and offered herself the time it genuinely takes to live intimately with the earth while she slowly rewrote her story, rebuilding the culture around her to become one of eco awakening. It's a fascinating story and one which many of us would not be brave enough to undertake. When I asked how others might begin this process in their own lives, she said, 'It starts with something as basic as an intentional "wander" or journalling and accepting awkwardness as we relearn the art of village-building using pan cultural tools like rhythm, percussion, scent, song, body movement, repetition, nature noticing.' She suggested we start outside, surrounded by the natural world and we start small – perhaps even on our own with repeated activity each day, like a sit spot.

Rituals can't be forced or curated. They need to evolve within community in the landscape they rest in. We need to be brave enough to begin the process of setting rituals in motion, because they will likely take generations to become entrenched in our way of being.

94

Ritualise towards a new culture?

How do we create a permanent culture? Honestly, we can't! Not deliberately anyway, like an artist with a palette. We can't predict the options or push back on intentional culture-building. This is not to say we can't do something worthwhile.

If we begin slowly we risk little when we fail, which we undoubtedly will. We can try and try again, nuancing it with every new attempt. The process of reconstructing ourselves into a new story, a new way of being will be painfully slow, and it will require an unpicking of our current culture in order to build a new one. This is multi-generational work and the transition is not defined. With new stories, new ideologies, new mythology and new ways of interacting with our world, we will inevitably mould the path.

Ritual will be the cornerstone of this rebuild. While we are still working out what this looks like, a great place to begin is by mimicking rituals from other countries, respectfully adapting it to our people and place and repeating it with intention.

At some point, what was new will begin to feel like an old sock that is familiar, comfortable and sought after. Once this happens the rhythms become widely accepted, entirely adopted and unquestioned because they 'just make sense'.

Take your signature for example. Signing something used to carry great gravity and it represented your stamp of approval, your authority. It had value and was guarded closely. Slowly, with the invention of online shopping and online subscriptions, the value of our signature has been eroded. Multiple times daily, with the click of a button, we are committed to something that will take our money, hold our details and be shared with complete strangers without so much as a handshake or a look in the eye from the person (or institution) you are now in agreement with. Our signature, which was once a ritualised mark of significance, is rarely even requested.

We didn't intentionally design the erosion of our individual mark. It's taken place over time with the evolution of culture. It's emergent, but these processes – not just our signature but many of the small, incremental changes that happen right underneath our feet – result in us becoming spiritual orphans who have opted for convenience and ease over intention and complexity.

The culture that dominates is the one that is allowed to emerge by virtue of a populace who have handed over the reins to the loudest narrative and the empowered decision-makers.

Storytelling ritual

Storytelling is crucial to the emergence of a new culture and the act of ritual-making plays a critical role in evolving this story. With ritual we can be launched into a new way of being, but we cannot design it. At best we can guide it and deliver a beautifully human outcome, which is interconnected with its surroundings.

When we engage our senses we step into myth and wilderness, avoiding the modern mentality of conquest, enabling us to be comfortable with relinquishing control. This is not to say that ritual can only embrace the wild. It can equally be precision and order. Think of legal proceedings or a medical process: both are rituals of knowledge and order of the highest degree.

Sad but true is the fact that even if we greatly desire it, we cannot expedite the creation of rituals and stories. There has to be a dissolving of the old story before the new one can take hold. Chaos sits between these two stories – the chaos that comes when losing control, when we surrender into the not knowing. On the other side of this chaos is room to create new narrative, new patterns and new rituals.

Under the cover of darkness

You can create memories while under the stars. The energy at night sets a different pace. It's safe and it holds you in silence, celebration, joy or distress. It's more tranquil and somehow, it's easier on the soul – a perfect stage for rituals to unfold.

When I was just venturing into this way of being, I was invited to a party at a friend's new property with a crowd I didn't know. I was nervous and nearly didn't go.

After a long, tall tree-lined, candlelit drive up the steep hill, we were greeted by a gathering of lantern-holding strangers who led us into the bush in murmured whispers. Over thirty minutes or so, we stopped at 'stations', where a self-nominated narrator read poems that reminded us of our humanity, the season we were in and the way our ancestors celebrated this time of year.

Once into thick paperbark scrub, our lanterns formed a circle. We clustered side-by-side and sang. The songs were new to nearly all of us, but they were repetitive and tuneful so even the melodically unpractised joined in. Together we made music in the night, under the stars while embraced by the cloaking trees and each other, a group of relative strangers who together created something that none of us could have conjured individually.

I recall walking back out of the trees and looking up to the sky and experiencing the distinct sense that I was walking above the ground.

It was my first taste of the power of ritual, and I knew that this was what I'd been looking for to push through my veins and fill all the pockets of air where emptiness sat.

Here are some ideas to kickstart night-time ritual building:

- **Moon gazing:** Observe the moon in its various phases. Reflect on its beauty, even with the naked eye. It's breathtaking.
- **Stargazing:** Find a quiet spot away from city lights, lie down and look up at the stars. It's inky and vast, but good to be minimised by its never-ending expanse. Within half an hour or so you are almost guaranteed a shooting star. Over time you'll learn to navigate the night sky and suddenly, the vastness will become familiar as you piece together the various markers up above.
- **Night walk:** Just as you do in the day, learn to navigate your world in the darkness. Your senses will heighten and, like all things, the more you explore at night, the more familiar the sounds, smells and ground undulations will be. I can still mentally navigate a summer camp I spent a few years in with my eyes closed.
- **Fire ceremony:** Fires are enigmatic without much effort at all, but when you wrap ceremony around them, they become central beacons to garner togetherness, release negativity, process grief and trauma, uplift and inspire.
- **Daytime things in the dark:** Normal everyday activities, like taking a shower, stretching and having a cup of tea, become altogether ethereal when you experience them in the dark. Try it.
- **Night-time gardening:** As strange as it sounds, gardening by moonlight can be done and is surprisingly tranquil. Try watering, weeding or planting.

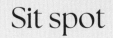

Sit spot

A few years ago I found a spot. Up near our dam under the gums in a soft bed of fallen leaves, with a fallen log to lean against. It's sunlit for most of the day, but the warmth is as dappled as the canopy is broad and thick. I call it my sit spot.

My sit spot is a salve! Sometimes I walk out the door and head for it three times a day. At other times a week will pass, but for a few years now it has been a place of tranquillity where the calm washes over me like I've dived into warm milk. Here, I've got to know intimately the deep, inky-black, tannin rich water, the family of magpies, including the overtly friendly white one, and watched as the fungi and moss interchange their growth at different times of the year.

Without fail there is always something to observe – slowly and deeply, without hurry or purpose. The treecreeper birds are my favourite, but I love waiting for the ducks to return to the water at dusk with their drawn-out 'waaaaaaark' as they come in to land. I've meditated, journalled, slept, daydreamed and had epiphanies in my sit spot. It's a balm in an otherwise overloaded life.

About six months ago, a feeling crawled under my skin. I wanted more from my sit spot. I wanted movement, more life, action and possibly noise – white noise. It occurred to me that this calm, quiet place wasn't able to take the never-ending thoughts away from me – gently or otherwise. Increasingly I was having trouble being still in my usual place of calm. The idea of building a relationship with another location as my sit spot was unshakable. During a meditation, the answer presented itself – it wasn't that I needed to replace my original, humble, but judgement-free sit spot. I simply needed a second one with moving water. A place where I could feel the energy flowing, pulling the thoughts and nagging from the outside world away from my overactive mind to be free for a moment.

Now, when I need the chaos in my body to be drowned out by white noise, flowing water, movement and life, I sit over a little creek not far from my original patch of dirt and dangle my legs close to the water. The water drowns out my thoughts and I take my worries downstream. For days when I need a deep, still, quiet place to wrap itself around me, I return to my original pad.

Being intimate with two locations now means I can read my mood and feed the desired outcome – no infidelity required. It's an ever-deepening interpretation of two similar, but ultimately very different landscapes.

Rites of passage

Can you identify the rites of passage you've experienced in your own life? How did each one set you up and what was left behind as you navigated to the next phase of life?

Every indigenous culture across the globe has curated their own rites of passage. Depending on the climate, landscape and patterns of the community, these symbolic rituals are like a dance of transformation, marking the threshold between phases of life.

They are sacred journeys, soulful initiations that take us beyond the boundaries of the familiar. A little like a caterpillar that weaves its cocoon before emerging a beautiful, winged creature, so too do we undergo profound metamorphosis during these transformative rituals.

The young men of the Maasai tribe in East Africa embark on a journey called the Eunoto, where they prove their courage and resilience through various challenges. They transition from boys to warriors, embodying strength and responsibility within their community.

Young women participate in coming-of-age ceremonies, like the quinceañera in Latin America or the bat mitzvah in Jewish tradition. Marking their transition into womanhood, they are honoured, supported and recognised as capable individuals ready to contribute to their communities.

These intentional stepping stones into adulthood are few and far between in our western world. Without facilitated rites of passage we will seek our own passage, and more often than not it can go awry, leaving us on the same late-teenage-step for the rest of our lives, unable to transition up the staircase of life.

This leaves us feeling individually inadequate, as we lack the opportunity to live life through a maturing lens. Ultimately, it makes that part of the staircase very overcrowded and results in an immature culture unwilling to move into later stages of life. A strong community requires a culture that consists of people at all stages of life. For only when we have a diverse and varied collection of thinkers and experience in a huddle can the group operate as it's supposed to.

These passageways are becoming thin on the ground, so we need to create our own rites of passage to mark significant transitions in our lives. Whether it's a solo pilgrimage to a sacred place, a communal gathering in nature or a heartfelt ceremony with loved ones, these rituals serve as anchors, guiding us through the turbulent waters of change.

By engaging in these transformative experiences, we forge deep connections within our huddles. We witness one another's growth, offering support and guidance along the way. The shared stories and challenges become threads that bind us together, creating a strong and resilient community.

Like the wise elders passing down their wisdom to the younger generation, let us create spaces where knowledge is shared, talents are nurtured and the torch of tradition is passed on. We honour the past, embrace the present and pave the way for a harmonious and interconnected future.

Charlie and my experience with undertaking intentional and facilitated passages with our children was different for each child – to be expected, but what we didn't expect was the impact that each experience had on the parent who guided them. Watching your child grow and evolve so significantly in such a short amount of time can be confronting. You watch as they push out of their childhood cocoon and spread their new-found wings ready to fly.

This is the way of things and being by their side as they emerge, while confronting, is as much a passage for the parent as it is for the child – go with it!

Even with a strong network to assist, it can be really beneficial to have an external guide to bring it to life and hold you through what can be sensitive and emotional.

Creative expression ritual: Create a personal ritual centred around your chosen form of creative expression. Writing, painting, dancing or even just moving.

Wilderness retreat: Embark on a solo journey into nature, disconnecting from technology and immersing yourself in the beauty and serenity of the natural world. Use this time for self-reflection, introspection and connection with the rhythms of the earth as your external, egocentric identity evaporates.

Life milestone reflection: Create a personal ritual to honour significant life milestones. Take time to reflect on the lessons learned, set new intentions and express gratitude for the journey so far.

Career transition celebration: When transitioning to a new career or embarking on an entrepreneurial endeavour, organise a celebratory event to mark the beginning of this new chapter. Share your aspirations, gather support and express gratitude for the opportunities ahead.

Vision board: Gather with loved ones and create a collaborative vision board or intention-setting activity. Share your dreams and aspirations, visualise your desired future and support each other in manifesting these visions.

Daily rhythms

While not as symbolic as a rite of passage, a women's circle or salami-making weekend, daily rhythms are not to be sneezed at. They guide us through each day with purpose. From the flick of the kettle at dawn to the hushed whispers of twilight where we breathe out – sometimes for the first time that day – these rhythms ground us, providing stability.

Morning rituals set the tone. The daily cadence of work and rest sustains us, balancing productivity and rejuvenation. Mealtimes become moments of connection and nourishment, gluing us together with our people. As the sun dips below the horizon, a gentle rhythm of winding down and rest embraces us.

Daily rhythms hold the power to honour our needs, nurture our relationships and cultivate a deeper connection to ourselves and our huddles. In their steady pulse, we find balance, growth and a bucketload of wellbeing.

Finding calm in repetition

Do you ever get overwhelmed by choice? When the offerings of possibility are as endless as they are in a society with so much, the human cognitive capacity is rattled. When this happens on a daily basis – through the endless messages of global disasters, opportunities, advertising, social media and networks of acquaintances, many of whom you've never even met – it spins our adrenals into a washing machine of excitement, empathy, hope, disillusionment, overstimulation and fatigue. Eventually it leads to a kind of stupefied stuckness where we can't stop scrolling.

If this happens to you, turn your phone notifications off, walk away from any screens and go outside. Scan for green. Count how many shades of green you can identify (there are hundreds, you know). Take five deep breaths while you come to your senses and consider this the beginning of your new-found ritual.

Repetitive rhythm can offer us the confidence to push back against relentless decision-making. It allows us to sidestep the habit of always saying yes, always wanting more and never finding deep contentment in what is already in our very full laps.

The most precious commodity we have is attention, which is probably why Netflix declared its biggest competitor was sleep. Each one of us has to guard our attention like a wolf, ready to defend against those corporate entities that make a meal of our rapt, and not altogether consensual, gaze. Rhythm really helps in this pursuit, because after one healthy action another follows suit.

103

HUDDLE ACTIVITY

CREATING RHYTHM IN CYCLES

For a week, capture your movements across your days in a journal. Once you have a week's worth of life documented, ask the questions:

• Where are the patterns?
• What is intentional and what has become a comfortable habit?
• Where is there room for more verve and purpose?
• What plays an important part in making your day flow as you need it to?
• What grounds you and fills your cup?

Gratitude sandwich: Upon rising, write down three things you're grateful for and three things you can do to make today great. At the end of the day, return to the same page and write three great things and one thing you could've done to make today just that little bit greater. It's simple enough, but will swaddle the whole day in gratitude.

Five for three: In for five, hold for five, out for five, hold for five. This box breathing rhythm is wonderful for resetting your nervous system or finding Zen if something's got you fired up. Can you pause for five rounds three times a day?

Sole food: Bare feet on the ground recharges our human 'batteries'. Through skin-on-skin contact with earth's magnetic field we find connectedness, peace and even immune enhancement. Make wiggling your toes in the grass part of your daily rhythm.

Candlelit reflections: The physical act of striking a match and lighting a candle can help signal to your mind that it's time to reflect. Treat yourself to a heavenly honey-scented beeswax candle and carve out ten or fifteen minutes before bed to pour your feelings onto the page.

Sultana meditation: Savour a single sultana for as long as possible, letting all the flavours, textures and subtleties melt on your tongue.

Vision quest

Clueless curiosity is how I describe that sensation of something catching your interest, calling your name – even when you don't know a scrap about it. This was my experience with vision quests. I wasn't entirely sure what they entailed, but when one-by-one my friends decided to 'quest', I knew by the butterflies in my belly that one day I too would take the plunge. I had so many preconceived ideas about how I might spend my time on quest and how I might emerge, but I soon learned that there are no rules. There is no control. If you surrender, you'll be broken down and remade in ways you'll never predict.

In the grunt of your bustling modern life, where distractions abound and the pace can be relentless, the idea of embarking on a vision quest might seem daunting and the degree of personal growth might feel like you'll drown. While not underestimating their potency, I'm here to suggest you might be pleasantly surprised.

What is a vision quest? On paper, it's a few nights in the bush entirely on your own in a small square, typically five-by-five metres, where you stay without food or entertainment. Quests are supported, meaning you have a few days leading up to the vigil to prepare yourself and set intentions in the company of others. And while someone will always know where you are once you're out on the land, it's a solo journey with just yourself for company.

How many of us have spent a night alone in the bush before, stepping out of our everyday routines and resting in the arms of nature? This kind of solitude may feel completely at odds with your social nature, or perhaps you relish the thought of being unfettered by kids, work or emails for a solid few days?

By embarking on a vision quest, you give yourself permission to step outside your comfort zone and embrace vulnerability. It's a powerful act of personal growth, allowing you to reconnect with your intuition, find renewed inspiration and cultivate a deeper sense of meaning in your life. It's a chance to return to your daily routine with a fresh perspective, revitalised energy and a profound sense of purpose.

While a vision quest may not be for everyone, if you feel a calling to embark on this transformative journey, take the leap. Trust in the process, embrace the unknown and allow yourself to be guided by the wisdom of the natural world. Your vision quest can be an empowering and life-changing experience, a sacred pilgrimage that helps you rediscover your true self and step into a more authentic and purposeful life.

Community ritual

Now it's time to talk about what it looks like to bring ritual to your community.

In my twenties I travelled through South America, doing my darndest to run from a broken heart. In a slightly dazed state I arrived at Semana Santa, or Easter Week, in Antigua, Guatemala. The streets had come alive with intricate carpets known as alfombras. Skilled artisans meticulously created these vibrant and temporary artworks using coloured sawdust, flowers, pine needles and other natural materials. The alfombras symbolise a sacred path for the processions and are a visual tribute to the religious traditions and cultural heritage of Antigua.

The process begins days in advance with community members and volunteers working together to design and outline the patterns. On Good Friday, the alfombras adorn the processional routes. Accompanied by music and incense, the procession makes its way over the stunningly crafted carpets, which often depict religious motifs, biblical scenes and intricate geometric designs.

Incredibly, I managed to find a bed in a house right in the heart of the city and I spent the night under the streetlights helping the family create their depiction. Our languages didn't co-regulate, so it was all curated by hand signals and affirmations.

We stood and stretched our backs just minutes before the several-hundred-human procession marched past in sporadic silence and singing, swinging their incense thurible, creating a smoky haze in the dawn light. Senses were saturated and the experience is now seared in my body to recall in vividity for the rest of time.

Watching the destruction of the alfombras and all that work created by the entire city was simultaneously horrific and strangely cathartic – a good reminder of there being a place for ephemeral things in this world. The festival is a celebration of community collaboration and devotion. It showcases the rich cultural traditions of Guatemala and provides a glimpse into the deep-rooted customs and religious practices of the region.

Building community rituals can take time, as you need to bring everyone along in what will ultimately become owned by each individual.

At Black Barn Farm we've launched headlong into winter wassails, but it might be that a simple solstice fire with friends is an easy place to start and can be repeated each year at someone else's house. Across the globe, there are fascinating annual rituals that run in the blood of entire communities. In the town of Buñol in Spain every year they host the annual La Tomatina Festival and revel in the world's largest friendly tomato fight, covering the streets in a sea of red.

The Festival of Colours – officially called Holi – in India is a vibrant celebration of spring. Participants gather in open spaces, smearing each other with brightly coloured powders and drenching one another with water. It symbolises love, unity and the triumph of good over evil.

The Lantern Festival in Taiwan illuminates the night sky with thousands of colourful lanterns. People release them into the air, representing the letting go of the past and embracing new beginnings.

The Day of the Dead is celebrated right across Mexico. Although it's celebrated on the 1st and 2nd of November, it lingers as part of their culture for the rest of the year. It's a joyful commemoration of loved ones who are no longer earthside. Families create elaborate altars adorned with photographs, candles and the favourite foods and drinks of the departed. It's a time for remembrance, celebration and honouring the cycle of life and death.

These annual rituals are a wardrobe of diversity and richness of our global cultures. They bring people together, foster traditions and create cracking memories.

106

Seasonal influence

It wouldn't be a ritual without some input from the mother herself. Some seasonally specific rituals that are easy to get in the calendar and invite your nearby crew to are:

Spring awakening: When new life emerges and the world is reborn, create a ritual to celebrate renewal and growth. This can involve planting seeds or tending to a garden together, symbolising the potential for growth and transformation in our own lives.

Autumn harvest: As the leaves change colour and nature prepares for winter, create a ritual to celebrate the harvest. Gather and preserve food, share a meal made from local produce or express gratitude for the abundance of the earth.

Get to know your seasons: How many are there? What are their traits? Give them names. Every part of the world is unique in its seasonality and getting intimate with the goings on in your patch is a beautiful way to begin your courtship of a more intimate relationship with place.

Create and revisit your emergency management plan: This is not just a summer activity, but an annual one for all manner of emergencies. Revisit your plan annually.

SEASONAL CELEBRATIONS

These celebrations can be in whatever form works for you based on where and how you live. Perhaps you are in the city and need to celebrate in a public park with a picnic. Make lanterns and take an evening walk through your streets. Do you have space to host an annual bonfire? There are a few dates to ritualise around: summer solstice (longest day of the year), winter solstice (shortest day of the year) and the spring and autumn equinoxes (when day and night are of equal length).

During the darkest time of the year (winter solstice), come together to reflect on the past seasons and set intentions for the coming seasons. This can be done through candlelight ceremonies, storytelling or creating a communal art project that represents the hopes and dreams of the huddle.

During the equinoxes, embrace the balance and harmony of day and night being equal. Engage in activities that promote balance and connection, such as yoga or meditation sessions, or create a ritual of sharing and exchanging gifts within your huddle.

If you think your kin are up for a little more depth with their ritual serving, try some of these:

Moonlight walk: Don head torches or carry candles and take a night-time walk under the full moon each season. Try it in silence.

Cleansing: Create a ritual of deep cleaning and decluttering your communal living spaces at the start of each season. Host a working bee, permablitz or town-wide garage sale.

Altar: Designate a small area in your home as a seasonal altar. Come together with your crew to decorate it with natural objects, symbols or items that represent each season. Encourage your community to use this space for reflection, meditation or simply as a reminder of the ongoing cycles of life.

Elemental ritual: Embrace the elements of each season through specific rituals. For example, in summertime swimming in a natural lake or gathering around a fire pit. In winter, sit by a cosy fireplace or take a mindful walk in the snow.

Potluck feast: Whoever hosts can set the rules but with seasonal potlucks, it generally needs to reflect what's in season and be locally sourced. Experiment with new recipes and congregate around a table heaving with collectively prepared food to feast on with your huddle.

These less obvious seasonal rituals allow us to attune ourselves to the subtleties of each season, deepen our connection with nature and create meaningful moments of reflection and celebration. They offer a chance to slow down, appreciate the beauty of the world around us and cultivate a sense of harmony and presence within our huddles.

A little repetition

Ritual by definition is a ceremonial act performed in a fixed order. This must surely mean that if I make a cup of tea in my favourite cup at 6 am every day or if I shake your hand or wave hello, I've just committed a ritual. I hope so, because ritual is the bricks and mortar of a life worth living.

During our WWOOFer (World Wide Opportunities on Organic Farms) seasons in spring and autumn, we beat to a drum dictated by repetitious daily patterns. Early starts wiping sleep from our eyes while simultaneously feeding groats into the turning wheel of the oat grinder to generate our morning meal and energise our morning tasks. Each day is the same: goat milking, hoop house watering, firewood chopping, chicken bucket tipping and sourdough starter feeding.

These rhythms have a certain cadence about them and while they are undertaken with limited reverence, they form the cornerstone of our pared back existence at Black Barn Farm. They offer consistency, stability and order, especially useful when managing the movements of many. They become second nature to all who live here. After just a few short weeks each season, tasks are completed without instruction and with a solid sense of community contribution oiling the farm cogs.

This is rhythm at work and when in a flow state it has a sweetness and virtuosity that's hard to describe.

Rituals are stamped with a higher degree of intention and their significance carries an unspoken weight. Each year we host our mid-winter wassail, as well as camp in a nearby valley, mark the date of our first dam dip of the season, the return of the striated pardalote and the bursting buds in the orchard. These events are significant and noted, even honoured and celebrated. They mark the passage of time and remind us of the passing year.

HUDDLE _____ HOW?

52 weeks of rituals

A new idea each week for a whole year to bed down.

—1—
Make three normally mundane things intentional.

—2—
Come-to-your-senses at least three times a day. Practise until it's embedded.

—3—
Find yourself a sit spot and visit it regularly.

—4—
Work up to a vision quest.

—5—
Sit by an open fire in silence.

—6—
Go outside, take off your shoes and listen to the earth through your feet.

—7—
Create a calendar of ritual-rich events.

—8—
Create a women's/men's group and meet regularly.

—9—
Contemplate a rite of passage process for your immediate huddle.

—10—
Share an evening meal together and each share a 'thorn and a rose' from your day.

—11—
Bring the outside in with a daily adorning of seasonal finds on the dining table.

—12—
Plan a seasonal community event.

—13—
Go outside at night and watch the stars.

—14—
Celebrate the big and small markers in your life – birthdays, anniversaries, promotions, health achievements – with handmade cards.

—15—
Acknowledge your privilege daily. Say it out loud with your morning coffee.

—16—
List your gratitude daily. Text it to a friend each day.

—17—
Spend at least ten minutes alone in your thoughts daily. Daydreaming is good!

—18—
Start a cake mates' or birthday girls' gathering to acknowledge your people.

—19—
Create a gratitude circle and gather regularly to share short stories of gratitude.

—20—
Begin journalling to make sense of your internal monologue.

—21—
Host a clothes swap at the change of the seasons.

—22—
Organise an annual passata, salami or pesto-making day.

—23—
Join a book club.

—24—
Do a daily seven-second hug to find co-regulation with someone else.

110

—25—
Make twice as much and gift meals to families who could do with a little leg-up.

—26—
Turn off all overhead lights after dusk. Let your body close down for the day with only lamplight, candles or nothing at all.

—27—
Dance before you walk out the door each day.

28—
Start a puzzle and place three pieces at the start and end of every day.

—29—
Acknowledge that each day may bring hardship or joy. Repeat this message while cleaning your teeth.

—30—
Learn a new word each week and incorporate it into conversation.

—31—
Rise with the birds each day and learn the owners of all the different sounds.

—32—
Fast together at different times of the year.

—33—
Seed swap each season.

—34—
Abundance swap each season.

—35—
Learn the moon cycles.

—36—
Learn new breathing techniques and build them into your daily practice.

—37—
Set intentions for the following day before you go to bed.

—38—
Visit the library every week.

—39—
Brew a pot with intention at the same time daily.

—40—
Wake up before others and watch the dawn to begin a new day.

—41—
Say goodbye to each day outside bathing in the twilight air.

—42—
Begin a garden so you can grow your own food. Start with some herbs to kick it off.

—43—
Keep chickens, ducks or quails and collect eggs daily.

—44—
Sing often and alone, but also when you are with others. Seek tuneful friends and create music at every opportunity.

—45—
Make group mandalas with nature's creations – a beautiful activity to do in silence.

—46—
Have a picnic under the largest tree you can find. Dedicate that day of the year to this tree and visit it annually with a packed picnic basket.

—47—
Take a very intentional meander with your afternoon cuppa. Make each step exceptionally slowly until you've finished your cup.

—48—
Count the shades of green from wherever you sit.

—49—
Engage with the commons and contribute to its wellbeing with regularity. Perhaps it's weeding, printing, making a seat or a bridge for the shared place.

—50—
Create a sourdough starter, which you feed each morning.

—51—
Let go of control and let chaos meet you. This is where you will find the courage to create rituals with your huddle.

—52—
Plan advent rituals during December.

Enoughness____

How do you define enough? Begin with your health,
your relationships, your sense of purpose, the
food you eat, the shelter you rest in and finish with
the way you interact with your huddle. Everything
else could be considered excess, could it not?

ENOUGHNESS

'When did two toilets, two ovens, two basins and walk-in robes bigger than the lounge become requirements for a life worth living?'

Jane Hilliard

I've spent the better part of the past few years asking people to define enough. One wise woman, who was surely a hipster of her time, ageing with a colourful flourish, told me, 'You may never be able to define "your enough", but don't let that stop you. Search for it and don't settle for what's obvious. Instead, take the time to explore your options. Rest your head on the earth, in different grasses and on different things – an old sheepskin, a cotton picnic rug, a sandy beach towel or a well-worn swag. Feel it, smell it, let your senses move you towards your enough.'

I was taken by her evocative description of the searching. While waiting for her to package and present her summary statement, I realised she had stopped talking. Slowly the dawning arrived. She was waiting patiently for me to realise that her enough sat squarely in the middle of the search, with her head resting in places that filled her cup.

116

How much do we need?

On an annual pilgrimage to a faraway bush camp without power or toilets, timeframes or rules but with tall trees, a clean river and a big fire, fifteen of us wandered down a bush track without a destination in mind. We stopped by the river's edge to watch the water. We slipped out of shoes; found patches of grass; rock piles were made; tic-tac-toe games were scratched into the dirt; patterns were drawn with stones; and the brave ones dipped. For hours we found small, gentle, unrushed ways to be entertained by little more than flowing water over beds of pebbles. Without a screen or manmade toy for either old or young, all ages interacted with each other and the place, this special place.

As I watched the scene and marvelled at the sense of unhurried peacefulness I thought to myself, 'This is my enough.' I slept beside my love in a tent with the sounds of the natural world around me. I'm surrounded by a group of humans who love, care for and are generous and kind to each other. My belly is full of food I've grown in my garden and shared with this motley crew. The sun is shining, the calendar is clear and I'm sitting on the earth in the sunshine with my feet in a mountain-top-cold river.

This was my enough moment where my cup did runneth over. I return to it often to remind myself of what it looks like.

What about you? How much is enough and what fills your cup? More importantly, if you had more than enough, would you be willing to share it with others to ensure they too could experience what you have?

HUDDLE ACTIVITY

SYMBOLISATION STONES

When next by a river, set your group on a hunt for their own symbolic stone. Popping a pebble in your pocket to remind you of a special time peps your step and reminds you of the things that really matter.

At that very same river, our huddle collected stones. Stones that represented something to each of us. We each hunted for our own perfect piece of rock. Some looked for colour, others weighed up the size. Pattern appealed to a few and feeling made the choice for one or two.

My advice for those wanting to pop a special rock in their pocket is that it must speak to you, feel right in your hand when it sits in your palm and it can't pull your pants down when it's in your pocket so the weight and size must be just right.

My perfect pebbles jumped from the millions of other pebbles to share a message. A simple message: keep the fire burning, but not to the detriment of balance.

In my mind, one of these stones is a fire stick to keep the coals alight even in times of distress and uncertainty, and one is to ensure that equal parts calm contemplation and action are both embodied.

To everyone else they're just two small pebbles, but to me they remind me of the paradox of our existence and my role in actively navigating this in everyday life.

Whenever I travel for work or am away from my place of stability, I pack these small but mighty stones, feeling their weight in my pocket. I am reminded of my enough!

Capitalism: friend or foe?

The relationship between capitalism and its impact on society is a complex and multifaceted one. When you realise that capitalism is the sea you swim in, it's even harder to be sure whether it's friend or foe. Capitalism, as an economic system, has undeniably brought about significant advancements, technological innovations and economic growth, lifting millions out of poverty and providing opportunities for prosperity. Okay capitalism, we'll give you that.

Thanks to its competitive nature, capitalism has people jostling to make discoveries and land innovations and flexing their entrepreneurial intelligence. This drives economic development and improves living standards in many parts of the world. It has provided incentives for individuals and businesses to create wealth, invest in research and development, and advance various sectors. Capitalism has also fostered freedom for lucky individuals like us – based on a fundamental ethic of freedom – to pursue our own goals. So, what if the unspoken rule is that they're economic?

But you don't get off that lightly, capitalism. Here come the critiques.

For starters, the unchecked pursuit of profit within a capitalist framework has led to several concerning consequences, collectively known as a *shit show*. It has perpetuated social inequalities by concentrating wealth and power in the hands of a few, exacerbating societal divisions and deepening disparities.

This unequal distribution of resources has led to marginalised communities, limited access to essential services and a lack of equal opportunities. Level playing field? More like match fixing.

Moreover, the profit-driven nature of capitalism has incentivised unsustainable, extractive practices, which are rapidly decimating the environment. The relentless pursuit of economic growth has come at the expense of natural resources, ecological degradation and the exacerbation of climate change. This has raised critical concerns about the long-term viability of our planet as a place for humankind to continue to live. Talk about messy teenagers!

The ethical implications of capitalism also loom large. By making money our god, we've prioritised short-term profit over long-term social and environmental stability. Anything is justifiable – whether it's exploitative labour practices, disregard for human rights, fracturing of traditional cultures or commodification of nature – it's going to make us richer, right?

Let's find common ground. Capitalism operates within a broader social and political context. Its outcomes and impacts are influenced by regulations, policies and cultural norms that shape its manifestation. While *unfettered* capitalism can amplify inequalities and externalities, appropriate regulations, social safety nets and ethical frameworks can mitigate its negative effects and promote a more inclusive and sustainable form of capitalism. In theory, anyway.

Ultimately, the question of whether capitalism is friend or foe depends on the values, priorities and goals of a society. Striking a balance between economic growth, social equity, environmental sustainability and human wellbeing is the key. By calling out the flaws of capitalism and singing the praises of alternative models, we can work towards a system that embraces fairness, ecological stewardship and shared prosperity.

Globalisation

Globalisation sits right next to capitalism as a system that, despite its flaws, has maintained domination in western existence. Initially championed by Thatcher and Reagan, it aimed to benefit all through increased interconnectedness and free trade. Remember 'a rising tide lifts all boats'? Hmmm, they didn't count on the regularity of tsunamis and king tides thanks to climate change doing more than rising boats; it's drowned them instead – perpetuated by the global system that has pushed for endless growth. Oh, the irony.

The reality is that the wealth gap has widened, and the middle class has suffered as a direct result. According to Oxfam, the world's richest one per cent of people have more than twice the combined wealth of the other ninety-nine per cent of the population. Globalisation has contributed to this disparity through outsourcing jobs to cheaper labour markets and favouring multinational corporations. The consequences include the hollowing out of industries and the erosion of job security for many workers. While globalisation has brought benefits, its unequal distribution of wealth and its impact on the middle class necessitate a more inclusive approach, which addresses these challenges and promotes equitable economic growth.

120

Collapse inevitability

This section nearly got the boot, because of its confronting nature. Then I remembered that it was the very first paragraph I wrote when *Huddle* was first penned, so here it is. It's too important not to include.

What is collapse inevitability? It's an abstract concept to many who cannot begin to fathom that our existence won't continue on its merry way as is forever more. The facade of this existence is beginning to show cracks and the things we don't see every day – our ecological fragility – are no longer able to endure the pretence.

Collapse inevitability is an acknowledgement we are drowning in the consequences of a western world that has perpetuated excess for far too long. We find ourselves at a critical juncture, where the ability to navigate an equitable and sustainable future is slipping through our grasp. The spectre of collapse looms before us; a stark reminder of the fragile balance we have disrupted. It is essential that we face this inevitability head-on, recognising that the path to resilience and transformation requires a fundamental shift in our values, behaviours and collective consciousness. Only by redefining 'enough' and embracing a new paradigm of sufficiency, harmony with nature and equitable distribution of resources can we hope to forge a path towards a just and regenerative world. This demands our collective commitment to deep introspection, radical change and a shared vision, which transcends the patterns of consumption and growth that have led us to the brink. Let us embrace the urgency of this moment, accepting the challenges we face while fostering hope, unity and a steadfast determination to build a future that thrives in harmony with the earth and honours the wellbeing of all.

And if collapse is indeed inevitable, what skills, networks, relationships and ecosystems do we want to be carrying into the aftermath?

122

Limits to growth

Amid the prevailing political narrative that remains wedded to an unsustainable, endless growth model, our collective trajectory is hurtling towards a precipice from which there may be no return. Urgency demands that we swiftly chart a new course, one that redefines our consumptive culture. Perhaps it's even more severe than this. Author Jeremy Lent believes rather than charting a new course that gives us false hope for continuation of this existence, our best chance is to look to the principles of deep adaptation. Whether you believe there is hope to maintain the status quo with some significant tweaks or that it's time to truly build a new way of being, now is the time to embark on this transformative journey. But how?

First and foremost, we must challenge the endless growth narrative and question the notion that unbridled consumption leads to prosperity. It requires a shift in mindset, valuing quality over quantity and recognising that true wealth exists where individuals, communities and the planet are thriving. We need to redefine success and progress, and embrace metrics beyond GDP that encompass social, environmental and human wellbeing.

Education and awareness play vital roles in this paradigm shift. By fostering a deep understanding of the interconnectedness of our actions and their impact on the planet, we can cultivate a sense of responsibility.

If you're reading this from the lands of academia, industry, government or finance, we need your assistance urgently. From where I'm sitting – a perch with views of both local and national systems of change – I see that government policies and funding have a pivotal role to play in steering us towards a limited growth model. It's bolstered by research and embraced by industry that are well supported by a non-extractive financial system.

We need our political leaders to unapologetically prioritise ecosystem regeneration beyond sustainability that merely maintains our current system of social inequity and short-term thinking. We need to implement regulations and incentives that enable deep cultural transformation, localised economies and regenerative landscape management practices to drive the necessary systemic change – or at the very least be the seeds of something new, which can sprout should the inevitable collapse unfold (more on that later).

It's time for our communities to get resilient, but what does that actually look like? I'm talking about more than just creating community 'phone trees' in times of disaster – although that is a good place to start. What's needed is localised economies. We could follow the lead of the town of Totnes in the UK by creating our own currency, supporting small-scale businesses more than once a year at Christmas and fostering regeneration – of the heart and mind. This reduces dependence on resource-intensive global supply chains and taps into community-led initiatives, such as cooperative models and regenerative agriculture. Not least, we can promote a sense of connection and ecological stewardship.

Individual action is also paramount, especially when collectivised at scale. With every decision you make, ask yourself: Will this result in a degenerative, sustainable or a regenerative outcome?

While transforming our consumptive culture and navigating a path towards limited growth is undoubtedly a formidable task, it is not insurmountable. It requires a collective commitment, bold leadership, systemic changes and individual responsibility. By embracing this imperative, we can forge a new narrative. One that fosters wellbeing, harmony with nature and a future where the needs of all living beings are met within the boundaries of our planet's finite resources.

Sidestepping 'shiny'

Every day we run the gauntlet of distractions – whether that's walking through a bustling city with its loud billboards and lusty shopfronts or being sucked face first into the universe of consumer temptation, which sits in the palm of your hand. However, you've got a secret weapon, even if it needs some sharpening ... and it's your focus.

Can you take a deep breath and remember what truly matters to you? Can you stay curious and ask questions? How about seeking substance over the superficial? Getting serious about gratitude, pausing to soak in life's simple pleasures (even if the word 'gratitude' gives you the self-help heebie-jeebies)? Notice cravings that arise for the next shiny thing, laugh a little and let them pass. Be intentional in your choices and find delight in a sense of purpose and the pursuit of meaning. Avoid shiny and discover the splendour of everyday grot, mess and texture. Focus.

Shiny not only generates obscene amounts of waste, but it strips us of our ability to learn skills like repairing – clothes, whitegoods and furniture. It overlooks those opportunities to meet our neighbours by taking them that extra loaf you baked or the abundance of zucchini you grew. It evaporates our creativity, robbing us of that problem-solving satisfaction of scavenging, fixing and upcycling – turning those ripped jeans into a carry bag.

I don't want to lose these moments that bring our humanness to the fore. They're small actions and endangered skills that make a big difference in tackling not only the waste problem, but our hollowing culture and collapsing ecosystems.

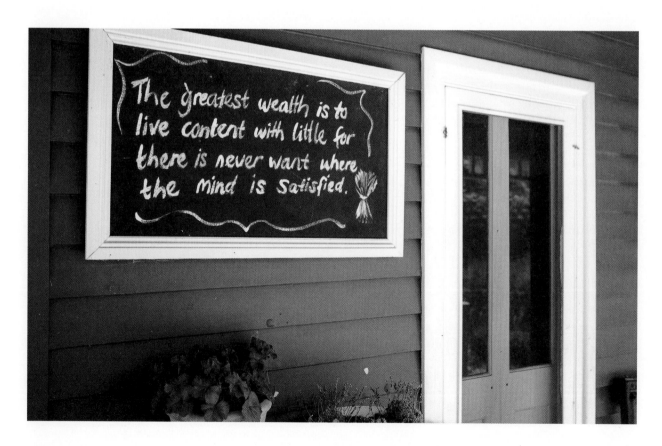

124

Consumption fatigue: waste not want not

'Only we humans make waste that nature can't digest.'

Charles Moore

Are you feeling the burn of consumption fatigue? It's like wearing a pair of shoes that are a size too small – uncomfortable and blister-inducing, but we keep shoving them on because everyone else is, and our desire to belong stops us asking why we wouldn't.

Despite no longer producing the vast majority of the things we actually consume on our own shores and with skills that exist in our huddles, each and every one of us is squirrelling more things into our lives than any generation before us. This is not just as a result of an increasing population, but per capita. With the prevalence of low-cost, low-quality products flooding our shores, we no longer buy things to last us a lifetime. We have decided that a warranty period is enough of a 'lifetime' – even if it's only 12 months – before we embark on an upgrade.

Every year, in the clothing industry alone, a whopping 92 million tons of textile waste are produced annually. That's 3.68 million Olympic-sized swimming pools worth of wasted textiles, which have been grown on cleared land as a monoculture crop – harvested, manufactured, exported, retailed and thrown away. Not to mention the transportation steps in between each stage of the supply chain. This is not entirely surprising when on average, every American woman buys sixty-four new pieces of clothing each year.

At home we generate approximately 2.1 billion tons of household waste each year. Construction and demolition waste makes up a staggering thirty-five to forty per cent of total waste generated globally, while the tourism industry generates around 1.3 billion tons of waste each year.

All this waste causes ecological heartache at every tier of the waste chain. We are using resources, underpaying wages and generating mountains of single-use products that will NEVER BREAK DOWN. Landfills also pose numerous environmental challenges of their own, because they contribute to greenhouse gas emissions as organic waste decomposes and releases methane. Landfills also contaminate soil and water, posing risks to ecosystems and human health.

In many ways, consumption as a pastime has replaced ritual, but of course its empty hollowness is never going to fulfil us in the way our hearts, bodies and souls want to be nurtured. Consumption versus ritualised lives simply don't compare, so naturally we fatigue.

The easiest solution is to stop spending, but nothing is that simple. Our culture has us by the short and curlies and doesn't want us to merely stop. Actually, stopping consumption would be a political and economic disaster for our current system of global capitalism. Our ecological and biological systems would rejoice though, and without them our orchestrated systems just might not have a leg to stand on.

One way of at least slowing the consumption fatigue is to do what I call sidestepping 'shiny' ...

Time vs money

So, this is apparently a representation of the modern human. I don't know about you, but there are definitely times when I don't have time, money or energy. It's quite a quandary that many of us seem to be getting to this state with greater frequency.

I don't need much of any, but I would like a little of each. To meet this balance I simply need to accept that I can't have it all. In fact, I can't have most, but I can have ENOUGH, and enough, when accepted graciously and humbly, is exactly how much I need. For all of us, enough is all we actually need. And when we only take enough, it results in there being enough for everyone.

Quite an ideological concept isn't it? Full of paradox and flaws, I know, but perhaps paradox is simply part of being human, and allowing both to be true at the same time actually allows us to get on with creating a new way of being.

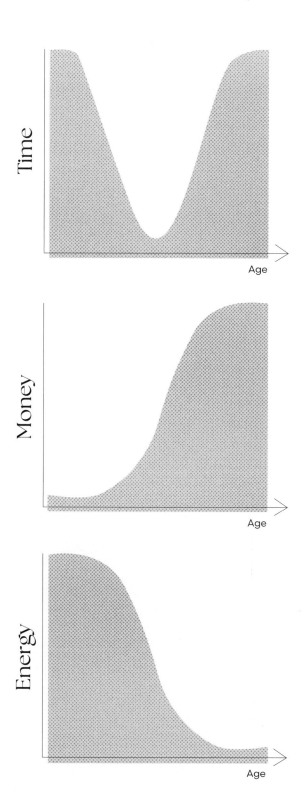

126

HUDDLE ———— *HOW?*

Time and money

This idea might be helpful. When you have a tight-knit huddle, something magical happens that alleviates the competition between time and money. Here's how your huddle can create a tap dance between the two.

Sharing the load, multiplying the joy: Within your close huddle you can join forces and pool resources. Together, you can tackle expenses, find clever cost-saving hacks and lend a helping hand whenever needed. The power of your collective support eases financial pressures and creates a sense of abundance.

Time becomes a treasure to share: With your huddle around you, time takes on a whole new meaning. You discover the joy of collaborating and coordinating schedules, making space for shared adventures and moments of rest. From carpooling to sharing household chores, you free up time for everyone to pursue their dreams without sacrificing precious moments together. Annabel Crabb, journalist and author of *The Wife Drought*, imagined a world where every household had multiple women to fill all the gaps. She was onto something. It doesn't have to be a wife – huddle!

Collective decision-making: We have a responsibility to couple our decisions and send them out into the world, for the sake of animal welfare, human justice, cultural vitality, waste stream minimisation and the endless squandering of precious resources. At the end of every decision is an outcome. By embracing collective decision-making, you ensure the needs and desires of each member are heard and valued. This inclusive approach harmonises your financial and time-related considerations, creating a beautiful balance.

If many hands make light work, many huddle hands redefine work altogether. With support and belonging, with agency and meaningful contribution, and with familiarity and interdependence, time and money no longer feel like adversaries. They become disco partners, thrumming together in a flow of community currency.

The art of wholeness

Could it be that enoughness is also wholeness?

Ever feel like you wear many different hats, but they rarely cross over? It's like each silo in your life is an individual city skyscraper. But imagine a different scenario: what if you could combine all those buildings into one ground-level community? A place where all your pieces come together, creating a vibrant and interconnected whole.

In this community, your personal and professional lives blend seamlessly; your passions, talents and relationships converge, fostering a sense of harmony and purpose. No longer confined to silos, you become a thriving neighbourhood of diverse experiences and aspirations.

Imagine the collaborations that could flourish when you bring your various roles and interests together.

The ideas that would spark, the connections that would deepen and the impact you could make. It's like transforming those towering silos into beautiful bridges that connect all aspects of your life.

By embracing the power of integration, you create a life where each part supports and enhances the others. It's like having a bustling town centre where all your passions, relationships and goals intersect. The sense of fulfilment and joy that comes from living in such a community is truly transformative.

So, let's all channel our inner Mahatma Gandhi, who was not only a political leader but also a philosopher, activist and spiritual guide. His approach to nonviolent resistance, combined with his deep spiritual convictions, allowed him to inspire and lead a whole nation towards independence. Step out of the silos and let your different hats come together in one little patch.

128

DEFINING YOUR
OWN ENOUGHNESS

Sidestep the noise and discover the power of 'enough'. What does it look like for you?

This can be quite a task. It requires serious reflection and brutal honesty with yourself.

Dig deep and ask yourself what 'enough' really means to you.

It's about prioritising your health, nurturing meaningful relationships, finding balance, embracing purpose and finding contentment in the basics. Strip away the excess and focus on what truly matters. Surround yourself with a close-knit huddle that uplifts and supports you. Let go of the chase for more and embrace a life where sufficiency brings true abundance.

What this process also asks is for you to consider what you will do with the excess of things that spill over your 'enough' cup. Inevitably, there will be more than you need and what you choose to do with this is perhaps the truest reflection of how impactful this activity will be for you.

A sobering place to ensure you get real with yourself is a cemetery. Yep, that's right. Take yourself off to your nearest cemetery and get comfortable with the fact that everything you know and love – including you – will see its ultimate end. None of us are capable of avoiding death, so let's get real about what matters while we're here.

If you're having trouble really formulating what your 'enough' statement is, ask yourself:

- Which possessions contribute significantly to my happiness and wellbeing?
- Which possessions are essential for my daily life and which ones are excess?
- What level of financial security and stability do I need to feel comfortable?
- What career goals align with my values and sense of purpose?
- How much success or recognition is enough for me?
- How do I prioritise my time between work, personal life and leisure?
- What level of work and career achievements bring a sense of satisfaction without sacrificing wellbeing?
- What kind of relationships and connections are essential for my happiness and development?
- How much time and energy should I allocate to building and maintaining meaningful relationships?
- What are my personal growth aspirations and when will I feel satisfied?
- How do I balance the pursuit of learning and self-improvement with contentment?
- What habits and practices contribute to my physical and mental wellbeing?
- When do I consider myself healthy and well enough?
- When do I feel I've made a positive contribution to society and how much can I give back?
- What spiritual or philosophical beliefs contribute to my sense of inner peace?
- How much does societal pressure influence my definition of enough?
- When do I catch myself comparing my life to others' and how does that affect my sense of satisfaction?

Once you've pondered these questions, create an 'enough' statement for you and for your household. Be sure everyone is involved, and it's well discussed before agreeing on what 'enough' actually looks like for your family. Acknowledge that it will require some level of sacrifice and commitment to maintain this degree of simplification. Agree on how you will check back in and assess success.

HUDDLE —————— *HOW?*

Redefining enough

Up for a challenge? Whether you frame these activities as games, explorations, rituals or household commitments, it helps to do them together and in the spirit of curiosity – no self-flagellation required.

To BE, not do: Drop the to-do list and create a to-be list. For example, calm, patient, rested, joyful.

Energy audit: How long since you eyeballed your energy usage? Looking into your household's power/gas/fuel consumption can be a fascinating exercise. It reveals hungry appliances, leaky spaces and accidentally-energy-expensive habits. Start with obvious sources of feedback, like bills (and backend usage graphs), before moving on to self-directed detective work that examines doors, seals, insulation, design and personal behaviours. Where can you economise? What can you shore up? How low can you go in the energy use limbo?

Waste-free challenge: Some people prefer making change incrementally; others go all in. However you roll, design a waste-free challenge for yourself, your household or your huddle. Can you go a week without buying anything packaged in plastic? Can you overhaul your pantry and join a local food co-op, committing to shopping in bulk? Can you reflect on your routines and habits to identify where you get stuck? Be patient, you're swimming against the tide.

'Enough' dinners: Cook a tasty meal and check in with yourself and/or your household around the theme of 'enough'. Everyone has a chance to be heard in this roundtable meeting, best held regularly. Questions may include: Are you receiving enough from the household? Are you contributing enough? How much yelling has there been this month? Are the limits of your patience being tested? Are we loving each other's company? Is there enough learning and growth? Are we spending enough quality time?

Are we having enough sex? What season are we in, individually and together?

New skills: Living with less will probably require a swag of new skills like food-growing, bread-making, soap-making, plant propagation and sewing. Can you learn (or at least, experiment with) one new skill each month for an entire year? Be generous and give yourself plenty of time to learn, bedding these new skills into your daily rhythm to hone over a lifetime.

Gratitude practice: Something changes when you switch from passive gratitude to an active practice. For me, there's magic and power in the deliberateness of morning gratitude, writing down those small and marvellous moments that make life sweet. Reflect on the things you are grateful for regularly, such as warm cups of coffee, kind gestures from friends or a beautiful sunset. Cultivating gratitude shifts your focus to the abundance already present in your life.

Unsubscribe and offload: Dive into decluttering your physical and digital spaces. Systematically unsubscribe to all those bothersome emails you don't remember signing up for. Let go of items that are cramping your style and revel in a new-found sense of space and lightness. Shoes are an especially good place to start. So is the third drawer down in the kitchen. Simplifying your surroundings can bring a greater appreciation for what truly matters and help you embrace a more minimalist approach to enoughness.

The pre-purchase pause: Haven't we all bought something new and shiny only to regret it later? So, pause for a jiff before buying. Ask: Do I really need this? Does this thing align with my values and truly make life better? If you can't upcycle or buy second hand, opt for quality over quantity and support local artisans over multinationals. Prioritise experiences rather than material possessions. Be intentional when you tap the plastic. Practise the pause.

Comparison detox: With social media forming a hefty part of our daily diet, it's easy to fall into the comparison trap. You're looking at a curated version of what someone wants you to see, not reality. I know you know this, but be quick to remind yourself lest you fall headlong into the comparison hole. Limit your exposure to social media – sometimes I literally put my phone in a box – and practise self-compassion. Embracing enoughness means valuing your own progress and finding joy in your own journey, free from toxic comparison.

Serious self-care: We all know about self-care, but what about the connection between self-care and enoughness, self-care and contentment, self-care and healing the wound that turns peaceful humans into problematic consumers? Self-care isn't just fluff, it's activism. Carve out time to nourish your mind, body and soul – and be deliberate about it. Engage in simple, grounded activities that bring you joy and calm, like yoga, wandering in nature, drawing, playing music, cloud-gazing, reading a book (during the day!) or spending quality time with good humans you love. Connecting with your own needs takes time, so go slow!

Protect your yes: In my experience, it's easier to give a sunny 'yes!' than a solemn 'no', but unless you get comfortable setting boundaries, the things that really matter to you may simply scatter into the forest. Practise saying 'no' to commitments, tasks or projects that don't align with your priorities or values. Establish healthy boundaries that protect your time, energy and wellbeing. Remind yourself that enoughness is just as much about what you lovingly decline as what you embrace.

Make regenerative decisions: When making decisions, ask yourself a few questions to be sure that life is ultimately the outcome:
• Will your action steal or heal the future?
• Will your decision or action create life or reduce it?
• Does it squash poverty or proliferate it?
• Does it make human life better or worse – for everyone?
• Will disease be prevented or create profit?
• Does it build vitality in communities or annihilate them?
• Will the land be improved on or extracted from?
• Does it contribute to the solving or causing of global warming ?
• Does it truly serve our needs or merely manufacture human wants?
• Do ALL humans have rights on the other side of this decision?
• In short, is the activity extractive or regenerative?

Embracing enoughness is a two-steps-forward-one-step-back kind of process. It's personal and ongoing. Ultimately, you are aiming to change the lens you look through every day, so of course this will take time. Bring a spirit of curiosity and playfulness to these activities and make sure they fit realistically into your life.

MAKE GOAT'S MILK SOAP

Bathroom and kitchen cleaning materials are one of the last bastions to combat in the waste war. In the name of enoughness, get together annually and make enough soap to last all of you the year. This way you can share the moulds, do the washing up once and mix and match different essences and botanicals.

Why goat's milk? It's rich in both saturated and unsaturated fats, making it ideal for soap. Saturated fats increase a soap's lather (the bubbles), while unsaturated fats provide moisturising and nourishment. If you can't access goat's milk easily, replace it in this recipe with tea or water.

Makes 10–12 bars

180 g (6½ oz) caustic soda
400 ml (13½ fl oz) goat's milk, frozen (or tea
    or water, frozen)
1.3 litres (44 fl oz) olive oil
200 ml (7 fl oz) castor oil (you can use any
    other type of oil)
your fave essential oils
your fave botanicals (such as rosemary, rose,
    green tea, calendula, fennel, dried citrus,
    thyme or oats), for infusing and decorating

To make the lye, put the caustic soda in a stainless steel bowl. Gently add the goat's milk (or tea/water). It will instantly be very warm. Mix together and let it cool to 38°C (100°F) – temperature is important.

Meanwhile, combine the olive and castor oils in a saucepan and heat to 38°C (100°F). Line a 2 litre (68 fl oz) mould with baking paper.

Tip the warm oil mixture into a plastic bucket then slowly add the lye and blend using a handheld blender until thick – it will take 3–15 minutes depending on the air temperature, so be sure to keep your eye on it and be ready to pour it quickly into the mould. Be careful not to splash it on your skin.

Stir through the essential oils and botanicals. Pour the mixture into the prepared mould and decorate with more botanicals as desired.

Cover with plastic wrap and store in a consistently warm place. Check every hour or so and once firm enough to cut (like butter), cut with a warm knife – this might be in 2 hours, 2 days or 2 weeks. Keep your eye on it. If you leave it too long it will become brittle and crack when cut.

HUDDLE

STORY

Enoughness as a design principle

A black sheep of the design industry, Jane Hilliard is pushing back on the bigger-is-better mantra so prevalent in the world of architecture. Instead, she is asking her clients when it became the norm to have two basins in the bathroom and three toilets, challenging them to think with a lens of enoughness. Even if the bank has offered them adequate money to have the extras, why not say no and enjoy more of life without a mortgage hanging over their head?

Just because 'you've worked hard and deserve it' doesn't mean you should aim for the biggest and shiniest.

'We stay in tents and shacks when we go away, and there's a romantic simplicity to this experience,' said Jane. 'Why can't we bring this spirit into our own house? How about an outdoor kitchen? Why not?'

Jane's enoughness exudes from her everyday existence. Despite being an architect capable of building herself the latest and greatest, she hasn't. Not because she can't but because she doesn't need to. Living in a humble home in Tasmania, she says 'enough' for her is being able to pick fresh food from her backyard and cook it for her next meal. It's also about having enough bandwidth to be patient with her children, interested in her community and having space to take the time she needs for her own wellbeing. She doesn't carry unnecessary debt for unnecessary things. It's also knowing that she can only take on so many projects at any given time if she wants to enjoy each and every one of them. Sure, it strokes her ego and fills her bank account faster, but what's the point in either of those things if her existence is highly strung, exhausted and miserable.

Once you frame life in this way, saying no to more than you can handle is easy, but it requires a need to be happy to live in a much simpler way. Who's in? It's harder than it sounds – given our cultural inclination to be influenced by the endless growth banter – but a great place to start is to turn off the noise and create your own 'enough narrative'.

She works a nine-day fortnight, lives in a house that doesn't have all the mod cons, doesn't bother with trends or fads, finds beauty in the very slow, simple, messy humanness of life and 'houses that are really lived in, are messy, creative, warming and capable of holding us'. Her weekends are void of to-do lists. Instead, she revels in unplanned downtime with family and friends, and enjoys taking a left-hand turn for a spontaneous opportunity should one pop up.

So, who's up for a life that has emotional, financial and clock time bandwidth for left-hand turns?

Let's

talk

When you can't go over or under, start talking. Face into the awkwardness that open communication requires. The simple answer often sits on the other side of complexity and the only way to reach it is through the very guts of it. It will take bravery, sincerity and vulnerability to yarn openly and honestly, but it's the skill that begins the pathway to deeper, more permanent solutions for humanity.

'You can speak well if your
tongue can deliver the
message of your heart.'

John Ford

Remembering how to yarn

Yarning: a term used by First Nations peoples all over Australia, and something we ought to do a little more of! This informal conversation style threaded with a little storytelling may sound casual, but yarning carries significant cultural and social importance. It's a way of connecting, sharing knowledge and building relationships, which goes beyond simple chitchat.

While it might not seem so, it isn't just an information exchange, but also a space for deep listening, understanding and collective wisdom sharing. Each person speaks from their own experiences, perspectives and cultural backgrounds, building a sense of respect and inclusivity.

The key to a good yarn is in its ability to create a safe, open environment where people can share personal stories, cultural traditions and knowledge. Yarning builds trust through active engagement, empathy and genuine connection. It leads to learning, challenges assumptions and shares insights that may not jump out in more formal settings.

Yarning is intergenerational communication for the passing down of wisdom. Elders and knowledge holders play a significant role in yarning circles, sharing their experiences and teachings with younger generations. This helps preserve cultural heritage, strengthen community bonds and nurture a collective sense of identity.

The power of yarning lies in its invitation for active participation and active listening, and it values everyone's voice. Yarning is not about hierarchy or dominance; it's about creating a space where diverse perspectives are honoured and celebrated.

By valuing a good ol' yarn, we tap into its transformative potential and build stronger, more inclusive communities where everyone's voice is heard and valued.

Raising our voices without shouting

There are voices everywhere. Not just in places with political pull, but in places where everyone can be heard, if we listen: workplaces, schools, universities, community groups, sports clubs, social groups, co-operatives, playgrounds. Now is the time for grassroots movements to gather and garner the murmurings so they can become rumblings. In turn they become coalitions of the unlikely, creating a unified vision for a new culture – one that is humble and huddled. The voices with these messages have been speaking for a long time, coming mostly from indigenous wisdom holders, but now we need to make a choice to start listening.

Spoken and written words are the dominant way we communicate. In addition to the sound that forms in our mouth when we speak and the flow of the pen when we write, there is so very much in the way we interact that cannot be taken for granted. Communication is so much more than simply talking or writing. Think about hanging out with a baby who has no verbal communication. With a little attention they can convey messages despite a lack of linguistic understanding. In return, they are listening to your voice, reading tone, pace and facial expressions – all non-linguistic cues that drive a connection for belonging.

All of these things are context and when layered on top of the written and spoken word, they complete the story. They allow us to really feel the communication, not just to hear or see it.

In fact, the shortcoming of the written and spoken word is that it minimises the depth of emotions and felt experiences associated with the world. When we undertook rites of passage experiences with our kids, the guides made a point of the experience not being talked about with those who hadn't attended. Not to keep it secret, but because of the magnitude of the experience, which was beyond the depth of words.

Limiting it to the spoken word would minimise the experience and make it less than it was.

Words often become singular and linear, which in turn ignores the 'whole'. For example, if I write or say the word 'leaf', you conjure an individual green leaf sitting on its lonesome. But a leaf is not just a leaf. Yes, it's a thing in its own right, but it's also a whole. When we talk about just a leaf we create an artificial boundary that limits the complete story. This is called a holon. In order to really understand the full context of the leaf, we need to also recognise the relationship that the leaf has to its parent tree or plant, and the tree's relationship with the earth, the landscape that surrounds it and the wildlife that interacts with it, and so on. To simply use the word 'leaf' to describe something fails to truly understand the leaf.

In order to really do justice to the topic at hand, we make an assumption that our listener or reader has a great deal of capability to backfill the details that contextualise and make the story whole. Given the pace our world beats, this is rarely given adequate time for deep understanding. It's precisely here that messages get misinterpreted and frustrations or sensitivities rear their head.

Knowing that language limits our thinking and is often causative in the compartmentalisation of knowledge is a potent place to begin. It's here we can learn how to communicate using other tools and in a way that stokes the fire of an emerging culture of huddles.

HUDDLE —————— *HOW?*

More than words

Two-way communication: To deliver and to receive. Both are fundamental.

Body awareness: Our bodies hold valuable insights and communicate strongly without saying a single thing. Being attuned to our own bodily sensations, representations and interactions helps us understand our own needs and read the situation as it unfolds around us.

Mindful presence: Being fully present enhances communication. Drop the distractions, judgements and preconceived notions. Instead, immerse yourself in the right-here-right-now.

Choose your language: Don't mince words and don't be ambiguous. The selection of words and the way we deliver them can be the difference between building and alienating your huddle. And only promise what you can actually deliver. It's not okay to simply say you'll contribute to something or work collaboratively, and then not make the effort to be available or not have the patience and willingness to listen to the needs, ideas and voices of everyone around the table.

W.A.I.T. (Why Am I Talking): Give conversation space before jumping in with answers or solutions. Let others have time to resolve for themselves in their own way. Willingly participate, fully show up, pay attention and don't be attracted or attached to outcomes. Conversation that is truly two way is free to meander where it needs to go and you're not in control of it. In some ways it develops its own pathway, and you are merely a participant in it.

HUDDLE

STORY

Talking to heal in the Amazon

The Amazonian people of Brazil actively use talking to heal wounds. When someone in their tribe finds themselves in a place of grief or trouble-making, the community doesn't banish or punish the individual. They recognise the gap that needs to be filled and each of them has a responsibility. The individual is brought before the entire community, who form a many layered circle of support around them. They ask the question: What hasn't been said that needs to be said? They then proceed to stand by the side of the person in need, holding them and hearing them until the talking that's needed runs dry.

Empathy

Step into the shoes of others to understand their emotions, experiences and needs. This involves not only recognising and validating their feelings, but also responding with kindness and compassion.

To do this we need to become an active listener. A what? An active listener. It's a lost art really, to know how to listen attentively without judgement or interruption, and it's powerful. It involves giving your full presence to someone else, understanding their perspectives and validating their experiences. Through active listening we create a safe space for open banter.

When surrounded by a symphony of voices it can be a challenge to stay connected. In the midst of bustling conversations we often find ourselves lost in our own thoughts, waiting for our turn to speak. But what if we shift pace, set aside our ego, relinquish the need to be heard and create a space for others to share what they need to? It goes beyond mere hearing; delving into the depths of emotions, perspectives and unspoken nuances.

   When we listen with empathy we forge connections that span the gaps of misunderstanding and judgement. It's an opportunity to feel the heartbeat of another and witness their joys, sorrows, hopes and fears. In this space of deep listening we acknowledge the profound value of each person's story.

   Empathetic listening is transformative as it's a force that fosters understanding, unity and a sense of belonging, validation and shared humanity.

   It's a big call but it could even be the cornerstone of community building. It transcends differences and builds bridges of connection. It allows us to dismantle the walls of isolation and creates a space where trust, compassion and collaboration thrive.

'It takes two years to learn to speak and sixty to learn to keep quiet.'

Unknown

140

CIRCLE TIME

Humans have been sitting in circles since the beginning of time. Today we call them yarning circles, sister circles, singing circles, fer-men-tation circles, gratitude circles, rewilding circles, community circles, ceremonial circles. In reality, they can be whatever suits you and your huddle.

Being 'in circle' carries a certain degree of ceremony. It's good to honour as it contributes to holding the group together. There are a few things to frame the gathering that, regardless of the group you are curating, will make for smoother sailing.

• Anything that happens in the circle stays in the circle.
• A theme makes the gathering stay focused, and clearly articulating this at the beginning of the circle helps to keep everyone on track. Use the theme to pose questions for group response and to curate activities.
• Regular (fortnightly to monthly) gatherings make for more powerful connection.
• Circles with four to twelve are ideal.
• Having a 'speaking stick' means everyone has the chance to speak if they wish.

• Placing something in the centre gives the group a shared focus area – perhaps a fire, candle or sculpture or an interesting seasonally relevant collection of foraged things like feathers, leaves, pine cones.
• It's not compulsory for everyone in the circle to speak.
• Always begin with a gentle arrival and check-in before you begin specific activities.
• Readings and singing are useful and beautiful ways to settle the group when they arrive.
• Arriving silently means the banter and conversation doesn't take off before you can reign it in.
• Neutral venues are more potent. Outside is wonderful too.

Although hosting the first one or two can feel awkward, it's new, so be patient and let the magic of the group's collective energy collaboratively bring intimacy and ideas to the table to be shared. Consider rotating hosts and venues and let the formal structure of the process emerge to suit the group. The circle will evolve quickly because of the intimate nature of these safe sharing spaces.

STORY

Truth talking

I found myself hosting a community gathering in a tourist town and our conversation meandered to their experience of housing shortages due to second homeowners jumping on the Airbnb holiday rental bandwagon, leaving locals without beds. A man in his fifties (one of only two men from forty in the room) stood up and very quietly talked about his 'enough'. He shared that he was a single dad caring for his young daughter. He had lived in this community for more than twenty years and was a generous contributor to the fabric of the town via his various volunteer roles in the fire brigade, on the school committee, fundraiser sausage sizzles and offering his tools and time to many working bees. He spoke of hardship with his ex-wife's mental health and how it ultimately led to him having to sell his house to cover costs. Eager to maintain stability for his daughter after his ex-wife took her own life, and recognising that his 'enough' was steeped in this place, within this township, surrounded by the people who had helped him through such difficult times, he stayed. But he was finding it progressively more difficult to find a home. The town was small and he had been retrenched from his stable job. By prioritising his daughter's needs he had found it hard to find another reliable job, so made ends meet with multiple part-time jobs. He did not have the money to buy another house in the now inflated local housing market. Having moved four times in five years as rental homes became holiday homes, he was on the brink of breaking.

The room was silent and everyone's eyes were facing down. It was overwhelming, actually. As I was mustering a response, a young woman stood and walked over to him. 'You used to work with my dad and he always said you were a good man,' she said. 'I'm so sorry this has happened to you. Thank you for sharing your story. In trying to set ourselves up, my husband and I have just bought our third house in town. Just as you say, we were planning to put it on the holiday rental market, but I can see that this thinking only hollows out our community and leaves the people who make it such a wonderful place to live – not just pass through as a visiting tourist – in a compromised position. I'd like to offer you our house. We have so much more than enough and you clearly don't.' He said nothing, just nodded and they both sat down.

About a month later, she contacted me to let me know that she had signed a five-year rental contract with him to ensure he was stable until his daughter finished high school. She had offered him a vendor finance option should he wish to buy the property from them on terms that worked for him. She finished her message saying, 'Thank you for encouraging our community to talk and to really listen to each other.'

142

Compromise

'Community cannot be treated like a supermarket, servicing your needs. You need to be willing to contribute through the ups and downs.'

Casper ter Kuile

Have you ever heard the quickly flung quip: compromise is an outcome that satisfies no-one? How about instead of seeing it as a grey no-man's-land where no-one is happy, we acknowledge that finding a middle ground is a very real way forward in creating communities that are inclusive, fair and more capable of existing into perpetuity.

Compromise can be challenging, demanding a willingness to let go of rigid positions and embrace flexibility. Through compromise, we seek solutions that honour the needs and aspirations of everyone involved. Sometimes progress over perfection leads us in the right direction rather than reaching a stalemate.

Death of division

To counter division in our communities we need to embrace diversity and actively seek common ground to bridge the divide. We need to open our ears attentively to diverse perspectives and offer understanding and compassion. Education on cultural competence and tolerance also plays a pivotal role. Encouraging respectful discourse and discouraging the spread of misinformation or stereotypes are essential. Additionally, promoting inclusive policies and practices within communities, workplaces and institutions all contribute to a more harmonious and united world.

In the past few years we've seen instability perpetuated by the deep division around issues like vaccination, lockdowns and government intervention. The opinions have been rife – often verging on fundamental – where labels were flung at anyone whose view differed from our own. Considering these complex issues as singular and in isolation is altogether unhelpful and reductionist. They are far from it. This simplified approach has been collected by the mainstream media narrative and is enough to drive cultural division – even in countries renowned for their political stability.

None of us are singular; humans are much too interesting for that. Accepting our contradictions makes us more capable. Life is a paradox where multiple realities can be true at the same time. Together they make up the many parts of a whole. The path to unity and collaboration ain't no walk in the park, but it's worth navigating it via practised compromise skills for the sake of collectivism and to build resilient relationships with our neighbours, work colleagues, schoolyard mates or community crew.

HUDDLE _____ _HOW?_

Say hello to vulnerability

Lead with love: Before you begin any inner work, be sure to check your internal monologue and judgement, and acknowledge that you are loved.

Self-awareness: Cultivating self-awareness is crucial in recognising and understanding our own vulnerabilities. Take time for self-reflection, explore your emotions and identify areas where you may feel guarded or resistant to being vulnerable.

Practise self-empathy: Empathy for others is great. On the same shelf of importance is a sense of compassion for yourself. This can actually be trickier than offering it to someone else, but its importance can't be underestimated.

Trustworthy relationships: Surround yourself with supportive and trustworthy mates who create an environment where vulnerability is accepted and valued. Seek out relationships that encourage open communication, empathy and no judgement. Equally, sidestep those who continue to draw you towards drama, self-deprecation and overcomplicated communication.

Start small: When learning how to do this, take small steps. Share personal thoughts, experiences or emotions with someone you trust to gradually build up your comfort level. Each small act of vulnerability will strengthen your courage to share more.

Accept imperfection: Recognise that vulnerability is not about being flawless or having all the answers. It is about embracing your authentic self, flaws and all. Embrace the idea that vulnerability is a strength, not a weakness.

Make mistakes: Mistakes and failures are opportunities for growth and connection as learning experiences rather than sources of shame. Sharing these experiences with others is often endearing.

Seek guidance: If you find it challenging to navigate vulnerability, seek support from those who know, such as professionals with a pocketful of insights, tools and techniques.

Courageous act: Remember that vulnerability takes courage. It requires stepping out of your comfort zone and creating a space for deep and meaningful connections to flourish.

Embracing vulnerability is transformative. While society may not always encourage us to lay our hearts on our sleeve, we can learn to unlock and share our vulnerabilities willingly by seeking out places that support it.

144

'Remember who checks on you
when you are quiet. Those are
your people.'

Unknown

Talker on paper

One of my best mates tells me I'm not an author. Rather she calls me a 'talker on paper' and right she is. In many ways, I write the way I talk: lyrically, creatively and in stories. It's something that has been honed via a lifetime of journalling, writing and public speaking for a living. Even if you've not had much experience with this, using this lens is a perfect way to kick off your love affair with the written word.

My grandfather always advised us to steer clear of writing anything down that could possibly be used against us at a later time. While it was sound advice, the opposite is also true. Writing down your thoughts can be the ideal way to unpack the complexity in your cranium and one of the best ways to communicate what's in your head and heart without the raw (potentially fraught) spoken word, which may fail you during delivery.

Journalling is an easy and accessible tool to stick in your toolkit. No-one else needs to ever see it, so your grammar and punctuation won't be judged and your heart and head can flow through your hand and into your pencil. All the while you are unpacking your problems, clarifying goals, boosting creativity, generating gratitude and offering a healthy emotional outlet. If the topic at hand generates a lightbulb moment and it feels celebratory, you might rip the page out and stick it on your fridge. Equally, if it was a swirling page of words, which poured incoherently from you but felt relieving to be rid of, you might burn it ceremoniously to symbolise letting something go.

We don't have to be our only audience for our written thoughts. Why not write a letter?

LETTER WRITING

Writing a letter gives you time to articulate without compromise and can be used for so many audiences. It doesn't need to be multiple pages long to justify the cost of the stamp or the time it takes. I promise the thrill it'll bring to the person on the receiving end will outweigh the time difference between sending a text and sending a written letter.

Love letter: Not just for 1940s movie stars separated by distance or circumstance, a love letter is a glorious gift of the heart. Poetic or pragmatic, poems left on the pillow, notes tucked in lunch boxes, posted prose or simple, speedy notes just because. Don't get stage fright. Rather, normalise it as part of your everyday dynamic with those in your huddle.

Gratitude letter: Relationships are complex – heck, sometimes beyond words – but don't let those words stay tucked in your heart. If saying I love you and I'm grateful for all you've done for me is too hard to form on your lips, get writing. Perhaps it won't be as rosy as I've suggested, but a letter is still a ripper place to document your thoughts and let your folks, friends, mentors or even strangers know you're grateful for them.

Letter to your future self: The way we think is shaped by those we spend our time with, the books we read, the jobs we have and the hopes we hold. Writing a letter to your future self is much like creating a time capsule of your current day persona. Share your thoughts of the day, aspirations, concerns and interpretation of current affairs. Seal it and save it for later.

Letter to your younger self: What guidance would you offer to your younger self? Insights gained with every year that passes can be the perfect way to really consolidate acceptance of where life has taken you. Acknowledgement that you've evolved your thinking can be a powerful way to rebuild patterns and behaviour.

Creative adventures: Write about a memorable adventure, even if it's a night in your own backyard. Get creative in the details of the sights, sounds and emotions. It's amazing how embedded the experience becomes when you mentally capture the sensorial experience as you live it with the intention of writing it down.

Book, movie or recipe review: Next time you watch a movie, read a book or eat out, write a review. Perhaps you could send it to a friend and kick start a two-way review series together.

Letters of encouragement: Why not! Letters of encouragement to friends or family members going through challenging times cost you nothing and mean the world. Offer support, share inspiring quotes and remind them of their magic.

Seasonal reflections: Let the seasons in the outside world be the perfect muse to document what you see. Share how each season impacts you, your favourite seasonal activities and ideas for rituals at this time.

Preserving memories: Penning personal experiences and sharing them with everyone who participated creates a tangible record and immortalises significant events, allowing the chance to reflect in later years.

Letter writing is a definite go-to for your huddle-building efforts. It's unmistakably deliberate and says a great deal before the words are even read.

How the arts can connect us

Yes, let's talk and write, but also let's create together using communication that doesn't involve words.

The arts hold a profound capacity to connect and bridge gaps between individuals and groups. This form of non-verbal expression – painting, sculpting, cooking, gardening, clothes creation, dance, music and performance – provides alternative means of communication, allowing individuals to express their emotions, experiences and perspectives without relying solely on words. It can transcend language barriers and reach a deeper level of understanding in a more subtle way.

A friend from my earlier life has a beautiful story to explain the power of the arts to communicate. She danced throughout her high school years and early twenties. She loved it. I marvelled at her commitment and watched her evolution from dancer to choreographer, never missing her shows. At her very last performance just before she graduated from university she came onto the stage for an interview. She explained that she had been estranged from her mum and extended family since she was twelve, and had danced all these years to be close to her mum, who had also danced as a child. Unexpectedly, her mum stood up in the audience and shared that while she had not been able to connect with her daughter since they were separated, she had anonymously attended every single show. She said she had felt closer to her daughter because she could see her mature and evolve through her dancing. It was a particularly emotional segue into the two of them forging a relationship as adults, independent of the complex family trauma of earlier years.

My own experience as an artist's daughter was similar, but the language was in the form of ink, chalk and pencil on paper. I was estranged from my dad for a number of years as a teenager. Having been particularly close before I took time out, his art was the world that we all orbited – for better or worse.

With the better part of a five-year separation under our belt, I was surprised to see him enter the homewares store I worked in casually on my eighteenth birthday carrying a framed artwork. He said virtually nothing, but handed me the work. I recognised it instantly. Years earlier, he had been teaching still-life classes and completed a range of uncharacteristic works on paper of flowers in a vase. The colour and movement of them had struck me as a twelve-year-old and I had longed for one on my bedroom wall. Alas it was to be included in the next exhibition and I let it go, imagining I'd never see it again.

My birthday gift was this exact piece. Without words, our bridge building to adult friendship had begun. Of course, it would be a number of years before we could fully mend our relationship. It was a painting trip of his that I attended in the outback that provided the greatest opportunity to bring to a head the issues that had been festering for a decade. Something about being on neutral territory – with him in his happiest of creative places and me brave enough to say all the things I'd been holding for a very long time. Art was central to the process of healing.

By engaging in artistic creations as a huddle, everyone can unleash their creativity, problem-solve collectively and learn from one another's unique perspectives. And this in turn opens up a dialogue for deeper understanding and empathy.

Building common language

If words are our primary tool then it stands to reason that it will be an easier process if we use a language understood by everyone at the table. Notwithstanding the fact that many don't speak English, a shared language serves as a unifying tool to facilitate understanding, cooperation and collaboration among individuals or groups. It helps eliminate barriers to communication, ensuring that messages are conveyed accurately and interpreted correctly.

This shared linguistic foundation fosters a sense of community and inclusivity, as everyone has equal access to information and can actively participate in discussions. In diverse settings, where people may have different native languages, establishing a common language promotes equity and minimises the potential for misunderstandings. Whether in business, education or any other context, prioritising a common language contributes significantly to the creation of robust and harmonious communication channels. Ultimately, it's not just the words used but the aligned values that attract people to be on the same page.

In defining your communication plan, start with the values you plan to appeal to, clarify the words that resonate with this and use metaphors and analogies to bring it to life. In some cases, it may be worthwhile developing a new language or vocabulary specific to a particular context or community. This can involve collectively creating terms, symbols or phrases that encapsulate shared values, goals or processes. It fosters a sense of ownership and promotes inclusivity among participants.

Futuresteading was exactly this. I couldn't find a word that was relevant to everyone and encouraged people to make decisions that lead to a stable future and value a home-based life.

Now I see it as the title for community groups and used in people's online profile descriptions and hashtags. It's fun and intimate to create a language of your own. Building a common language is an ongoing process. Encourage open dialogue and provide opportunities for feedback to ensure that the language used evolves and adapts to the changing needs and dynamics of the community. Regular check-ins and discussions can help identify areas where clarity and alignment can be improved.

149

SACRED READING

Given the depth and range of written material available, it would be sacrilege to become so lured by the screen in our hands that we no longer use the old-school book.

One way of making it collaborative and connecting you to your kin is to turn it into shared or sacred reading material.

Over the years, Charlie and I have refined a double act on the reading front. By both reading different books then discussing them at length with each other, we voraciously inhale books. It's quite incredible how many books you can get through this way AND how much more you absorb when you discuss each passing chapter.

Literally anything can be a sacred text and generate deep conversation. Read it together, a paragraph or page at a time, then interact by finding ways to connect the text to your own life. It's a gift waiting for us if we pay attention and give it the time to be considered.

The way to go deeper is to make the connection between the text and our lives. This breeds a capacity to really listen and really respond. When many voices participate in the sacred reading process, across many generations and in many locations, it ensures we step outside our bell jar of safety. By using the text as a guide and reading aloud, deep conversations – where opinions differ and contradictions present themselves – can unfold safely.

MAKE AND USE TALKING STONES

With your crew, collect a range of stones that are small and flat. With simple acrylic paints, add a small symbol to each stone and let them dry in the sun. These symbols can be anything you like, but be sure they are easily recognisable and will prompt conversation or storytelling.

Around a fire, picnic rug, talking circle or coffee table, pass the bag of stones around, with each person taking one stone in their hot little hand. One by one, each person will tell a short tale prompted by the stone they hold. It might be make-believe, it might be a joke, it might be a riddle or it might be a story about their own life. Limit the time each person has so everyone gets to have a turn.

HUDDLE ———— *HOW?*

More chatter

If you can't find the words yourself: Find them in music or books written by someone else and gift a copy or make a mixed tape – okay, so these days it's a Spotify playlist.

Go bushwalking or take a drive: It's amazing how much easier it is to get through the tricky topics when you're side-by-side and not making eye contact.

Take ownership over your power of attention: Observe how others respond to your attention on them. Attention leads to intimacy. Without it we are deleting the relational and increasing the demand of a commoditised attention reality – hello screens and apps.

Turn your listening ears on: Challenge yourself to become an active listener.

Create reasons and ways to get talking:

- Light a fire under the stars and raise the subject in the dark under a dwarfing sky. It'll keep things in perspective and wrap the conversation in a blanket of safety.
- Create a sacred reading book club. Start with an easy read while you get used to the idea of reading aloud to one another and discussing it 'in circle'.
- Join or begin a circle. Women's rewilding circles, full moon circles, men's circles, menstrual circles – you choose the theme and create the rules as you go.
- Host a fer-men-tation gathering. The concept is as simple as inviting men in your life to join a regular catch-up with their fermented goodies playing their part as props: bread, beer, kraut, kimchi, salami. With beers in bellies and bread broken together, the conversation will flow. Add a fire for good measure and you've got yourself a fer-men-tation group.

Community heartbeats

Not one community is alike and getting to know them takes time, humility and curiosity. Each one is as individual as our handwriting style, but learning their language, tone, pace and expectation provides a window into its soul, and in time, enables entry provided you have the courage to tell the truth. Truth is raw and contagious, bringing connections which enhance hopefulness and dilute apathy. Communities are both blood and chosen, but they need to be understood. Once you understand yours, spring into action and get involved.

152

'Imagine a future where most of your food comes from nearby farmers who are committed to producing delicious, healthy nourishment for your community. Imagine children running, playing and exploring freely and safely under the watch of friends and neighbours. Imagine the money you spend on everyday goods helping a local business owner pay for their family's healthcare, instead of enabling a distant CEO to buy their fourth home. Localisation is that future.'

Local Futures

As the man with the legendary beard, TV host and landscape architect Costa Georgiadis said, 'It's those little practical things that are able to take the urgency and turn it into real, active change. And go ahead, call it "activism", because it's people getting "active".'

Finding a way to be in service comes naturally to some and is actively learned by others, but it's certainly crucial when creating a path that builds community. A place to begin is by developing an interest in the way humans connect, offer kindness, build acceptance and create equality and justice.

'Ask yourself, for the sake of community, would you rather be right or happy?'

Charlie Showers

154

Sacrifice for the greater good

'There's a finely tuned balancing act required when curating a plan for our community. It can't be so planned that we disable the ability for emergent ideas and individuality, but it can't be so fluid that it leaves everyone feeling ambiguous and paralysed.'

'Kids and parenting styles are surely one of the hottest potential bones of contention and so too is the degree to which one contributes or is perceived to contribute. A sense of imbalance can rift groups irreparably if not addressed. The key to allowing points of difference to exist in one community is to learn how to address rising tensions as a group. This takes practice, time and sometimes help from an objective outsider.'

My small but long and insightful observations of quite a few friends living in intentionally collective places fill me with admiration for their gumption and willingness to endeavour along this path. They share their experiences and learnings openly as they navigate the twists and turns, steep climbs and deep chasms of what it means to rebuild a culture that operates collectively.

Without dropping my friends in it as they all still live in their communities, I collected a few comments from them to share with you – I'll keep them anonymous. While I know most of us don't have plans to live in an intentional community in the immediate future, their stories are really important to hear. In many ways they are providing us with the results from the Petri dish that tells us what will or won't work when we inevitably have to collectivise.

'It would be so much easier to exist as a nuclear entity, but if we don't begin relearning these collective skills now, we will be yet another generation away from embedding the necessary knowledge. This is multigenerational work, so the time to begin was yesterday.'

>>>

156

'Living communally has taught me more about myself than I ever would have learned if I'd continued to exist in my own nuclear world. The need for self-reflection is fundamental. There's no time for apathetic behaviour because the consequences are too great.'

'The interaction of humans is far more time-consuming and emotional than the creation of the physical infrastructure we need to house us all. I can swing a hammer with my hands, but I have to converse and interact with my heart.'

'Living collectively at a time when people are still building their identity around land ownership and outward displays of success takes courage and bravery because it's bloody hard. When living in community, there's nowhere to hide, so you are in your truest form and on show for many to witness. While they can indeed offer support, they also hold you to account.'

'Slowly I've learned to make my decisions based on the needs of the collective as a priority over the needs of me. Of course, I can't always guarantee this, but if I do decide to suit myself, I have to justify and explain myself to my community. For this you must learn empathy, humility and cracking communication skills.'

'Interestingly, one of the most potent traits required when living communally is a strong sense of self. In my experience, it's those who actually don't NEED the community who find their place most seamlessly.'

'It took a long time for me to decide on the balance of alone time and communal time. In a collective community there is ALWAYS someone available to play with, but while this can fill all your days and enhance your sense of FOMO if you don't engage, it's really important to seek solitude so you don't lose yourself in the "everyone".'

157

Their commitment to this way of life is a profound contribution to the greater good, particularly at a time when so few are willing to challenge the status quo. The western world maintains a facade of business as usual, fuelled by 'abundance', allowing many to comfortably retreat behind their very own fences, inside their own four walls and participate in the things that interest them only at the times that suit them.

This self-indulgent way of life is far from representative of a collective existence. Our ability to enjoy this independence stems from the aftermath of a short-lived experiment extracting resources from the natural world. The influence of the dollar in this narrative allows those with sufficient means to effortlessly bypass what would otherwise require negotiation, compromise, empathy and interaction.

Despite the existence of complexity and challenges that those in my sphere living in these communities have acknowledged, all of them have continued to live this way. Opting for shared daily child rearing, food growing, songs of gratitude in ceremony ahead of meals, willingness to face the hard conversations and acknowledgement of the differing views and needs.

I've sat at potluck dinners in these communities – even during times of turbulence where the examples of difficulty are piling up – and still felt an unexplainable pull to this way of being. I know we can't click our fingers and have the skills, rituals, rhythms, communication capability, ceremony and selflessness to adopt such a different way of existence, but I'm grateful to those who are working on it and sharing what they learn as they go.

The seeds of community are going to be different in each environment and be influenced by the individuals involved, the culture that emerges from the group, the model chosen and the pace and tone. But there's no doubt that learning the good, bad and ugly from those already trialling it is a great place for us to begin the collective returning.

Community leadership

It takes a special person to put their hand up to be a leader. It's hard to swallow the oxymoronic need to seek community input while also being capable of making the final decision. Good leaders empower individuals within the community to find their niche and bring all the pieces together to form the whole.

Community leadership can, at times, be difficult but in the pursuit of decentralised localisation, relying on local leadership becomes crucial. However, the presence of diverse voices and potential conflicts can pose challenges. Identifying leaders, supporting them and fostering unity despite the presence of unwilling coalitions is the challenge our communities face.

Skilled leaders create shared vision and values of the collective, with a true desire to nurture wellbeing through collaboration and the finding of common ground. Leaders who can bridge gaps and navigate conflicts effectively are essential for fostering unity.

Trusting their judgement takes time to establish but ultimately, they need to be enabled to make decisions autonomously in case of a collective stalemate. It's easy to be a leader when times are grand, but when times get tough, true leaders show their cards. Trust within the community helps solidify support for leaders and encourages unity.

158

Ego let go

Within the collective huddle is the dynamic combination of many individuals. What a glorious pot of potential this offers, but ONLY if the individuals are united in their commitment to the collective. In many ways this requires us to get out of our own way. Perhaps a tad challenging in our hedonistic modern western world, but it's a crucial step towards building a community that beats in unison. Stepping aside so others can shine gives space for everyone's unique brilliance to be offered to the collective.

Getting curious and staying open means you ask more questions than you offer answers for. My stepdad must surely be one of the most well-read men I know, but when he first meets people, he has this knack for saying nothing about himself and queuing questions back-to-back. Even when it's a subject he knows a great deal about, he never offers an opinion or interrupts. The open curiosity and space offered evokes an open book from his conversation partner and they share overtly. 'There's always something you can learn,' he says. 'If they don't know anything about me, they don't curb what they tell me.'

Shutting your mouth and attuning your ears is only one part of the puzzle in getting out of your own way. Channelling humility goes a long way too. This doesn't mean doubt yourself; it means mentor your internal monologue to say I love you but remain humble. It means keep yourself in check. Drop the performance and acknowledge your shortcomings. Take time to create a genuine openness to learning, a willingness to acknowledge and learn from mistakes, and an understanding that everyone has something valuable to offer.

Perhaps it's time to let people get to know your soul, even if they don't know what you do for a living.

Finding balance: setting the pace

Community-led organisations are rarely anything but all consuming, so it's important to set a pace in keeping with the capacity of the community you are part of.

As co-founder of a community food co-op I had this obnoxious idea: if I could just set the pace and lead by example, others would follow and between us we would fill all the gaps for the things that needed doing. But this approach led to a few things that could have possibly been avoided had I moved at the pace of the community.

By moving at my pace, I didn't allow time for the community around me to get to know each other, formulate a united vision or build trust. By moving at my pace, I was leading from the front rather than by everyone's side, which meant my ideas were yet to land with others and I inevitably had to deliver initiatives single-handedly. By moving at my pace, I alienated others who didn't feel they could bring value to the efforts in the same way, so they didn't participate at all.

Pace also tends to be linear, but communities are not linear. They are intricate and dynamic networks of interconnected relationships, shared values and diverse interactions. Rather than following a straightforward path, communities exhibit complexity, adaptability and a continuous surging and strangling of ideas, contributions and efforts. They are vibrant and evolving ecosystems shaped by the collective endeavours and experiences of their members. The rhythm of collaboration mirrors the natural ebb and flow of a living, breathing entity.

In fairness, our community co-op existed for eight years. It was a really strong voice in developing a local food action plan, local government food strategy, school education programs and grow-the-grower initiatives, and was a foundational brick of community for a really engaged group of locals who were committed to eating locally-grown food.

It was a wild ride and many of my closest comrades are still my closest women folk, but there's no doubt that not only did the approach cause me to suffer incredible burnout, but it often resulted in the complete opposite of what I desired.

Just like any relationship, getting to know your community takes time and it really does need that time to build trust, share experiences and get a sense of who your people are and where you can contribute.

Things you can do while courting your community:

Find your community's rhythm: Get in tune with the unique pitch of your community. Understand its needs, capabilities and passions. This will help you find a rhythm that matches the beat of your collective crew.

Be purpose made: Prioritise your goals and focus on initiatives that bring joy and make a meaningful impact. Choose projects that ignite excitement and align with the community's capacity. Then, stay true to your purpose and be careful not to aim to be all things to all people. Stay in your lane.

Share the spotlight: Everyone who deserves it should have time in the sun. Let different voices and talents shine and encourage everyone to take the stage. It's all about creating a symphony of ideas and contributions, where more participation and less load on individuals becomes the norm.

Keep chattin': Maintain open and flowing communication channels. Celebrate achievements, listen to concerns and hop to the rhythm of transparent and inclusive dialogue. Communication is the ultimate tool for maintaining balance.

Look after thyself: Ask, will doing this be nourishing or neglectful to what my mind and body needs right now? It's okay to let others take the lead if you need a break.

Partner up: Seek partnerships that align with your mission and amplify your impact. Collaborations will bring fresh ideas, spread the reach and dilute the pressure. This stuff is hard, so find others to share the challenge with.

'You're only as strong as the community that holds you and you can only move at the pace that it sets.'

Stephen Morris

Flex: There's value in being adaptable. The community landscape might change – it's likely it definitely will – and that's okay! Stay nimble, adjust yourself and be ready for the unexpected. Flexibility keeps the rhythm alive and the community spirit vibrant.

Celebrate like rockstars: This stuff is tough, so celebrate it! All of it, even with simple festivity: show pictures of your group's experiences, spread a picnic, sing a song, dance. Let the cheer flow as you recognise and applaud the collective awesomeness.

Honour volunteers: Goes without saying that the efforts of those who give up their time need to be seen and honoured. Yep, even if you did it too and you're tired. A regular morning tea with a spread of cakes always puffs up your people, and when you thank them publicly it's the icing on the cake.

I clearly remember the day I decided to evaporate my expectation on others and shift my view from 'it's a community organisation, so community should contribute' to 'my ability to give to community at this point in my life is strong, so I'll give for as long as I can and if anyone else can give too – even just a little bit – I'll be so, so grateful. The pace we deliver on our vision will be what it's supposed to be.' This subtle shift in thinking totally reinvigorated our community enterprise because the pressure was off. Without expectation, people were drawn to the organisation, not pushed away by the obligation.

Get your eyes off that end game and enjoy the detail of the day-to-day highs.

161

Factions

It's been said that slowing down, respect and diversity are the greatest challenges faced by humanity.

Factions speak to this. I recall my dad referring to these as a kid and thinking he was simply being difficult. In my naive mind, everyone was good and no-one was going out of their way to be antagonistic. As is often the case, we were both right. Everyone is good and no-one really wants to be an aggressor unnecessarily – at least that's the way we were born into this world. Then, slowly but surely, with a tug to the left and a shove to the right, a lurching forwards and a brick wall backwards, we evolve. We become our adult selves in response to the individuals we meet, the experiences we have, the love we are shown, the grief we experience.

Our identities are formed and our beliefs wedge us into camps that make us feel as though we belong. Once we belong, our opinions are reiterated and the 'faction' we are part of argues its case as a collective. The modern-day media pounces on these distinctions and highlights the divisions, deepening the narrative that we are different. There's so much to learn that one could not possibly unpack all the knowledge in just one lifetime. In light of this I now think, how do I arrest myself at the crossroads of a faction that might be nestling around me and how do I ensure that I don't let it deepen my division, but rather empower me to work towards unity?

Remember, unity doesn't mean erasing differences or suppressing individual voices. It means finding ways to collaborate, respect one another and work towards a shared vision. By openly understanding, embracing diversity and seeking common ground, we can unite at the crossroads and build a stronger, more cohesive community.

Sociocracy: Socio ... what?

Illustrator and sustainability educator Brenna Quinlan has lived in all manner of shared communities, and when I asked her for her must-have tool in her kit for this way of living, she said, 'Sociocracy.'

What the heck is this? Sociocracy, in its most basic form, is a dynamic governance system that flips the script on traditional top-down structures. Instead of the usual bureaucratic maze, sociocracy empowers every voice in the room. It's about talking and walking in true collaboration. Imagine a living, breathing organisation where decisions are made efficiently, hierarchies are flattened and creativity isn't stifled by the same old power plays. Sociocracy is the rebellious shout against the mundane, injecting innovation and responsiveness into the veins of life.

Let's try a garden analogy (see right). Imagine a community garden where people come together to cultivate a vibrant and flourishing space. Sociocracy is like the framework that guides how the garden is organised and decisions are made.

By applying sociocracy principles, the community garden thrives. People have a sense of ownership and responsibility for the garden's success. They work collaboratively, sharing knowledge, resources and tasks. The garden becomes a symbol of collective effort, where everyone's contributions are valued. In this way, sociocracy creates a framework for community decision-making and collaboration, which mimics the interconnectedness and growth found in a flourishing garden. It fosters a sense of unity and empowers individuals to participate actively in shaping the community they want to be a part of.

162

Steps in sociocracy

Planting seeds: Just like in a garden, sociocracy starts with planting seeds of ideas and aspirations. People in the community come together to discuss their shared goals and values, envisioning what they want the garden to be.

Feedback and adaptation: Similar to tending a garden, sociocracy encourages regular feedback and adaptation. Gardeners share their experiences, offer suggestions for improvement and make adjustments as needed to nurture the garden's health and productivity.

Garden circles: Sociocracy organises the community into different circles, just like dividing the garden into smaller sections for various plants. Each circle has a specific purpose or area of responsibility, such as gardening techniques, community events or sustainability initiatives.

Consensus decision-making: Sociocracy emphasises consensus decision-making where ideas and proposals are discussed among circle members. It's like the gardeners coming together to decide which plants to grow, where to place them and how to maintain the garden collectively. Any apprehension is raised early to ensure it has been aired and acknowledged. Rationale for concern can be offered and counter-communicated, and a vote may be needed at this point before further action is taken.

Role distribution: Within each circle, roles are assigned to individuals based on their skills and interests. Just as different plants have different roles in the garden ecosystem, people take on roles that contribute to the overall functioning and growth of the community.

Mutual aid

Tyson Yunkaporta said if you are part of an effort that is doing good things for each other, then don't shout it from the rooftops. Instead, get stuck into doing more of it – at whatever scale, in whatever way.

His point being that as soon as we use our small wins as a marketing exercise, we increase the chance of them being interrupted by nosey bureaucracy. Instead, just hunker in with your people and let your genuine reciprocity and mutual aid continue to flow between your huddle.

We could learn a thing or two from the First Nations Elders. Their culture is deeply rooted in the principle of genuine mutualism and mutual aid. This way of existing acknowledges that humans are naturally inclined to seek reciprocal relationships and interconnectedness.

In these communities a deep understanding exists about the interconnectedness between our figurative neighbours, as well as the natural world. Rather than positioning ourselves as masters, they embrace the role of stewards and live harmoniously with nature.

At the heart of these communities lies a commitment to collective wellbeing, fostering cooperation, sharing and reciprocity. Resources are not individually owned but collectively shared, nurturing a spirit of mutual support to meet everyone's needs. This extends beyond material possessions to the exchange of knowledge, experiences and skills – a practice vital for preserving cultural heritage and fortifying community bonds.

Within this cultural framework, the wisdom of Elders holds a special place. Intergenerational Elderhood relies on the acknowledgement that each generation bears the responsibility to learn from and honour the knowledge passed down by their ancestors. This exchange of wisdom fosters a deep sense of mutual respect and understanding, ensuring the continued preservation of cultural traditions and teachings.

Ceremonial practices are woven into the fabric of First Nations cultures, embodying their belief in mutualism. These ceremonies serve as moments of gratitude, reciprocity and renewal – whether it be honouring the land, expressing thanks for bountiful harvests or seeking harmony within the community. These rituals stand as powerful reminders of the interconnectedness between individuals, their communities and the spiritual world.

Collaborative decision-making is the traditionally practised consensus-based decision-making process in these communities. This approach ensures that everyone's voice is heard and decisions are made collectively. The focus is on finding solutions that benefit the community as a whole, rather than prioritising individual interests. This inclusive and participatory approach strengthens social cohesion and fosters a sense of shared responsibility, mirroring the holistic principles woven into the fabric of this way of living.

In essence, genuine mutualism reflects the understanding that humans are an integral part of a larger interconnected web. It emphasises harmonious relationships with nature, a sense of communal support, the preservation of ancestral knowledge and inclusive decision-making.

HUDDLE

STORY

Trade with me

While picking raspberries, my English friend Billy and I chatted about all the ways individuals can do our part: localising, sharing, being active and not passive, simplifying. All the usual things were threaded through our conversation when he said, 'Before I retrained for my current outside job, I used to earn big dollars as an editor, but I was miserable. I spent all day inside without windows, the tech-filled room heating my bones. I became more and more miserable living an existence I hadn't evolved to live. With each pay cheque I began to resent the money, feeling like it owned me and was keeping me on a wheel of minimum-monthly-repayments. I was existing rather than living, and I found myself spending the money to get rid of it so I didn't feel so dirty for having traded my happiness for something as benign and soul-destroying as cash.

'While at the depth of my money misery, I did a job for a friend, but as payment we negotiated to trade our services. He was a tailor and agreed to make me a handmade set of pants in return. The value of our trade wasn't discussed specifically but it felt fair. The timing of the return took many weeks, so it wasn't as clean or as simple as an invoice being paid, but the simple act of trading with one another was, we decided, a forgotten tool with a magnificent ability to sidestep the faceless but blameable system that is holding us ransom in so many ways. It felt virtuous to have avoided paperwork, be presented with something made with me in mind and to have negotiated with a human I intrinsically care about to achieve an outcome that was fair, respectful and reflective of compromise that worked for both of us. I'd found my way of "doing business", and while it couldn't be applied to all aspects of my life, it forced real consideration of my decisions, has deepened my commitment to localising, built stronger networks and greater trust. One simple trade has led to me feeling like I actually have a community around me.'

Turns out trading is a heartbeat within communities. In asking around, I discovered in my huddle alone I had friends trading massages for chiropractic adjustments, lawn mowing for sourdough bread, childcare for artwork, herbal tinctures for goat milk, garden design for music performance, retail space for essential oils. As I unpacked the world of trading, I realised it is a transformative act. It leads us to talk, listen, ritualise, simplify, localise, collectivise and rebuild culture within our huddles.

HUDDLE ——————— *HOW?*

Get in there!

Righto, I promised practical ideas on sinking your teeth into community, so here goes. Some of these ideas are as well worn as old socks; some are new to me but come proven from other lands; some are good for small communities; some are better in cities; some will take little effort on your part but deliver virtuosity in spades; and others will feel like hard work only to eke an inch of dripping gold from your offering.

Find your crew and band together: Once you have each other – even if there are only a couple of you – it's easier to navigate your broader community.

Reimagine success: Flip the script by embracing a new definition that emphasises collective wellbeing, resilience and environmental regeneration.

Stand in solidarity: Raise your voice! Join rallies, sign petitions and advocate for policies that promote social justice, equity and a fairer distribution of resources. Together, we amplify our impact.

Skill up and share: Be a beacon of knowledge and share what you learn via workshops, social media posts or neighbourhood gatherings. Empower others with the tools and inspiration to make change.

Embrace give-and-grow: Offer support when you can and accept help when you need it.

Support those in need: Things like backyard permablitzes, meal trains and childcare rosters are all practical and gentle ways to offer a helping hand to those who need it most. Everyone's time of need swings around at some stage.

Create a relationship covenant: This is a simple but unifying statement that can be created with anyone you intend to be in relationship with, professional or personal. Not unlike wedding vows, a covenant is poetic and explanatory of what you both hope to contribute and agree on together. It's a sacred agreement between you both and can be referred to during times of difficulty with the support of those around you. It can stand for as long as you both wish and be formally accepted and then renounced when the relationship is no longer serving its purpose.

CREATE A 'PERSONAL COMMITMENT TO COMMUNITY' PLAN

Sasha had intentionally moved from the city to a smaller rural town so she could build a community around her and her kids. I met Sasha while working on the creation of a local food action plan. She was a confident voice in the group. At the end of the session, I asked a few probing questions about all the participants and how they came to be involved, assuming that this woman had lived there all her life. Another woman piped up and said, 'Oh, Sasha has only just arrived, but it doesn't feel like it. She seems to be everywhere I go, and it feels like she's part of the furniture.' I looked to Sasha for explanation and she said, 'When I moved here I sat down and created a "personal commitment to community" plan and I committed twenty per cent of my time to causes that aligned with my values and could use my skills. It took me a while to figure out where I was needed and what really sparked my interest. It also took a while to build the trust of the town, so I did a lot of listening and a lot of volunteering small simple things to find my feet, but after about a year I had a good sense and I stepped up – sometimes to assist, but sometimes I began things from scratch. It's ever evolving but I check in regularly with myself and others and rearrange as I go. I couldn't expect the community to wrap itself around me without getting into the trenches with them, so here we are.'

If creating a plan feels daunting, try these simple steps:

- **Reflect on your values:** What's most important to you?
- **Assess your skills and passions:** What do you enjoy doing and how can it contribute to the wellbeing of others?
- **Define your community:** Who do you want to impact? Your neighbourhood, a local organisation or a broader cause?
- **Set clear objectives:** What are you hoping to achieve from being involved? What or who will your gift of time benefit?
- **Commitment:** Determine how much time and resources you can realistically commit. Be mindful of your existing commitments and responsibilities.
- **Research opportunities:** Explore existing community initiatives, organisations or projects aligned with your values and goals that may need assistance.
- **Build relationships**: Establish connections with individuals and groups in your community. Attend local meetings, events or volunteer opportunities to better understand their needs and dynamics.
- **Create your plan:** Based on your reflection, skills and community needs, create a detailed action plan. Break down your goals into specific, actionable steps with realistic timelines.
- **Adjust and evolve:** Nothing stays the same, so check in regularly. Life circumstances may change and community needs may evolve. Stay flexible and be willing to adapt your commitments accordingly.
- **Celebrate:** Acknowledge your achievements – whether big or small – and the positive impact you're making on the community. Use these successes to fuel your ongoing commitment.

Creating the plan is the easy part, but committing to action can be a tad harder. Go gently.

167

HUDDLE ———— *HOW?*

The rhythm of the heartbeats

Even small actions have a ripple effect in the place you call home. When you glue those small actions together, the result is cataclysmic in all the right ways.

Localise: Have your holidays closer to home; send your kids to the local school; buy gifts from local artisans; walk or ride and avoid the car; use the library and neighbourhood centre; promote local initiatives, events or causes; help amplify by using your own social media platforms to share the efforts of local organisations and individuals working to make a positive impact.

Connect to your food: Join the local co-op and get to know where your food comes from; eat seasonally available food predominantly; join the local community garden; seed save and swap; share seedlings if you have too many; buy direct from farmers where you can; grow your own; swap abundance; attend community dinners; host potluck gatherings; and calculate your food miles and set goals to decrease them.

Share your knowledge: What skills do you have that others might like to know?

Participate in community events: Attend No Lights No Lycra events, tree planting days, festivals, panel discussions, book talks, working bees, clean-up projects and workshops. If someone local is making an effort, support by at least attending.

168

Shop from local stores: Boycott the multinationals.

Volunteer your time: Committees, driving lessons, op shop, reading at school.

Play cross-generational card games: It's about the company.

Hike a hill as a group: All ages, all abilities, all distances. Even a 200-metre walk with a view is rewarding. When you walk it shoulder-to-shoulder and stand on the summit watching the world below for a sunrise or sunset, the collective rises.

Be a good neighbour: Extend a helping hand with jobs and keep them company.

Define your love language and the language of those in your closest huddle: How do you navigate the differences with those you love?

Join a book club: It's more about the chatter and connection than the book.

Participate in citizen science: Like the Aussie backyard bird count.

Build a community cubby in the commons: Cubbies are for adults too.

Participate in local decision-making: Attend town hall meetings, community forums or local government sessions to voice your opinions, concerns and ideas. Active participation helps shape the future of your community.

Open your garden: A day of solidarity with other garden lovers. Share seeds, offer cuttings, sell plants.

HUDDLE

STORY

Creating community with cake
Written by Josephine Ackland, AKA Lady Jo

When I first moved to Tasmania in 2016, I didn't know anyone at all. After a few months, the glitter of the relocation settled, and it soon became rather lonely navigating my new move. One day on my Instagram, I put out a shout-out to see if anyone was interested in meeting up at a local cafe. Four of us got together and it was brilliant. For the first time in months, I felt I had people to chat with. At the end of it, we decided to meet up again the following month. From then on, it became a monthly thing, snowballing into a large group and graduating to the local cider house. Willies set aside a table for us.

There are no rules or RSVP. You can turn up for ten minutes or the full two hours. Depending on what's happening in your life, some people stay all day and drink on! There could be four people or forty. It's generally the first Friday of the month, but it's been other days too. Sometimes I miss for months, and COVID stopped everything for a while. We often bring things we want to share that we have been making, and little prearranged swaps often happen. This little gathering has grown into 'Cakemates'.

I find that sometimes life gets tough – there's a phase around the two-year mark of living in Tasmania where it tests you in ways you can't predict. If you know a few people who have been on the same journey, it can be easier. I've noticed that if you haven't found your 'group' by the four-year mark, people often start leaving for various reasons – whether it's work or money, but mostly loneliness. Over the past eight years, hundreds have passed through Cakemates. Personally, I've never found it hard to chat with people, but I see that others do. Many have made lifelong connections through our gatherings.

I remember one day walking back in the car park, a lady approached me with tears streaming down her face. Although new to the group, she shared that she had been in Tasmania for three years, and today was the first time she had made friends and felt incredibly happy. Making friends in Tasmania can be challenging; many people are busy, and in the coldest winter months, they tend to stay indoors, only venturing out for necessities, like the doctor, supermarket or chemist.

Moving to a new place is daunting and overwhelming. Cakemates is a space where you don't need to buy or eat cake – it's just an excuse to catch up. However, if you do decide to order cake, know that we don't judge, whether it's one slice or three. There's no cake shaming here.

170

Mangroves or the ocean?

Collective action is no more than the aggregation of individual actions, yet while that sounds simple enough, the nuance comes in our ability to work collegially with others. Some of us are comfortable in the deep and unpredictable ocean, but we can only exist out there if we have relationships with those in the mangroves. We can work our magic, build big ideas and navigate the chaos using the bond we hold with those who find their place in quieter, more methodical and predictable places. Which are you? Perhaps a little of both depending on the situation. Communities need both to function cohesively. It's a matter of finding where you fit and being okay to wade in as deep as you're comfortable – or maybe a tad more just to bring the opportunity of growth to the fore.

Hardscape designing for community heartbeats

The Cairo Flats in Fitzroy, Melbourne were designed in the 1930s for young single folk to have their own space, but to ultimately live in cohesion with one another. They originally didn't even have kitchens. Rather there was a communal kitchen and food was delivered to tenants via special food delivery hatches. Each apartment was just 23 sqm (248 sq ft) but had great amenity and intentional connection with line of sight to each other. Living like this can create a huddle in a way that someone on a quarter acre block never could.

Developed as a cooperative, Urambi Village in Canberra was never built to be sold for profit. It wasn't designed by developers, but by the people who wanted to live there. The designer removed the car as a focus and returned seventy per cent of the green space back to the people with paths, trees, gardens and nooks. Fences are limited, so gardens merge into large common spaces.

Nourishment_

Feast with your kinfolk! Be tickled from nose to toes, filling your cup and your belly at once. Food has connected us since the beginning of time, building friendship, memories, wellness and culture through conviviality and sharing. It's a language all on its own yet requires no words. It says, 'I love you. I want to care for you. I value all that you are and I want to make memories that bond us for a lifetime.' Now that's a language to huddle into!

173

I've saved the very best chapter till last and taking the idea of huddling past our tastebuds and into the seat of connection and wisdom: the gut. It's time to feast!

The language of food requires no words. It speaks to multigenerational ways of being, and it tells the stories of who we are as individuals and in the community. Our community is only strong if we ALL have enough, and food is no exception. As permaculture expert Su Dennett asked, 'Can you sleep straight in a king-sized bed of luxury when your neighbour can't put food on their plate?' How right she is!

The best part of huddle feasting is that you can begin today, and you'll learn with every single recipe, experiment and gathering. It's almost impossible to get it wrong. Even if the food itself doesn't go to plan, when you have company on your travels to building rhythm and ritual in this way of being, everything is all the better for it.

We are all eaters regardless of our age, sex, house size or politics. We are connected by food across generations and countries, and because these boundaries are crossed, it provides us with an opportunity to reconnect and rekindle a nourishing local culture. The way we choose to eat has a profound impact!

A few things that go without saying:

- **Eat what's in season:** Sure, this might mean a lot of repetition, but with good company and a range of sauces and chutneys, you'll still feast like a royal and your body will thank you for feeding it what it needs at the right time of year.
- **Get comfortable with foraging:** It'll connect you to your landscape, the season and set you on a slow and tasty path away from the long supply chains of our unwieldy supermarket systems.
- **'From scratch' is the ideal:** Of course, but you're a busy human holding a lot, so don't run out of gas trying to make everything yourself. Set an intention to routinely cook up a few key staples that slot easily into your life. Perhaps granola once a month and a batch of chutney or sauce each year. Slowly add to your repertoire as you have the time and inclination.
- **Do one thing:** Introducing lots of new ideas at once into your way of being is rarely sustainable. To spare yourself the overwhelm, focus on one thing at a time, inhabiting the fullness of each new ingredient, method or idea and savouring the slowness.
- **Simple is super:** A boiled egg on toast IS dinner.
- **You're not alone:** Bring your people with you and share in the ups and downs of growing food, swapping abundance, preserving, potlucking and making it up as you go.
- **There are no rules:** You do you and love the heck out of whatever it is that unfolds.
- **Localise:** Know where your food comes from and how it was grown. Buy directly from those stewarding the soil with their growing practices and ask, with genuine curiosity, how it's going on the farm.

174

Love your farmers

The challenges posed by lengthy supply chains – casting farmers as mere price takers – paint a grim picture for farming communities and put our nation's food security at risk. Over the past century, the consequences have rippled through various facets of our lives:

• A fading canvas of seed and soil biodiversity.
• Farmers stuck in an increasing debt cycle with pressure to get big or get out.
• Heart-wrenching spikes in farmer suicides.
• Lengthened journeys to market, testing the endurance of our growers and changing the varieties on offer.
• Obesity and health issues burdening our health system.
• Mountains of wasted food – a stark contrast to the simultaneous scarcity crisis.
• Overuse of chemicals impacting soil and river health.
• Continuation of land clearing, resulting in erosion and topsoil loss.
• A sense of growing disconnection in our hollowed out, corporatised farmland communities.

Our long food supply chains are a recent convenience. While supermarkets are able to satiate our every whim and desire at any time for a price below the true cost of production, it is a system that is fragile and operates on a three-day-just-in-time approach. If we face unexpected calamity, our ability to guarantee food is impacted. Remember those empty shelves during COVID and the rush on seedlings and seeds?

Yet, within these challenges lies an opportunity – an opportunity to cultivate local, secure and sustainable food systems, which not only nourish our bodies but heal our soils and reconnect us to the very essence of community. Using our food-purchasing decisions

we can be in step with our regenerative farmers and together we can embrace and champion food systems that prioritise local, sustainable and social inclusivity; nurture concerns for human health, animal welfare, agricultural and ecological sustainability; and foster food justice and political empowerment. This heartfelt movement stretches its roots across borders, resonating with both political influence and societal significance.

The hope for this book is to build skills and appetite for a somewhat different way of interacting with the world – the way we feast is no different. While many of these recipes are currently able to be made from store-bought ingredients, careful consideration has been given to re-skill us with tools that allow us to feast outside of our reliance on the convenient option.

176

Huddles beyond your own backyard

When scrutinising my own huddle, I was amazed to realise it was much broader than those in my own backyard. As much as I pride myself on being hyper-relational, there is actually a very large contingent of folks who I don't see very often – some I've never even met face-to-face.

Given the beating heart of this book, I took a good hard look at myself and decided to remedy the situation. I packed my bag and headed off. Some folks lived close, others further afield, but I did my best to turn up on the doorsteps of the many good eggs who had become my huddle – whether in person from long ago, more recent relationships or online. There's nothing like spending time with your people, is there? The feeling of familiarity, warmth and connection is beyond compare. Having spent the first seven chapters talking about the vital need to be in physical proximity to our people, having that belief reinforced and resonating in my deepest recesses was a beautiful thing. On these travels I had the incredible honour of meeting people who I had previously only known by their 'handle' or interviewed for the podcast over Zoom or not seen for more than a decade. I also collected a pocketful of gifts from each of them to share with you.

There's something about sharing a special recipe from your world. It tells your story; it captures moments spent with your nearest humans; it opens the doors to family history; and it lets us look inside your cupboards, figuratively speaking. It's intimate. I requested a recipe from any who were willing to fill these pages with warmth and nourishment, like a big, old community potluck.

This chapter shares food perfect for huddle feasts – whatever they look like. Of course, seasonality is our eternal foundation, so these pages are broken into the six *Futuresteading* seasons of Awakening, Alive, High heat, Harvest, The turning and Deep chill.

HOW TO STERILISE JARS AND BOTTLES

To help extend the shelf life of your preserved goods and stop any nasty contaminants, it's important to sterilise your jars before using.

Preheat the oven to 110°C (230°F). Wash the glass jars and their lids in hot soapy water. Without drying, place the jars and lids on a clean baking tray. Transfer the tray to the oven for about 15 minutes until the jars are completely dry.

WATER BATHING PRESERVED FOODS

Water bathing jars or bottles of your preserved goodies will keep them shelf stable for years.

Use a Fowlers Preserving Kit, if you have one. If you don't have a dedicated preserving kit, simply use a stockpot. Line it with a tea (dish) towel and enough water to fully submerge the jars you want to preserve. Add the jars to the pot, making sure they don't touch the sides of the pot or one another. Slowly bring to the boil over a medium heat. If you have a thermometer, check you reach at least 60°C (140°F) and hold it at that temperature for 40 minutes, adding more boiling water if necessary, so the jars stay completely submerged at all times.

If you have more than seven jars, you'll need to work in batches, but don't add cold jars to the pot of boiling water or the jars might crack. Between batches, remove some of the boiling water and replace with cold water to bring down the temperature to match the temperature of the jars. Then add the jars, making sure there is enough water to completely submerge them.

Remove a little water from the pot so you can then lift each jar out and rest them on the bench overnight – their lids will pop as they cool slowly, confirming they are vacuum sealed. If the lids are not concave by the next day, jars should be stored in the fridge and the contents used within 2 weeks. Sealed jars can be stored in a cool, dark place for up to 2 years.

Note

This book uses 20 ml (¾ fl oz) tablespoons. Cooks using 15 ml (½ fl oz) tablespoons should be mindful of slightly increasing the amount with their tablespoon measurements. Metric cup measurements are used, i.e. 250 ml for 1 cup; in the US a cup is 8 fl oz, just smaller, so American cooks should be generous in their cup measurements.

Additionally, the recipes in this book were cooked in a fan-forced or convection oven, so if using a conventional oven, increase the temperature by 20°C (35°F).

Awakening

A time to wake gently from your winter hibernation. Let the fire go out and throw open the doors to catch the warmth from the new season's sunshine. The morning frost has packed up for the year and new growth pushes through the mulch, preparing to break the hungry months with spring greens. Asparagus and eggs are plentiful, while the last of the winter kraut adds zest to most meals. The days are getting longer, so spread a blanket, make a cake, brew a pot and invite friends for afternoon tea.

180

NOURISHMENT

Gluten-free foraged five weed tart

BY CATIE PAYNE, RESKILLIENCE
PODCAST HOST

If you can find five different wild greens to add to this tart, all (nutritional) power to you! But don't worry if not – it's perfectly delicious with whatever greens you've got in your garden or fridge. I love this recipe because it's so forgiving, taking seasonal variations in its stride. I've made it with spinach, silverbeet (Swiss chard), warrigal greens, beetroot leaves, carrot tops, chard, dandelion, mallow, fat hen, plantain, comfrey leaves, borage and more. It never fails to work. So long as you have a giant bushel of glistening leafy goodness to cook down for the filling and a medicinal amount of cheese, you're set.

Serves 6–8

2 tablespoons olive oil
1 garlic clove, minced
10 cups roughly chopped edible greens and weeds, roughly chopped
1 teaspoon fine sea salt
3 eggs, lightly whisked
handful of crumbled feta
35 g (1¼ oz/⅓ cup) finely grated parmesan cheese
35 g (1¼ oz/⅓ cup) blue cheese (optional)
green salad and toasted seeds dressed with Creamy cashew lemon dressing (page 198), to serve

PIE CRUST
190 g (6½ oz/2 cups) almond flour
65 g (2¼ oz/½ cup) buckwheat flour
½ teaspoon fine sea salt
45 g (1 ½ oz) cold butter, cubed
1 egg, lightly whisked
2 tablespoons cold water (optional)

Line a 22.5 cm (9 in) round tart tin with baking paper.

To make the pie crust, use a fork to combine the almond flour, buckwheat flour and salt in a large bowl. Add the cold butter and rub into the flour mixture with your fingertips until it resembles fine crumbs. Mix in the egg and bring the dough together with a fork or your hands into a ball. If it's too dry or crumbly, add the cold water, 1 tablespoon at a time, until the dough sticks together.

Press the dough into the prepared tin, working it evenly across the base and up the side for full rustic coverage. (You can roll it out between two pieces of baking paper first, if you prefer.)

Prick the dough all over with a fork for even cooking.

Heat the olive oil in a frying pan then fry the garlic for a few minutes until golden. Add the greens and salt. Give a little stir then let them sizzle for a few moments. Add a splash of water, cover with a lid and cook down for 10–20 minutes, adding more water along the way as it absorbs into the greens. (You don't want any liquid sloshing about at the end, so if there's any left in the pan let it evaporate.) Transfer the cooked greens to a bowl and set aside for 5 minutes to cool.

Meanwhile, preheat the oven to 180°C (360°F) or a wood stove to mid-range flames.

Stir the egg and feta through the greens then scatter over the tart base and top with the parmesan and blue cheese. Bake for 45 minutes until golden on top.

Serve with salad.

Wholewheat sourdough bread

BY COURTNEY YOUNG, WOODSTOCK FLOUR

Woodstock Flour has been a legend in our 'local food sphere' for the better part of a decade, with our lives crossing paths erratically via our efforts to localise food systems. Owners Courtney Young and Ian Congdon have bitten off one of the greatest challenges in their commitment to localising grains, but hats off to them as they've grown from strength to strength.

'Ian, my now husband, and I met at uni through a wine-tasting class,' said Courtney. 'We learned about terroir, different viticultural practices, the beautiful process of fermentation and how it all influences a bottle of wine. This class was the beginning of a long conversation and experiment in regenerative farming and local food. We were excited about the prospect of approaching farming in the way that viticulturalists do: producing something that tastes delicious, is proud of its roots and worth sharing. And so, we started Woodstock Flour.

'We bought organic grain from Ian's parents' farm and started milling it into flour. We now sell to bakers, restaurants and homes. Alongside this foray into milling has been our journey of learning how to farm and bake. We will never stop learning, but we feel really proud to be able to ferment and transform grain grown by our family into loaves to share with loved ones. Bread for us is a story about our relationship, the landscape we live and farm on, our family and our community.

  'We often double this recipe so we can gift a loaf to a friend.'

Makes 1 loaf

425 ml (14½ fl oz) slightly warm water
500 g (1 lb 2 oz) freshly milled, high protein wholewheat bread flour (such as Spitfire, see Tip), plus extra for dusting
12 g (¼ oz) fine sea salt

SOURDOUGH LEAVEN
20 g (¾ oz) active starter
50 g (1¾ oz/⅓ cup) wholewheat flour
60 ml (2 fl oz/¼ cup) slightly warm water

To make the sourdough leaven, the night before or morning of the day you want to make bread, combine the leaven ingredients in a small bowl. Cover and set aside at room temperature for 4–6 hours to rest. Test its readiness by dropping a spoonful of the mixture into a bowl of room-temperature water. If it floats, it's ready.

Combine the slightly warm water with 75 g (2¾ oz) of the leaven in a large bowl. Add the flour and use your hands to mix until combined. Cover with a clean tea (dish) towel and set aside for at least 1 hour at a warm room temperature (26–30°C/79–86°F) to hydrate and ferment.

Use wet hands to fold the salt into the dough. Cover with a clean tea towel and set aside for 3 hours to prove, folding the dough with wet hands every 30 minutes (six times in total). To do a fold, dip one hand in water, pick up the underside of the dough, stretch it up and fold it back over itself. Turn the bowl by one-quarter and repeat fold for the three remaining corners. After roughly 3 hours and six folds, the dough should feel aerated, billowy and softer and should have increased in volume by 20–30 per cent. If this isn't happening, fold once or twice more over another hour.

Gently tip the dough onto a lightly floured surface. Work it into shape by drawing your hand around the dough in a circular motion. The dough will anchor to the bench, creating tension. Lightly dust the top of the dough with extra flour, cover with the tea towel and set aside for 30 minutes to rest.

184

Line a bread proofing basket or bowl with a floured tea towel.

Flip the dough over so the lightly floured top is now on the bench. Pull the bottom of the dough up and fold into one-third of the round. Do the same with the other three sides. Flip the dough back over, seam side down, and round your hands over the dough to tuck the corners in and make it less square. Set aside for a few minutes to seal the seam.

Place the dough, seam side up, in the prepared basket or bowl. Cover with the tea towel and rest at a warm room temperature for 3–5 hours or overnight in the fridge if necessary.

Preheat the oven to 260°C (500°F) or as high as your oven goes. Place a cast-iron Dutch oven with its lid on in the oven to preheat.

Once the Dutch oven is hot (about 20 minutes), tip the dough gently into the Dutch oven, seam side down. Use a knife to score the top of the dough. Place in the oven. After 20 minutes of baking, turn down the oven to 230°C (445°F). Bake for another 10 minutes then remove the lid. Continue to bake for another 15–20 minutes until dark golden.

Turn the loaf onto a wire rack to cool. Once cool, take to it with a bread knife.

TIP
If you can't source a freshly milled, high protein wholewheat bread flour, use a combination of baker's flour and wholewheat flour.

HUDDLE ACTIVITY

KRAUCHI-MAKING

Nothing like a good-for-your-gut and ripe-on-the-nose brightly coloured food to wake you and your huddle from your winter slumber. Because this will keep in the fridge for a long time – six months at least! – this is great to make en masse, BUT there is loads of chopping so it's a great awakening activity.

This is Charlie's not-quite-kimchi but more-than-kraut recipe – we call it 'krauchi'. It's delicious beyond words and can be easily adjusted according to taste preferences.

Makes 1 kg (2 lb 3 oz)

1 medium green cabbage
1 medium purple cabbage
5 carrots
2 medium whole beetroot (beets, optional – it gives a very earthy flavour)
2 tablespoons non-iodised coarse sea salt
2 tablespoons honey
2 tablespoons fish sauce
2 tablespoons minced garlic
1 tablespoon finely diced ginger
caraway seeds, juniper berries, dried chillies or other spices, for flavouring (optional)

Clean all the vegetables, discard outer leaves and peel. Thinly shred the cabbages using a mandolin or sharp knife and grate the carrot and beetroot, if using, then transfer to a large bowl.

Add the salt and massage for 5–10 minutes. (The salt will draw out moisture from the cabbage, creating a brine.) Add the honey, fish sauce, garlic, ginger and your chosen spices, if using.

Mix well, cover and leave to sit for 10 minutes.

Transfer the mixture and brine to a sterilised wide-mouth glass jar (page 178) or ceramic fermentation crock and pack it down well to remove any air bubbles. Place a weight on top to keep the mixture submerged in the brine. This could be a smaller jar filled with water or a purpose-made fermentation weight. (The cabbage must be fully submerged to prevent mould.) Cover with a cloth or lid that allows gases to escape but prevents debris from getting in.

Everyone can take their krauchi home at this point and let the fermentation take shape in their own pantry. Allow the krauchi to ferment at room temperature, ideally between 18–24°C (65–75°F). Check it every day or two, skimming off any scum that forms on the surface.

Taste the krauchi after a week and continue fermenting until it reaches your desired flavour – up to 4 weeks. Once ready, remove the weight, seal with a proper lid and store in the fridge for up to a year.

TIPS

- **Ensure all equipment is clean to avoid unwanted bacteria.**
- **Use non-iodised salt, as iodine can inhibit fermentation.**
- **The fermentation time depends on personal preference and temperature. Taste as it ferments to find the flavour you like.**
- **If you see mould, skim it off immediately. The krauchi beneath the brine is still safe to eat.**

186

NOURISHMENT

Slap-together picnic sausage rolls

BY BLACK BARN FARM

These are perfect if the fridge feels bare and the day still has a little chill so you're seeking something warm.

You can use store-bought pastry for this as it saves time and stays true to being a slap-up meal. It's particularly handy to have these up your sleeve in the freezer when unexpected extras arrive on the doorstep.

Makes 2 large rolls to feed 4
or about 25 party-sized rolls

1 kg (2 lb 3 oz) minced (ground) meat (we use lamb because that's what we have stacks of, but any mince will work)
2 cups finely chopped mixed greens (anything from the garden, such as bolting brassicas, outer cabbage leaves, carrot tops, silverbeet/Swiss chard)
4 spring onions (scallions) or 1 onion, finely chopped
155 g (5½ oz/1 cup firmly packed) grated carrot (a good way to use up the last haul from the carrot patch in late winter/early spring)
80 ml (2½ fl oz/⅓ cup) passata (page 234 if eager for homemade)
2 tablespoons your favourite mustard
1 tablespoon savoury yeast flakes
1 egg
2 sheets frozen puff pastry, thawed
sauce (such as Smoky blackberry barbecue sauce, page 274), to serve
salt and freshly ground black pepper, to taste

Combine all the ingredients, except the pastry and sauce, in a large bowl.

Place the pastry on a lightly floured surface. Shape the filling mixture into two logs and lay over the pastry along the edge closest to you. Roll the pastry over the filling to enclose, pressing the seam to seal.
Cut into party-sized pieces or keep as big fat meal-sized sausage rolls (see Tip).

Preheat the oven to 180°C (360°F). Line a baking tray with baking paper.

Place the sausage roll/s, seam side down, on the prepared tray and bake for 25 minutes until golden. Serve with sauce.

TIP
After rolling and cutting (if making party size) you
can freeze for a rainy day. Place on a lined tray and
in the freezer until frozen. Transfer to a freezer bag
and store in the freezer for up to 6 months.

Green tahini sauce

BY CHARLIE SHOWERS

Based on a recipe Charlie found years ago, this has become a mainstay in our fridge as it can be used on absolutely EVERYTHING! We make up a batch every week or so and it gets spread on pasta, pizzas, eggs and toast or drizzled over salads. It's never quite the same from one batch to the next as it evolves throughout the year depending on what's in the garden and what we need foraged.

Makes 500 g (1 lb 2 oz)

4 garlic cloves
250 ml (8½ fl oz/1 cup) olive oil, plus extra for drizzling
270 g (9½ oz/1 cup) tahini
juice of 4 lemons
2 tablespoons apple-cider vinegar
4 cups mixed greens (our favourites, if we can get them, are sorrel, lemon sorrel, coriander/cilantro, rocket/arugula and flat-leaf/Italian parsley. We've also tried mint and wild radish)
fresh or dried chilli, to taste (optional)
salt and freshly ground black pepper, to taste

Preheat the oven to 170°C (340°F).

Place the garlic on a small baking tray, drizzle with extra oil and roast for 30 minutes.

Transfer the garlic to a blender along with the remaining ingredients. Blend, adding water as necessary for desired consistency. If the oil and the water separate to begin with, it requires a longer blend to emulsify. Store in a jar or airtight container in the fridge for up to a week.

Pickled magnolias

BY ANNA MATILDA, THE URBAN NANNA

If you long for spring during the cold, dark months, the sight of a gnarled, bare magnolia tree peppered with flower buds will make you skip. These voluptuous, headily perfumed flowers have remained largely unchanged for millennia. They have a long history of being used as food throughout China and Japan. Their aromatic, gingery flavour makes them excellently suited to tea, dumplings, salads, in baking and more. These pickled flower buds taste like the pickled ginger you eat with sushi.

Makes 2 × 250 ml (8½ fl oz/1 cup) jars

20–30 unopened magnolia flower buds, about 8–10 cm (3¼–4 in) long (see Tip)
500 ml (17 fl oz/2 cups) rice vinegar
110 g (4 oz/½ cup) white granulated sugar
large pinch of salt

Gently wash and dry the flower buds. Remove any brown papery bracts. Trim any stems right to the base of the flower bud. Firmly pack the flower buds into sterilised jars (page 178).

Place the vinegar, sugar and salt in a saucepan over a medium heat until the sugar dissolves then simmer for 5 minutes.

Pour enough of the vinegar mixture over the flower buds to cover. Use a flat knife or chopstick to press down and dislodge air bubbles. Top up with more vinegar mixture until submerged. Seal quickly with the lids then invert the jars for a few minutes to test and improve the seal.

Set aside to cool then store in the fridge for up to 6 months.

TIP
All magnolia varieties are edible, but they definitely don't all taste the same! Magnolia soulangeana (saucer magnolia) or magnolia stellata (star magnolia) generally have the best flavour. Taste test before picking lots of flowers to make sure you like their flavour enough to pickle them.

Banana pocket bread

BY LADY JO, TASMANIAN WOMAN OF MYSTERY

'This cake floods back memories of snowboarding in Canada at Whistler Hill, where I worked as a chalet girl in my twenties,' said Lady Jo. 'As an early riser I used to love doing the powdery "first tracks" on the mountain in the dark. After a few runs I'd pop into the mountain cafe, buy coffee and a slab of banana bread, eat half then tuck the rest into a hidden pocket. But I'd often forget about that hidden banana bread until a few days later. On the slopes again and ravenous, I'd be delighted to find that hidden, mangled slab of banana bread. It was utter joy as a little extra fuel meant I could spend more time on the slopes.

'I generally use the bananas that have taken a beating in the school bag or the ones that have been neglected in the fruit bowl. I freeze them until I have enough to make one loaf.'

Makes 1 loaf

350 g (12½ oz) ripe banana (about 4 bananas), thawed
    if frozen, cut into pieces
130 g (4½ oz) unsalted butter, softened, plus extra
    to serve
150 g (5½ oz) caster (superfine) sugar
2 eggs
220 g (8 oz) plain (all-purpose) flour
2 teaspoons baking powder
1 teaspoon bicarbonate of soda (baking soda)
pinch of table salt
100 ml (3½ fl oz) buttermilk
2 teaspoons natural vanilla extract
90 g (3 oz/½ cup) milk or dark choc chips

Preheat the oven to 180°C (360°F). Grease a loaf tin with butter then line the base and sides with baking paper.

Whiz the banana in a food processor or blender then add the butter and sugar. Blend for another 10 seconds until combined. Add the eggs and blend for another 10 seconds. Add the remaining ingredients, except the choc chips. Blend until combined. Scrape down the side of the processor or blender then blend again until smooth, for about 20 seconds.

Pour the mixture into a bowl and stir through the choc chips. Transfer the mixture to the prepared tin and bake for 1 hour until a skewer inserted into the centre comes out clean.

Serve it warm or completely cooled with slabs of extra butter.

TIPS
• To freeze, cut the cold loaf into slices. Place them in a recycled bread bag with baking paper between each slice.
• Two toasted slices with ice cream sandwiched between them is the best quick dessert.

'Smoko' crunchy chocolate slice

BY JANE SMITH, THE SHADY BAKER

'For as long as I can remember, smoko – particularly morning smoko – has been a part of my life,' said Jane Smith. 'As a child growing up on a sheep station in outback NSW, we would always take a break midmorning for a cup of tea, something to eat and a quick pause before the workday resumed. My paternal grandmother would pour strong tea from a pot and serve shortbread or chewy Anzac biscuits on a proper serving plate.

'Nowadays, with a farming family of my own, smoko is still a daily ritual. If we are mustering sheep, the supplies and thermoses will be packed up and taken to the paddock. The back of the work ute becomes the table, and everyone serves themselves while keeping an eye on the sheep. If it is particularly cold we might light a little fire to warm cold hands. If it is hot we will take shelter under a shady tree. At shearing time smoko is served in the woolshed, among the wool bales, sheep dogs and the busy rhythm of the woolshed.

'This short break is a time for everyone to reconnect, share some news and enjoy something sweet before the day continues.'

Makes about 20 pieces

50 g (1¾ oz) butter
200 g (7 oz) icing (confectioners') sugar
200 g (7 oz) Dutch (unsweetened) cocoa powder
hot water, for thinning
hundreds and thousands,, for decorating

BASE
250 g (9 oz) butter
225 g (8 oz) plain (all-purpose) flour
30 g (1 oz/¼ cup) Dutch (unsweetened) cocoa powder
175 g (2¾ oz) soft brown sugar
100 g (3½ oz) shredded coconut

Preheat the oven to 180°C (360°F). Line a 33 × 23 cm (13 × 9 in) slice or brownie pan with baking paper, allowing the paper to overhang the sides (this will make it easier to remove the slice once cooked).

To make the base, melt the butter in a small saucepan over a low heat. Remove from the heat. Sift the flour and cocoa into a large bowl. Mix in the brown sugar and coconut until combined. Pour in the melted butter and stir until well combined. Press the mixture firmly and evenly over the base of the prepared pan, ensuring it gets right into the corners. Bake for 25–30 minutes until it starts to bubble around the edges. (It may feel soft at this stage, but it will become firm as it cools.) Set aside in the pan until firm enough to remove. Turn onto a wire rack to cool completely then chill in the fridge while you make the icing.

Melt the butter with 2 tablespoons water in a small saucepan over a low heat. Remove from the heat.

Sift the icing sugar and cocoa into a bowl. Pour in the melted butter mixture and stir until smooth. If the icing seems too stiff, gradually add small amounts of hot water and continue to mix until an icing consistency.

Spread the icing evenly over the cold base and top with hundreds and thousands. Cut into pieces to serve. Store in an airtight container for up to 3 days (in the fridge in warm weather).

192

Avocado chocolate mousse

BY MARCO, OUR BOLIVIAN FARM VOLUNTEER

A vegan from Bolivia named Marco appeared on our doorstep like an apparition one grafting season – we were running weeks behind. Quite delightfully, he happened to be a professional grafter and he whipped our nursery into shape in a matter of days. It was spring and we were enduring our hungry months – living on eggs, asparagus, kraut and meat from the freezer. While this might have been tricky given he was vegan, he sidestepped the problem by taking to the kitchen and teaching us all manner of meal ideas we'd never considered. Not only did he graft like a magician, but he also rebuilt our spring eating habits by adding a couple of incredible flavour bombs to our repertoire – saving us from the repetition of spring eating.

While this could be a dessert in its own right, it can also be used as a rich chocolatey sauce instead of custard, cream, jam or ice cream. The thinner you make it, the saucier it is. The thicker you make it, the more desserty it is. It's delectable served with fresh berries.

Serves 4 as a full dessert or 10 as a topping

2 avocados
1 × 400 ml (13½ fl oz) tin coconut cream
125 g (4½ oz/1 cup) cacao powder
175 g (6 oz/½ cup) rice malt syrup or honey or 95 g
  (3¼ oz/½ cup) rapadura sugar or soft brown sugar
1 teaspoon natural vanilla extract

Blend all the ingredients in a blender until velvety smooth. For a runnier consistency, add a little water and blend again.

Alive

This is the season of blooming with an abundance of verdant green growth before your very eyes. Having gently woken over the past month or so, life vibrantly ups its pace. So, strap in as you tap-dance your way through this jaunty time, where seasons flip quickly from one gentle sun-kissed spring day to scorching skin-burning heat in a blink. Hike in the hills with your huddle and haul in new-season berries. The soil is now warm, the sun reliable and moisture still plentiful, so get seeds in the ground for plantings of everything you can muster. Everything suddenly feels ALIVE.

194

Herby chevre

BY BLACK BARN FARM

My beautiful goat, Sunday, produces 1–3 litres (34–101 fl oz) of milk each day. Even with a family of five, farm volunteers and lots of visitors, it is simply too much milk to just drink, so I use the milk to make cheese. Each week I use the oldest 10 litres (338 fl oz) to make haloumi and chevre.

While the haloumi takes a little longer and requires a few extra pieces of equipment, the chevre is super fast and anyone can make it using things they have in their kitchen.

This recipe speaks to my weekly 10-litre (338 fl oz) quantity, but you can make this with as little as 3 litres (101 fl oz) at a time. I use goat's milk, but you could easily use cow's. If buying your milk from the store, buy full cream, unhomogenised milk.

Makes 3 cups

10 litres (338 fl oz/40 cups) milk
125 ml (4 fl oz/½ cup) white or apple-cider vinegar
  or lemon juice
2 cups mixed fresh herb leaves, finely chopped
finely minced garlic cloves, to taste
olive oil, for drizzling
salt and freshly ground black pepper, to taste

Slowly heat the milk in a large saucepan or stockpot over a low heat until 90°C (195°F). This will take about 30 minutes if the milk came from the fridge. Check the temperature regularly as you warm it so it doesn't burn.

Remove from the heat and mix in the vinegar or lemon juice. The curds and whey will start separating. Set aside for 15 minutes to separate further.

Put a clean tea (dish) towel or muslin (cheesecloth) over a fine sieve and set over a bucket or large bowl. Pour the curds and whey through the sieve (see Tip).

Once the bulk of the whey is separated, tie the towel or muslin with kitchen string and hang from a height over a bowl to drip for the next hour. The longer you let it drip, the drier the chevre will be.

Tip the ball from the cloth onto the herbs and garlic and roll the ball until covered. Drizzle over the oil and season to serve.

TIP
The whey caught in the bucket is a brilliant antifungal and can be used in diluted form (1:100) for plants that are susceptible to fungal rot, such as apples and raspberries. Pot plants will also thank you for a splash.

196

197

Creamy cashew lemon dressing

BY MARCO, OUR BOLIVIAN FARM VOLUNTEER

This dressing is perfect on a green salad. It's also a cracker on roast chicken, rice, couscous and anything else you think could do with a spritz.

Makes 250 ml (8½ fl oz/1 cup)

15 cashews
80 ml (2½ fl oz/⅓ cup) olive oil
juice of 1 large lemon
handful of fresh coriander (cilantro) leaves
1 garlic clove
salt and freshly ground black pepper, to taste

Soak the cashews in a bowl of water for an hour or so to soften.

Drain the cashews, then whizz them in a food processor or blender together with the remaining ingredients and a splash of water until creamy. For a runnier consistency, add a little water and blend again. Store in the fridge for up to a week.

TIP
If you have a dehydrator, feel free to use that instead of baking.

Foraged green chips

BY BLACK BARN FARM

Remember when kale chips were the go? Well, we loved 'em and I tried my darnedest to keep a solid store of them in the pantry – even the kids loved the tanginess of the marinade, so we went through a tonne of kale. Inevitably, we ate more than we could grow, so I found a way to extend the season by foraging greens found readily in the paddock. You could hunt for these greens in your own backyard, on riverbanks or in parks – seek out wild spots infrequently traversed and not likely to have attracted a peeing dog. Be sure to only take the greens you can identify.

I particularly hunt out borage, plantain and rocket (arugula) as they have big strong leaves that hold lots of marinade. You could also use dandelion, but it can be a tad bitter (healthy, but not everyone's taste).

Makes a big bag's worth

40–50 leaves foraged greens, washed

MARINADE
juice and zest of 1 large lemon
80 g (2¾ oz/½ cup) toasted cashews
2 tablespoons tahini
2 tablespoons olive oil
chilli flakes, to taste (optional)
salt and freshly ground black pepper, to taste
Preheat the oven to 80°C (175°F, see Tip). Line a baking tray with baking paper.

To make the marinade, blend all the marinade ingredients in a blender until smooth. Taste and add more of any ingredients and blend again.

Toss the greens and marinade in a large bowl until well coated. Spread over the prepared tray in a single layer. Bake until hard and crispy. The time will depend on the oven temperature, but expect it to take at least 2 hours. Set aside to cool completely before transferring to a large jar or airtight container. They will keep for up to 6 months (but I bet they only last 6 minutes!).

199

GO GREEN WITH PASTA

Just as the days begin to stretch and gain a little warmth, the greens appear back in the garden, as do the eggs in the chicken nesting boxes. It's also the time that we are waking up from our slumber and getting social again. What a perfect opportunity to coincide the two with a pasta making gathering. This must be one of the most fun create-with-a-crowd dishes – if a little likely to coat the kitchen in a thin layer of flour.

You can make enough for a one-off communal feast or, while you've got many hands on deck, you can make enough to keep you all going for a few more months.

This recipe can be multiplied as many times as you require, and results in vibrant, flavourful fettucine strips.

Serves 4

2 cups spinach leaves
525 g (1 lb 3 oz/3½ cups) plain (all-purpose)
   flour, plus extra for kneading
3 large eggs
pinch of fine sea salt
your favourite pasta sauce or a drizzle of
   olive oil, to serve
finely grated parmesan cheese and/or fresh
   herb leaves, to garnish (optional)

Prepare a bowl of iced water. Blanch the spinach in a saucepan of boiling water for 1 minute until wilted. Transfer the spinach to the bowl of iced water to cool. Drain and squeeze out any excess water then finely chop. Puree the spinach in a blender or food processor until smooth.

Pour the flour into a mound on a clean surface and make a well in the centre. Crack the eggs into the well and add the salt. Pour the spinach over the eggs. Use a fork to gradually incorporate the flour into the wet ingredients until a dough forms.

Knead the dough for about 8–10 minutes until smooth and elastic. (You may need to add extra flour if it's too sticky.) Wrap the dough in plastic wrap and set aside at room temperature for at least 30 minutes to rest. (This allows the gluten to relax.)

Divide the dough into smaller portions then use a rolling pin or pasta machine to roll out each portion into thin sheets. Cut the sheets into your desired pasta shape – fettuccine, tagliatelle, etc.

At this point you'll need to decide if you're eating it right away or keeping it for another day. To store it, hang or coil the pasta into nests and leave overnight to air-dry hard. Once completely dry, it will store in an airtight container or in the freezer for up to 6 months.

If it's time to feast, get cooking! Bring a large saucepan of salted water to the boil. Cook the pasta for 2–4 minutes (depending on the thickness of the noodles) until al dente. Drain and toss with your favourite pasta sauce or a simple drizzle of olive oil. Garnish with parmesan and herbs, if using.

NOURISHMENT

Oh my goodness granola

BY BLACK BARN FARM

As a teenager my best friend lived next door and her mum used to batch-make the most delicious granola I'd ever eaten. We found a reason to eat it at all hours of any day.

I tried to replicate her dish, but never quite nailed it. Years later, my stepmother gifted us a huge jar of her own version, then more recently my next-door neighbour presented us with her own chocolatey take. It inspired me to revisit the challenge of mastering our own rendition, as the incentives for having this in your pantry are plentiful – not least of which is having a ready-to-go stash should I need a last-minute gift. That's if I can keep it out of sight of the teenage boys!

This is a brilliant recipe to make a big batch of as it lasts for at least a year if kept in a cool, dark place in an airtight container. Double, triple, quadruple to your heart's content.

Makes 1 kg (2 lb 3 oz)

125 g (4½ oz) butter
90 g (3 oz/¼ cup) honey
1 teaspoon ground cinnamon
30 g (1 oz/¼ cup) cacao powder
½ teaspoon ground nutmeg
100 g (3½ oz/1 cup) rolled oats (freshly rolled means
   they won't have any bitterness or rancidity)
60 g (2 oz/1 cup) shredded or flaked coconut
280 g (10 oz/2 cups) roughly chopped mixed nuts
   (I use almonds, walnuts and hazelnuts)
30 g (1 oz/¼ cup) pepitas (pumpkin seeds)
30 g (1 oz/¼ cup) sunflower kernels

Preheat the oven to 160°C (320°F).

Melt the butter and honey in a saucepan over a low heat. Remove from the heat then mix in the cacao, nutmeg and cinnamon.

Combine the remaining ingredients in a large bowl. Pour the butter mixture over the oat mixture and mix well until everything is well coated. Spread the mixture over a large baking tray in a thin layer. Bake for 20 minutes, checking about halfway through to make sure it doesn't get too brown.

Set aside to cool completely before decanting into a large jar or airtight container.

TIP
This is a fruit-free blend, but if I want a batch with a little extra sweetness, I add 65 g (2¼ oz/½ cup) dried apple, finely diced, and 60 g (2 oz/½ cup) dried cranberries. I add these after the granola is cool.

203

Cumquat marmalade

BY PAMMY WALPOLE, ONE OF MY MOST
PRECIOUS FRIENDS

Marmalade has eluded me since the beginning of time; I've over- or under-simmered it every time I've tried, and in the end I concluded it wasn't my love language. I adore the bitter-sweet-jelly-with-bits though, especially on homemade sourdough with lots of salty butter, so I wasn't willing to accept defeat.

I have a very special friend who I've had in my corner my whole adult life. We drifted apart once until one day she sent me a handwritten letter and I knew she was a keeper, and drift we did no more. This friend happens to know the secret to marmalade-making and every year she shares.

Pammy reminisced, 'In my twenties I purchased a small standard Nagami cumquat tree in a terracotta pot. It must have been dragged through twenty share houses and rentals before it finally put roots into soil. Periodically, it would require careful resurrection, but it survived! It never fruited much back then. Now, it is still compact but is the most productive and beloved tree, planted right in between garden beds.

'Every year I make a large batch of cumquat marmalade. It's a bit of a Zen ritual really. The cumquats are sliced ridiculously fine, which of course is not necessary and takes absolutely forever, but looks strikingly beautiful once cooked.

'The ritual also involves displaying the filled jars on the kitchen bench for several weeks. They give a sense of joy, which is hard to explain. During this "display period", many jars are given away to friends, neighbours, family or those who just look in need of a hug. Happiness grows as the number of jars diminishes.

'Preserved fruit and vegetables always remind me of my mother's resourcefulness and how she could feed a family through winter from pantry cupboards filled with Fowlers Vacola jars. Back then, being resourceful was a necessity. Now it's more about the connections we make.'

Makes 10–15 × 300 g (10½ oz) jars

2 kg (4 lb 6 oz) ripe but not overripe cumquats (can be much more or less than this, just however many you can get your hands on)
juice of 4 limes
soft brown or white granulated sugar of the same weight as the fruit and liquid

Wash the cumquats and remove the stems. Finely slice (or quarter if you don't want the Zen journey) and remove all the tiny pips. Put the pips on a clean, cotton handkerchief and tie firmly.

Put the fruit, lime juice and pips in their handkerchief in a large bowl. Cover with cold water until just submerged. Set aside overnight to soak.

Transfer the fruit, pip handkerchief and soaking liquid to a large saucepan (see Tip), counting the quantity in cups. Cook the fruit over a low heat until it is just tender. Add 1 cup of sugar for every cup of fruit and soaking liquid. Increase the heat to high and boil for 30–40 minutes until the marmalade reaches setting point, when the cooking marmalade starts to stick on the side of the pan. (Alternatively, put a teaspoon of the mixture on a cold saucer in the freezer for a few minutes then check to see if it is holding together.) Don't panic, marmalade tastes excellent runny or thick.

Meanwhile, sterilise the jars (page 178).

Remove the pip handkerchief from the marmalade. Use a small ladle or large spoon to fill the hot jars, putting the lids on while still hot to ensure they seal. Label the jars and include the year – good marmalade seems to improve with age, and it will keep for years unopened. Give them away freely and with love.

TIP
An enamel saucepan works beautifully if you have one or use a stainless steel pan.

204

Marmalade in tea

Strange but true, marmalade in tea is a wondrous thing. Discovered quite by accident by the 13-year-old in our house who was sniffing for a sweetener to no avail. Not averse to giving new things a go, he dolloped a full spoon of the sticky citrus stuff into his cup and a new family favourite was discovered.

PS I prefer mine without milk, and it's especially good in rooibos tea.

Rose petal syrup

BY BLACK BARN FARM

I took to making rose syrup en masse for Christmas presents when the kids were small and we were not financially flush but wanted to gift. Damask roses are colourful and aromatic, but any rose petals will work – except white, as they turn brown.

Use this syrup as a cordial, in teas or cocktails. It's also lovely drizzled over desserts and pancakes or used as a flavouring in various recipes.

Makes 4–6 × 250 ml (8½ fl oz/1 cup) jars

2 cups fresh, unsprayed rose petals (see Tips)
500 ml (17 fl oz/2 cups) boiling water
440 g (15½ oz/2 cups) white granulated sugar
1 tablespoon lemon juice (optional, see Tips)
1 cup dried rose petals (optional)

Gently rinse the fresh petals under cold water to remove any dirt or bugs then transfer to a large bowl. Pour over the boiling water. Set aside for 45 minutes to steep, allowing the water to absorb the floral essence.

Strain the rose petal-infused water through a fine sieve or muslin (cheesecloth) set over a bowl, discarding the petals.

Pour the rose-infused water into a saucepan. Add the sugar and place over a medium heat, stirring until the sugar is completely dissolved. Add the lemon juice, if using. Reduce the heat to low and simmer for 10–15 minutes until the syrup thickens.

Remove from the heat and set aside to cool to room temperature. Pour the syrup into sterilised jars (right). Add the dried petals, if using, then seal the jar.

Water bath the jar to make the syrup shelf stable for years (right) or store in the fridge for up to a month.

TIPS
• Make sure your fresh rose petals are free from pesticides. Harvest them early in the day when the oils are most concentrated.
• Lemon juice adds a zesty flavour and helps preserve the colour of the syrup.

Gran's plum sauce

BY GRAN AND BLACK BARN FARM

This is my gran's recipe, so it's cherished beyond measure and the taste takes me immediately to the 5 pm (not a minute later) 'tea' she served in her little cottage in Bunyip – inevitably meat and three veg every. single. night! Having three generations at the table was a regular experience, and more often than not there were cousins from multiple families perched either side of Granddad at the green melamine table. He'd butter his bread thickly while we waited in silence under his somewhat intimidating gaze for the plated meals. Gran had more often than not grown the food herself and dug it up just hours earlier before boiling it to various shades of grey to be laid in front of us.

The house was beyond tiny and decorated sparsely, but it was full of kids daily who needed to be fed, loved and smacked (we released his ferrets and hunting dogs all too often and swung on the clothesline at every opportunity). Poor Granddad had his first of six children at seventeen, as well as twenty-three grandchildren and twenty-four great grandchildren under his feet until the day he died at eighty-seven. We flipped the furniture upside down to make forts for battles, used his brill cream to 'soften' the vinyl on the Kingswood bench seat and ate his apricots straight from the tree before they even had a chance to fully ripen. The threat of his belt was legendary, but with each passing generation it moved from reality to folklore.

He'd dollop this plum sauce in great quantities on his evening meal and in turn, the grandchildren would follow suit.

At fourteen when walking home from school, I foraged plums from the local park and rang Gran for her recipe. I've been using it ever since – with a few tweaks – to put roadside plum harvests to good use. This recipe is for 2.5 kg (5½ lb) of fruit, but can be multiplied with ease. To make it worth the effort you'd really want at least 3 kg (6 lb 10 oz) of fruit.

Makes 8–10 jars

3 teaspoons cloves
3 teaspoons whole allspice berries
3 teaspoons black peppercorns
2 teaspoons ground ginger
2.5 kg (5½ oz) plums (any variety), pits removed
1.5 litres (51 fl oz/6 cups) brown vinegar
6 teaspoons fine sea salt

Place the spices in a small muslin (cheesecloth) bag. Place in a large heavy-based saucepan along with the plums, vinegar and salt. Cook, stirring occasionally, over a low heat for 2–2½ hours until the mixture is thick.

Remove the spice bag and any stray pits before bottling in sterilised bottles (page 178). Water bath the bottles to make the sauce shelf stable for years (page 178). Once opened, store in the fridge for up to 6 weeks.

TIP
I use roadside foraged plums (small yellow and red). They are VERY pit heavy, so you'll need to be patient when pitting.

Plum sauce.

6lb plums, 2 lb sug. 6 level teaspoons
salt. 3 pints brown vin, 3 level teasp.
cloves. 2 level teasp. allspice, 2 level
teasp. whole black pepper 2 level teasp.
ground ginger.

Put spices in muslin bag and
boil all together for 2 - 2½
hrs or until mixture is
thick. Strain & bottle

209

High heat

The days are long and the nights are warm. High heat is a top 'n tail kind of season to avoid the blistering guts of the day until the cooler twilight fun with roadside foraging, riverside antics and an abundance of fresh food feasts. Berries are everywhere and the veggie patch is turning out tomatoes, basil, beans and greens aplenty. Stone fruit is performing its short-lived ritual, so put them to good use while at their best. This is the season of socialising with your broadest huddles – dust off your conversation capabilities and fill your cup with folks from far and wide.

210

NOURISHMENT

Pickled nasturtium, the poor man's capers

BY BLACK BARN FARM

We have nasturtium planted in all the places that need a helping hand with pollination and where frost can't touch her. When left to her own devices she climbs the walls of our hoop house in an attempt to conquer the world. Generally, I leave her to her ways as the further those little crawling vines go, the more seed pods – AKA poor man's capers – we get. In the name of using things in abundance, these little flavour bombs have become a firm favourite at Black Barn Farm and feature in every potluck dinner we have.

Towards the end of spring each year, you'll notice there are nasturtium seeds appearing all over your plants – pounce immediately!

Use as you would capers, but remember they have a slightly more peppery kick than capers. You can multiply or halve this recipe with ease.

Makes 2 cups

1 cup nasturtium seeds (see Tips)
250 ml (8½ fl oz/1 cup) apple-cider vinegar
1 heaped tablespoon rapadura sugar or
  soft brown sugar, plus extra to serve
1 heaped tablespoon fine sea salt, plus extra to serve
3 garlic cloves
2 teaspoons black or white peppercorns
dried herbs (such as dill or tarragon), to taste

Combine all the ingredients, except the garlic, peppercorns and dried herbs, with 125 ml (4 fl oz/ ½ cup) water in a saucepan and bring to a gentle simmer over a very low heat. Taste for salty and sweet, adding more sugar or salt if you prefer.

Divide the garlic and peppercorns among sterilised jars (page 178). Top with the nasturtium mixture, ensuring the seeds are completely covered with the brine. If any seeds float to the surface, use some dried herbs as a 'follower' to keep them under the liquid. Seal the jars.

Water bath the jars to make the pickle shelf stable for years (page 178) or store in the fridge for up to a year. Allow them to pickle for at least a week before using.

TIPS
• When harvesting the nasturtium seeds, discard any that are brown or soft.
• Every part of the nasturtium is edible. As well as the seeds for pickling (this recipe), we use the flowers for salads and the leaves for a peppery addition to the Green tahini sauce (page 190).

Fresh-pick-quick-pickle

BY SU DENNETT, MISTRESS OF MELLIODORA

When completing my permaculture design course, I slept in my swag and often had the luck of eating with the teachers. On one such evening, David Holmgren (co-founder of Permaculture) and Su Dennett were staying, too. Su is an elder that everyone needs in their life. She's frighteningly practical, eternally youthful and matriarch of Melliodora (the permaculture display property in Hepburn, Victoria). That evening she taught me the art of the fresh pickle - now a kitchen mainstay at Black Barn farm.

Eat as a side or add a boiled egg and half an avocado for a simple lunch.

root vegetables (you can use any vegetables really, but carrots and beets are heavenly)
fresh soft herb leaves and stems (any you like, such as fennel, flat-leaf/Italian parsley, coriander/ cilantro, basil)
olive oil
apple-cider vinegar
nigella seeds, sunflower kernels and pepitas (pumpkin seeds), to sprinkle
salt and freshly ground black pepper, to taste

Grate the vegetables and finely slice the herbs. Combine in a bowl then douse with the oil and vinegar. Sprinkle with the seeds.

Season and set aside for 20 minutes to pickle before eating fresh. If you make too much, it will store for up to 24 hours in the fridge without losing its crunch.

Adult elderflower icy poles

BY BLACK BARN FARM

When elderflowers are abundant – as they are at this time of year (and they can be found in abundance in public places) – make cordial and icy poles!

Makes 10–12 depending on your moulds (which could just be small glasses with spoons for handles)

250 ml (8½ fl oz/1 cup) Elderflower and rhubarb cordial (page 224), plus extra to taste
250 ml (8½ fl oz/1 cup) gin, plus extra to taste
375 ml (12½ fl oz/1½ cups) tonic water
60 ml (2 fl oz/¼ cup) lime juice, plus extra to taste
thinly sliced lime and cucumber or fresh edible flowers, to garnish

Mix the cordial, gin, tonic water and lime juice in a jug until well combined. Taste and adjust – add more cordial for sweetness, more gin for a stronger kick or more lime juice for acidity.

Pour the mixture into icy pole (popsicle) moulds, leaving a little space at the top as the liquid will expand as it freezes. Pop a slice or two of lime and cucumber or a couple of flowers into each mould before adding the sticks.

Put the moulds in the freezer for at least 4–6 hours until completely solid.

214

Summer apricot jam tart

BY MICHELLE CRAWFORD, HOST OF THE BOWMONT
EVENTS AND GUEST HOUSE

I swooned when this human wrote her book, *A Table in the Orchard*. Before we even had an orchard of our own, I met her fleetingly at a Deep Winter Agrarian Gathering and was surprised to realise she is quite shy. Finally, I was beyond flipping delighted by an invite to join her at The Bowmont in Franklin, Tasmania for an afternoon of Futuresteading conversations. It's a space to make even the most travelled talkers feel comfortable, and the upstairs B&B feels like home.

Michelle Crawford is whip smart, gentle and quietly spoken. She's somewhat of an enigma really. Spending time in this glorious old building, which had been a bank, maternity hospital, administration building and now a home and event space, was heaven. We talked until it was almost dark, surrounded by her piles of books, plotting a potential project or two together.

'This is my go-to recipe for using the glut of summer stone fruit,' she said. 'I love apricots, but plums are good, or peaches – any stone fruit really. You can use regular jam in a pinch, but I like to make a low-sugar, jammy puree so the tart is not too sweet. A slice of this is my perfect summer breakfast, eaten outside in the garden with a black coffee, collecting my thoughts for the day.'

Serves 6–8

250 g (9 oz) ripe apricots
55 g (2 oz/¼ cup) white granulated sugar,
  plus extra to taste

PASTRY
250 g (9 oz/1⅔ cups) plain (all-purpose) flour,
  plus extra for dusting
100 g (3½ oz) icing (confectioners') sugar
pinch of table salt
125 g (4½ oz) unsalted butter, cut into cubes
1 large egg, lightly whisked

Halve the apricots, discarding the kernels. Transfer to a small heavy-based saucepan. Add 1 tablespoon water and heat gently over a low heat, stirring, until the apricots start to release their juices. Cook for about 20 minutes until soft. Add the white sugar, bring to a gentle simmer and cook, stirring occasionally, until thick and jammy, about 10 minutes. Remove from the heat and set aside to cool slightly. Taste the apricots – you may need to stir through a little extra sugar if they are very tart.

To make the pastry, whisk together the dry ingredients in a large bowl. Add the butter and rub into the flour mixture with your fingertips (being nimble-fingered so as not to melt the butter) until just combined. Mix in the egg, adding a little water if the dough feels too dry. Tip the mixture onto a lightly floured surface and quickly bring it together to form a smooth dough. Shape pastry into a flat disc and wrap in a beeswax wrap or plastic wrap. Chill in the fridge for at least 30 minutes.

Meanwhile, use the extra flour to lightly dust a 28 cm (11 in) tart tin with a removable base.

On a well-floured surface, gently roll the dough disc into a 30–40 cm (12–14 in) circle and line the base and side of the prepared tin, carefully trimming the excess and reserving any scraps. (You can make a shape or lattice for the top with this if you fancy.) Put in the fridge for 30 minutes to rest.

Heat the oven to 180°C (360°F).

Smooth the jam over the pastry case. Bake for 30 minutes until the pastry is golden..

Set aside in the tin to cool slightly then serve warm. This is great for morning tea with strong black coffee.

Summer berry trifle

BY BLACK BARN FARM

Here's another recipe that began with a version my gran used to make for every special occasion during the summer months, when berries were abundant. I have tweaked and changed this as my adult tastes have changed and my kitchen capabilities have evolved.

The decadence of this is beyond measure, so it's a once-or-twice-a-year performance. Because of its infrequency, we go all out and ensure that each of the ingredients is the best version of itself so when combined, the sum of the parts knocks your socks off.

This will feed a crowd as it's very rich, so not much is needed per serve.

Serves up to 20

1 homemade or store-bought chocolate cake, cooled and cut into 1 cm (½ in) slices
250 g (9 oz/2 cups) fresh raspberries
260 g (9 oz/2 cups) fresh blackberries
500 ml (17 fl oz/2 cups) chocolate custard (made from scratch or combine store-bought vanilla custard and 4 tablespoons cacao powder)
375 g double (heavy) cream mixed with a handful of thinly sliced fresh mint leaves
Raspberry jelly (page 242 or use a box of store-bought jelly crystals)
sifted icing (confectioners') sugar, for dusting

It's as simple as layering the ingredients, except the icing sugar, on top of each other in a glass trifle bowl. To minimise the smeary run that comes from the custard and cream, try this order: some of the cake, berries, custard, more cake, cream mixture, all the jelly, more berries, the remaining cake, cream mixture and custard. Finish with the remaining berries on top. Dust with icing sugar.

Raspberry and rosemary jam

BY STEPH, WOODSIDE FARM PRODUCE

Steph has been making this jam for a long time. Given we don't grow strawberries, but we do grow raspberries, I've adapted this little gem accordingly and it adds an intriguing and delicious twist.

This recipe has been devised around 1 kg (2 lb 3 oz) quantities, but it's very easy to multiply.

Makes 4–6 × 300 g (10½ oz) jars

1 kg (2 lb 3 oz) white granulated sugar
4 fresh rosemary sprigs, leaves picked
1 kg (2 lb 3 oz/8 cups) fresh raspberries

Blend the sugar and rosemary in a food processor until the sugar takes on a greenish shade and you can't see any bits of rosemary. (If you leave larger bits of rosemary, the taste will still be great but the texture will be compromised.)

Transfer the rosemary mixture to a bowl. Combine with the raspberries, cover and set aside for 12–24 hours at room temperature. You want the mixture to be quite liquid by the end.

Gently heat the raspberry mixture in a heavy-based saucepan until it reaches 90°C (195°F) then cook at a rolling boil for at least 10 minutes until it forms a skin when you place a spoonful on a cold plate from the freezer.

Pour the jam into sterilised jars (page 178) and seal with lids quickly. Leave to cool on the bench at room temperature before labelling and storing for as long as you need to devour it or in the fridge for 6 weeks once opened.

TIPS
- Undercooked jam is always better than overcooked. Soft-set jam is delicious, spreads well and is delicious in yoghurt. Overcooked jam is like eating a jam lollipop.
- Make more rosemary sugar than you need. It's beautiful in a plain cake or use it day-to-day.

Crabapple jelly

BY LUCY ETHERIDGE, MATE FROM
UNIVERSITY DAYS

This glorious mother hen has been in my life since uni when we travelled through Europe during the summer break. While now geographically separated, our lives have strong parallels: with three kids and strong connection to community, our hands are calloused and our days are often tractor bound.

Crabapple jelly is synonymous with Luce, gifting jars when she visits and when she hosts.

When I asked her to share, she responded with, 'Funny you emailed about the Crabapple jelly when you did, as I had only just this week found a poem I wrote to Nana not long after she died in 2002. It went a little something like this ...

'Wooden spoons, condensed milk
Sausage rolls and "squeeze"
St George and Margaret Fulton
Soup of ham and peas

Macaroons and white tea
Sixpence in the pudd
Saccharine and Styvos
New Idea a should

Roses in the garden
Rain to fill the gauge
Macrame, sewing, cross-stitch
Knits for any age

Crosswords and an HB
Books of scorn and glee
Crabapples, pommies, medlars
Jams and jellies please'

'Note that I rarely use a recipe for this; instead working on visual cues for quantity and water and lemon initially, but always measure juice to sugar.

'My nana, Joan Etheridge, had a couple of enormous crabapple trees in her garden. She was always one to make the weird and whacky jellies and jams from things like medlars, persimmons and crabapples. I took cuttings from her tree and now have a little hill of crabapple trees of my own, which I love dearly but pay very little attention to until it's later summer/early autumn when I harvest and make crabapple jelly, syrup and cider vinegar. It's become an annual cook-up, mainly for gifting to others but the kids always assume there's a jar in the larder for their use too. They grew up with an after-school staple diet of pikelets with lashings of butter and crabapple jelly, so it's become a bit of a comfort food condiment over the years.'

Makes 10–12 250 ml (8½ fl oz) jars

2.5 kg (5½ lb) crabapples, washed, stems removed and halved
caster (superfine) sugar (500 g/1 lb 2 oz for every 500 ml/17 fl oz/2 cups of juice)
80 ml (2½ fl oz/⅓ cup) lemon juice

Put the crabapple in a stockpot, cover with water until just above the fruit line then bring to the boil over a low heat. Simmer for 30 minutes until soft.

Pour the fruit into a jelly bag or a muslin (cheesecloth) lined sieve set over a large bowl. Set aside to strain overnight. Do not press the fruit. This step makes it a slow food but is important to ensure the clarity of the jelly at the end.

Measure the liquid in the bowl then pour it into a heavy-based saucepan. For every 500 ml (17 fl oz/ 2 cups) liquid, add 500 g (1 lb 2 oz) sugar. Add the lemon juice and stir over a medium heat until the sugar dissolves. Increase the heat to high and boil rapidly for 20 minutes until at setting point. (To test, dip a wooden spoon in the jelly and run a finger over the back of the spoon. If a skin forms, it's ready.)

Meanwhile, sterilise the jars (page 178).

Pour the jelly into the warm jars. Store at room temperature for as many years as it takes you to use or gift it. Once opened, store in the fridge for up to 6 weeks.

TIPS
- **Enjoy on a cheese platter or with ham, pork or turkey, on pikelets or straight from the jar!**
- **For a crabapple syrup, use this same recipe with a little less cook time after adding the sugar and juice. Cook until the sugar dissolves. It's delightful in drinks, as a kombucha topper or glaze.**

Stone fruit galette

BY BLACK BARN FARM

Living in orcharding country means there's never a shortage of summer and autumn fruits. Using the abundance of sweet sugar bombs that are pregnantly heaving on the tree branches is the challenge, but one of the best ways to put it all to good use is this simple galette.

The joy of this recipe is that you can make baby individual galettes or you can create one large family-sized pie AND you can use whatever fruit you can get your hands on. Apples, peaches, plums, nectarines and blackberries are all easily found in summer and early autumn, either roadside-foraged or from friends or farm gates. Abundance is a reality for those with trees in their yard, so putting the fruit to use will be doing them a favour.

Serves 8

3 cups of your chosen fruit, cut into chunks no larger than the size of your little finger
55 g (2 oz/¼ cup) of your preferred sugar (I use rapadura for an added caramelised flavour)
1 teaspoon natural vanilla extract or 2 vanilla beans, split lengthways and seeds scraped
1 teaspoon ground cardamon (optional)
1 egg mixed with 2 tablespoons water
vanilla ice cream or yoghurt, to serve

SWEET SHORTCRUST PASTRY
335 g (12 oz/2¼ cups) plain (all-purpose) flour
80 g (2¾ oz/⅓ cup) caster (superfine) sugar
175 g (6 oz) cold unsalted butter, chopped
2 egg yolks
2 tablespoons chilled water

If making the pastry in a food processor, it's as simple as throwing it all in together and mixing until a well-combined ball of dough forms. If mixing by hand (which is a lovely tactile task if you have the time), place the flour the bench, make a well in the flour and add the remaining ingredients, except the chilled water. Working with your fingertips (being nimble-fingered so as not to melt the butter), rub together until it resembles breadcrumbs. Add the water to bring it all together into a ball. Be sure to work fast so the butter doesn't melt. Chill the dough in the fridge for 30 minutes.

Meanwhile, combine the fruit, sugar, vanilla and cardamom, if using, in a large bowl. Set aside for 30 minutes to marinate gently.

Preheat the oven to 180°C (360°F).

Roll out the dough into a rough circle and transfer to a baking tray. Put the fruit mixture in the centre and fold over the edge of the dough so the cooking juices won't escape. Brush the pastry with the egg wash then bake for 45 minutes.

Serve with ice cream or yoghurt.

Elderflower and rhubarb cordial

BY TRESKA JAMES, RYTHDALE COTTAGE

Given the upwards appeal of non-alcoholic drinks, this is a cracker to serve when you want to avoid the grog but you have guests midsummer and still want to feel a little bit fancy.

This recipe is from the good (and clever) Treska James at Rythdale Cottage in Picton, NSW. She has won first prize at the Moss Vale Show, with a judging comment: 'Just needs gin.' We've got you covered on that with the Adult elderflower icy poles (page 214). She created this adaptation from a basic elderflower cordial recipe after deciding the original was too bland – controversial, I know. Like lots of us, she had a surplus of rhubarb around the same time the elderflower comes into flower, and the tart rhubarb flavour nicely balances the fruity sweetness of the elderflower.

The affection for this recipe comes from the seasonal ritual that sits alongside its making: in the secret window that appears after school finishes for the year and before the new year begins. The elderflowers are in full bloom where we live, so the sweet drink captures summer days to perfection. It also bottles the hard-to-explain feeling of freedom, the long, unplanned days which are only ours for a few weeks of each year.

Treska's words of advice: 'I am not fussy in my cooking – more of a "chuck it in" kind of girl – but I have found as I have learned to distil botanical waters how the properties of flowers change throughout the day. As such I am pretty stubborn around ensuring the elderflower is picked right as the sun hits the garden on a dry day. Also, I suggest popping the picked elderflower immediately into a bowl with some lemon slices to ward off any critters that might be hidden in the petals.

Makes about 1.7 litres (57 fl oz)

1 kg (2 lb 3 oz) white granulated sugar (see Tips)
6 rhubarb stalks, roughly chopped
zest and juice of 2 lemons
50 g (1¾ oz) citric acid (if canning)
20 or so elderflower heads (see Tips)

Put the sugar and 1.5 litres (51 fl oz/6 cups) water in a large saucepan that you won't need to use for anything else in the next 24 hours! Bring to a gentle simmer over a low heat, stirring, until the sugar dissolves. Add the rhubarb and lemon zest. Cook over a low heat for 10 minutes until the rhubarb has infused the water and gone stringy. If preserving, stir in the citric acid until dissolved. Remove from the heat.

Add the elderflower heads and lemon juice. Cover with a lid or clean tea (dish) towel. Set aside to cool completely.

Use a fine sieve, a muslin (cheesecloth) set over a sieve or a colander to strain the cordial (see Tips). The cordial can now be bottled.

If not canning, pour into sterilised bottles (page 178) and store in the fridge for a month.

If canning, can for 20 minutes once bottled (or to around 85°C/185°F, see Tips).

TIPS
• You can reduce the sugar, but you must use the quantity specified if canning.
• Canning does heat the contents, which pasteurises the elderflower, so make the cordial with the citric acid, chill what you will drink in a month then can the rest.
• To prep the elderflower heads, remove as much of the stem as possible – fiddly, I know, but important.
• If you don't have 20 elderflower heads, pick what you have and decrease the rhubarb proportion accordingly. The cordial will be lighter in flavour but still worth making!
• If you have a worm farm, they will love the strained solids.

224

NOURISHMENT

BLENDING TEA

Yes, we live in a caffeine culture! But more frequently than ever before, I'm hearing friends and farm gate visitors quip that they are not drinking coffee at the moment or indeed at all.

Because of my own aversion to coffee, I love herbal tea. Don't get me wrong, I love the smell, ritual and social-ness of coffee, but it makes me really crook. Once full of caffeine, my adrenals just don't cope. Instead of missing out, I've taken to making a vast array of herbal tea and now host regular tea-blending gatherings for others to learn and experiment. This is a great activity for a group because if you all raid your own gardens it expands the range available to everyone. Together you can experiment with different blends and provide feedback on medicinal impacts.

You can dry a massive range of leaves and flowers. During the months they are in full bloom, simply cut into bunches then hang — above a doorway, on the verandah, from a ladder — for 2–5 days. Keep them away from direct sunlight and if hanging outside, be sure to bring it in at night to avoid the evening air moisture. It needs to be bone dry before you blend with it.

On the right and over the page are some to experiment with.

It's important to note that while herbal teas are generally considered safe, individual responses can vary. Pregnant or breastfeeding women and individuals with specific health conditions or those taking medications should consult with a healthcare professional before consuming herbal teas regularly. Additionally, moderation is key, as excessive consumption of certain herbs may have adverse effects.

INGREDIENTS	MEDICINAL PROPERTIES
Peppermint leaf	Known for its ability to soothe digestive issues, alleviate headaches and relieve stress. It has antimicrobial properties and may help with respiratory conditions.
Chamomile flower	Often used to promote relaxation and improve sleep. It may also have anti-inflammatory and digestive benefits, making it a popular choice for calming the stomach.
Lemon balm leaf	Associated with calming effects, stress relief and improved mood. It may also have mild antiviral properties and be used to support digestion.
Lavender flower	Has calming properties and may help with anxiety and sleep disorders. It also has potential antioxidant and anti-inflammatory effects.
Eucalyptus leaf	Often used to relieve respiratory issues and congestion. It has antimicrobial properties and can provide relief for symptoms of colds and flu.
Nettle leaf	Rich in vitamins and minerals, it's believed to have anti-inflammatory properties and may be used to alleviate allergies, improve digestion and support joint health.
Rooibos leaf	Caffeine free and rich in antioxidants, it's associated with potential benefits for heart health, digestion and skin conditions.
Hibiscus flower	Known for its vibrant colour and tart flavour. It may help lower blood pressure, support heart health and provide antioxidant benefits.
Green tea leaf	Rich in antioxidants, particularly catechins. It's associated with numerous health benefits, including improved metabolism, heart health and cognitive function.
Dandelion leaf	May support liver health, act as a mild diuretic and provide potential anti-inflammatory benefits.
Gotu kola leaf	Known for its potential cognitive benefits, including improved memory and concentration. It's believed to have adaptogenic properties, aiding in stress management. Additionally, it may support wound healing and promote healthy skin.
Thyme leaf	Rich in thymol, a compound with antimicrobial properties. It may be beneficial for respiratory health, helping to ease coughs and congestion. It also contains antioxidants and may have anti-inflammatory effects.

INGREDIENTS	MEDICINAL PROPERTIES
Birch leaf	Traditionally used for its potential diuretic properties, promoting the elimination of excess fluids. It may also support detoxification and provide mild anti-inflammatory benefits.
Ginkgo leaf	Often associated with cognitive benefits, including improved memory and concentration. It has antioxidant properties and may support circulation, potentially benefiting conditions like tinnitus and mild cognitive impairment.
Oregano leaf	Rich in compounds like carvacrol and thymol, which have antimicrobial properties. Oregano tea may support digestion, boost the immune system and provide antioxidants. It is also used traditionally to alleviate respiratory issues.
Calendula flower	Has anti-inflammatory and antimicrobial properties, making it beneficial for soothing skin irritations and promoting wound healing. Calendula tea may also be used for digestive support and immune system enhancement.
Borage flower	Contains gamma-linolenic acid (GLA) and is traditionally used for its anti-inflammatory properties. It may support skin health, reduce inflammation and provide potential benefits for respiratory health.
Rose petal	Rich in antioxidants and has anti-inflammatory properties. It's known for its calming effects, promoting relaxation and stress relief. Also associated with potential benefits for skin health and digestion.
Citrus rind (orange or lemon)	Rich in flavonoids, antioxidants and essential oils. It may have anti-inflammatory and antimicrobial properties. In particular, the rind of orange and lemon contains compounds like limonene and citral, which contribute to the fruit's aromatic and potentially health-promoting qualities. Its high vitamin C content can support the immune system.
Rosemary leaf	Contains compounds like rosmarinic acid and essential oils, such as cineole, as well as antioxidants that contribute to overall immune support. Its anti-inflammatory properties may support joint and muscle health. Also linked to improved cognitive function and memory, and may help alleviate indigestion and support digestive health.

228

229

Harvest

The baskets fill themselves and the benches pile high with the abundance of fresh food in this season. It's time to sharpen your preserving skills so you can slice 'n dice 'n chop 'n dry your way to a pantry full of goodness to get you through winter. This must surely be the pinnacle of shared huddling activities with passata-making, fruit-leathering, herbal tea-blending, potato-harvesting and fruit-bottling all on high rotation. More fun with many, so huddle up and get chopping.

230

Baked breakfast eggs with fresh basil and chevre

BY BLACK BARN FARM

When friends stay over and you want a flashy but fast and fuss-free breakfast to serve a crowd the next morning, this is your guaranteed go-to.

You can use fresh, just-in-season tomatoes, or last year's passata (page 234) is just as delicious. It also makes the most of basil, which is just coming into season as well.

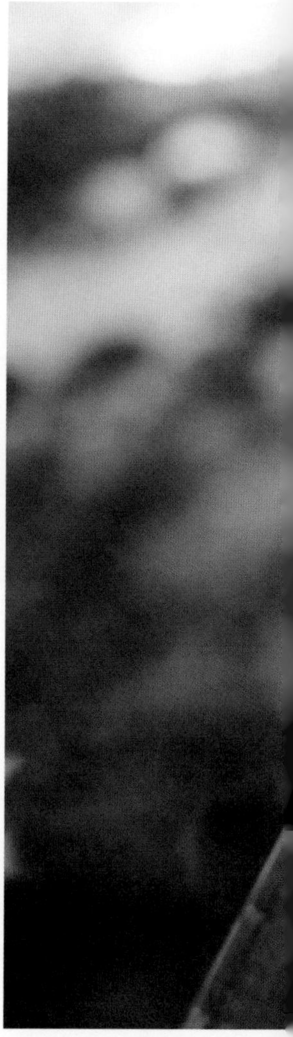

Serves 4

1 cup diced fresh tomato or passata (page 178)
8 eggs
Herby chevre, to taste (page 196)
1 red onion, diced
½ cup fresh basil leaves
olive oil, for drizzling
salt and freshly ground black pepper, to taste

BASIL TOPPING (OPTIONAL)
1 cup fresh basil leaves
3 garlic cloves
juice of 1 lemon
2 tablespoons olive oil
rock salt and freshly ground black pepper, to taste

Preheat the oven to 180°C (360°F).

To make the basil topping, blend all the topping ingredients in a blender until roughly chopped.

Divide the tomato or passata among four small ovenproof ramekins. Crack two eggs into each ramekin. Crumble in some chevre, sprinkle over the diced onion and fresh basil leaves, then drizzle with a little oil. Bake for 20 minutes. When the whites are completely cooked and the yolks are to your liking, remove from the oven and crumble a little more chevre over the top.

If you prefer your yolks softer, keep a close eye on them and remove at around the 15-minute mark.

Spoon the basil topping over, if using, and drizzle with a little more oil to serve. Make sure you have good rock salt and pepper for folks to add.

TIP
This is also great when you use baked beans instead of the tomato. Use any tinned baked bean – my favourite is JimJam Foods' beans.

232

233

PASSATA PARTY

Eager for a quintessential huddle experience? Passata-making days are exactly this. It's hard to put a date on it if you're all growing your own tomatoes, as it'll depend on the season. If you've not got a willing tomato grower in your group, find a farmer or a local grocer who sells in bulk and get your order in early. Aim for late harvest season to set a date that repeats each year.

It makes for a beautiful ritual to meet under one roof in the same kitchen and create your winter stores of food. Spend your year saving jars or finding them in op shops. Share the cost of the mouli and large pot, so you don't all have to purchase. Come together to get your production line creating red sauce for the year.

This recipe comes from the glorious Alex Elliott-Howery, owner of Cornersmith. This firecracker was interviewed for the *Futuresteading* podcast, and her spirit is contagious and frank. She has an unpretentious energy and doesn't take herself too seriously – traits I adore in others as they help to balance an inclination towards earnestness in me. This is her go-to recipe for the red sauce that can get you through any meal emergency.

Makes 10–20 jars

5 kg (11 lb 3 oz) ripe red tomatoes, halved
500 g (1 lb 2 oz) onions, chopped
1 garlic bulb, cloves separated, peeled
*   and bruised*
125 ml (4 fl oz/½ cup) olive oil
1 bunch fresh basil, leaves torn
salt and freshly ground black pepper,
*   to taste*

Preheat the oven to 180°C (360°F).

Spread the tomato, onion and garlic on oiled baking trays and season well with salt and pepper. Drizzle over the oil and roast for 45 minutes until the tomato has blistered and the onion is soft. Set aside for 30 minutes to cool before stirring through the basil.

Meanwhile, sterilise the jars (page 178).

Transfer the mixture to a bowl then blend with a handheld blender. Pass it through a mouli or sieve into a bowl, extracting as much juice as possible. Discard the solids, which will mostly be seeds and skin, as these make the mixture bitter.

Pour the passata into the hot, sterilised jars. Tap the jars on a hard surface and run a clean knife around the inside edge to remove any air bubbles. Wipe the rim with paper towel then seal.

Water bath the jars to make the passata shelf stable for years (page 178). Store in a cool, dark place.

235

Sweet and sour bean soup

BY MARIA KONECSNY, GEWÜRZHAUS

'Of all the things my mum has cooked in her time, this soup has endured,' said Maria Konecsny from Gewürzhaus. 'She made it for my sister, Eva, and I when we were kids, all that time back in Germany. She continues to make it for her grandkids now, dropping off a big pot full to feed and nourish us every other week.

'The soup is a surprising combination of sweet, sour and saltiness, harking back to the Eastern European ancestry in my mum's family. It is deeply satisfying on a cold day where these contrasting elements wake you up and remind you of the beauty and paradox of life; sometimes sweet, sometimes sour, sometimes salty. I find so much comfort in knowing that I can hold this paradox in my huddle, just like the soup holds it in perfect symphony in its ingredients. Life is not easy by design. Yet having a place that is home – both physically but mostly in our hearts and among our humans – makes it a journey of richness and beauty. This soup reminds me of that.'

It's gluten and dairy free too!

Serves 6

olive oil, for frying
200 g (7 oz) speck, rind removed and reserved, meat finely diced (see Tips)
1 large onion, finely diced
7 potatoes (Dutch cream, nicola or desiree), peeled and cut into 1 cm (½ in) cubes
2.5 litres (85 fl oz/10 cups) salt-reduced chicken stock
1 kg (2 lb 3 oz) green beans, trimmed, cut diagonally into 2 cm (¾ in) lengths
2½ teaspoons dried summer savory leaves (see Tips)
¼ teaspoon freshly cracked black pepper, plus ¼ teaspoon extra
salt, to taste
3 tablespoons white vinegar
2 tablespoons white granulated sugar

Cover the base of a stockpot or large saucepan with oil and place over a low–medium heat. Add the speck and fry for about 5 minutes. Add the onion, reduce the heat to low and sauté for 5 minutes until translucent.

Add the potato, cook briefly then increase the heat to high and deglaze the pot with the stock. Cover with a lid, bring to a simmer then reduce the heat to low and cook for about 20 minutes.

Add the beans, savory leaves and pepper. Season with salt. Stir in the reserved speck rind then bring to a simmer. Cover and cook for 30 minutes.

When the potato is soft, remove from the heat and use a potato masher to carefully mash the potato just a little (maybe fifteen times, so you have some mashed and some chunks). This thickens the soup a bit. Set aside for 15 minutes to cool, then remove and discard the speck rind.

Taste the soup. Start to season by adding a little of the vinegar, sugar, extra pepper and salt (see Tips). You are looking for a punchy broth, which is sweet, sour and salty.

TIPS
- If you don't have speck, use fatty bacon or pork belly instead.
- Summer savory, known as Bohnenkraut (bean herb) in German, is the perfect partner to green beans and the secret weapon of this soup. The herb is most similar to thyme.
- Don't be tempted to leave out the sugar or swap the white vinegar for a more mellow one – this soup needs the sharp aspects of both of these ingredients.

236

Traditional potato salad

BY INGRID GLASTONBURY, OTTI MADE

Potato salads speak to Christmas in South Australia's Barossa Valley, explained Otti Made pottery maker Ingrid Glastonbury. 'Go to any share-table Christmas party or barbecue and you will inevitably find six different potato salads; all a variation on a given set of ingredients that have been grown or farmed here since European settlement.

'Potatoes, onions, dill gherkins, cream, smoked bacon, boiled eggs, white-wine vinegar – these were all readily available ingredients in the Barossa in the 19th century. Over the years, families developed their own signature variation, and these recipes were then faithfully passed down through the generations.

'My mother, Irma, grew up on the old Henschke property at Keyneton, where the winery, vegetable garden, chooks, pigs and cows provided the ingredients, and it is her recipe that we share here.'

Serves up to 10

1.8 kg (4 lb) potatoes, peeled and cubed
2 onions, diced
5 bacon rashers (slices, as smoky as you can get your
    hands on), rind removed, bacon diced
350 g (12½ oz) Polski Ogorki dill gherkins (Zimmy's,
    if you can get them), diced
sliced boiled eggs and fresh or dried dill, to serve

SALAD DRESSING
450 ml (15 fl oz) pouring (whipping) cream
3 teaspoons caster (superfine) sugar
⅓ teaspoon ground white pepper
100 ml (3½ fl oz) white-wine vinegar
4 teaspoons flaky sea salt

Put the potato in a large saucepan and cover with plenty of cold, well salted water and bring to the boil over a medium heat. Cook for 25 minutes until soft but not broken down. Drain.

Meanwhile, gently fry the onion and bacon in a frying pan until the onion is lovely and golden and the bacon is crispy. Combine all the dressing ingredients in a bowl.

Transfer the hot potato to a large serving bowl and toss through the dressing so the potato absorbs it. Gently stir through the onion, bacon and gherkin. Chill in the fridge for an hour before serving (so that the flavours can mingle).

Garnish with boiled egg and dill to serve.

237

Apple and berry pie

BY BLACK BARN FARM

When touring through New England in the US on a research trip to learn about local food systems, we peppered the journey with visits to you-pick orchards to keep the kids interested. Along the way we built a vision for what would ultimately become our own Black Barn Farm. The added appeal of just about every small-scale family-owned farm was an offering of fresh apple cider doughnuts and homemade apple pies. Each family we visited had their own recipe and each pie was just a little different. The idea of creating our own version one day felt like a very distant dream. When we returned to Vermont later for an East Coast book tour, we were hosted by a vibrant woman called Tammy White at Wing & A Prayer Farm. Mid *Futuresteading* talk in her quintessential red barn, Tammy served her apple and berry pie. Alongside it were thickly cut slices of homemade cheddar cheese. Apparently, it's a Vermont thing, but what has continued to whip around my head was her cute little saying: 'Apple pie without cheese is like a kiss without a squeeze.' Who doesn't love a little squeeze?

Our own apple pie recipe, which we now make for our farm gate, has evolved over the past few years, but it definitely has its roots in Vermont.

Serves 10

30 g (1 oz) butter
4 large apples, peeled and chopped (see Tips)
150 g (5½ oz/1 cup) mixed fresh berries (blueberries, raspberries and blackberries, see Tips)
1 vanilla bean, split lengthways and seeds scraped
1 teaspoon ground cinnamon
½ teaspoon ground cardamon
grated zest and juice of 1 lemon
1 tablespoon rapadura sugar (or soft brown sugar)
freshly grated nutmeg, to garnish
double (heavy) cream or vanilla ice cream, to serve

CINNAMON PASTRY
375 g (13 oz/2.5 cups) plain (all-purpose) flour (see Tips)

180 g (6½ oz) cold butter, cubed
95 g (3¼ oz/½ cup lightly packed) rapadura sugar (or soft brown sugar)
1 teaspoon ground cinnamon
2 egg yolks, lightly whisked
1 teaspoon chilled water

To make the pastry, put the flour in a large bowl and rub the butter into the flour with your fingertips (being nimble-fingered so as not to melt the butter) until it resembles fine crumbs. Use a spoon to mix in the sugar and cinnamon then the egg yolk. Add the teaspoon of chilled water to bring the dough together and ensure the pastry won't break when rolled out. Wrap in a clean, damp tea (dish) towel and chill for 20 minutes.

Meanwhile, melt the butter in a large heavy-based saucepan over a medium heat. Add the apple, berries and vanilla beans seeds, and cook for 10 minutes. Once soft, add the vanilla, spices, lemon zest and juice. Mix gently then remove from the heat.

Preheat the oven to 160°C (320°F). Grease a 20 cm (8 in) pie dish with butter.

Set aside one-third of the dough and roll the remainder into a circle about 3 mm (⅛ in) thick.

Use the dough to line the base and side of the prepared dish, pressing into the base to remove any air pockets. Tip the fruit mixture over the dough then top with strips cut from the remaining dough (plait, if you like). Bake for 1 hour until the pastry is golden.

Serve warm with cream or ice cream.

TIPS
• Use different varieties of apple, so you have some that turn soft and others that hold their shape.
• Again, variety is good for the berries too, because some are tart while others are sweet. Together, they are delicious.
• To make this gluten free, replace the flour with ground almonds (125 g/4½ oz/1¼ cups) and brown rice flour (220 g/8 oz/1¼ cups).

238

240

Iced chocolate, beetroot and raspberry slice

BY BLACK BARN FARM

Everyone in charge of kids looks for ways to bury extra veggies into every meal. Slices are no exception. Beetroot is earthy so you wouldn't imagine it is suited to a sweet treat, but when cooked it has a delicate sweetness, and the colour makes this slice dark and rich.

We grow beets of all shapes and colours, and while I preserve as many as I can for the winter months, they are so darned diverse that we stick them in anything we can.

Because this is simple to make, it's as well suited to an arvo tea as it is for a fancy shindig. It's gluten free, so it's a good one to have up your sleeve for gatherings to be sure everyone can partake in sweets.

Makes 14–18 5 × 5 cm (2 × 2 in) pieces

CHOCOLATE LAYER
30 g (1 oz/¼ cup) Dutch (unsweetened) cocoa powder
2 eggs
300 g (10½ oz/3 cups) ground almonds
140 g (5 oz/1 cup firmly packed) grated raw
    beetroot (beet)
55 g (2 oz/¼ cup) white granulated sugar
dash of natural vanilla extract
1 tablespoon olive oil

PINK LAYER
2 × 400 ml (13½ fl oz) tins coconut milk
15 large fresh mint leaves, plus extra for
    garnish (optional)
185 g (6½ oz/1½ cups) fresh or frozen raspberries
55 g (2 oz/¼ cup) white granulated sugar

CHOCOLATE DRIZZLE
2 tablespoons Dutch (unsweetened) cocoa powder
1 tablespoon icing (confectioners') sugar
1 tablespoon boiling water

Preheat the oven to 180°C (360°F). Line a 20 cm (8 in) square cake tin with baking paper.

Blend all ingredients for the chocolate layer until well combined, adding a little water if the mixture is not sticking together. Press into the prepared tin and bake for 30 minutes. Set aside in the tin to cool completely.

Meanwhile, blend all the pink layer ingredients in a blender until smooth.

Pour the pink layer mixture into the tin and spread evenly.

Combine the chocolate drizzle ingredients in a small bowl then pour over the pink layer. Top with extra mint, if using, before popping in the freezer for at least 3 hours to set. Remove from the freezer when ready to slice and serve.

From-scratch
fruit jelly

BY BLACK BARN FARM

When our twins were young, we were lucky enough to have very active grandmothers and their friends eager to spend time with them. On one particular excursion, the boys returned from a day with one of these women with cups full of homemade jelly. I remember thinking, 'I can't believe I don't know how to make jelly from scratch.'

I know it can be bought with ease from the shop and it's quick and easy to do, but I couldn't shake the idea that I really should have a basic jelly recipe in my back pocket. So, I set about learning how to do it using fresh fruit and juice rather than a packet mix full of colourings and sugar.

Apple juice jelly is without a doubt the easiest. With two ingredients (500 ml/17 fl oz/2 cups apple juice and a 12 g/¼ oz gelatine leaf) you can't go wrong. Simply heat the juice until it just begins to boil then add the gelatine. Mix until dissolved and pour the mixture into moulds and set in the fridge for 2 hours. If you're keen to get more adventurous, try this raspberry version – still very hard to go wrong, I promise.

Serves 6

1 kg (2 lb 3 oz/8 cups) fresh raspberries
100 g (3½ oz) icing (confectioners') sugar
5 × 12 g (¼ oz) gelatine leaves

Combine the raspberries and sugar in a large saucepan. Bring to a very gentle simmer over a low heat for 1 hour until a consistent thickness and all the raspberries have broken down. Remove from the heat and set aside to cool completely.

Lightly oil your jelly moulds – different sizes are good (see Tips).

Strain the mixture through muslin (cheesecloth) in a sieve set over a bowl, discarding the seeds. Return the liquid to the pan and bring to a gentle boil over a low heat. Add the gelatine leaves, stirring, until dissolved. Pour the mixture into the prepared moulds and set in the fridge for approximately one hour.

TIPS
• To ensure the jelly comes away cleanly from the mould, you need to lightly oil the mould. This step is not necessary if you are intending to use the jelly in another recipe, such as the Summer berry trifle (page 218). You can also serve it in the moulds.
• This makes a perfectly clear jelly mixture, so it can be really lovely to add some fresh berries to the bottom of the mould.

242

Gluten-free lemon and berry tart

BY BLACK BARN FARM

At EVERY single workshop, school group or bus tour we run, I whip up this little number – sometimes two or three at once. It's gluten free and can easily be made dairy free (just serve with coconut yoghurt or omit the cream/yoghurt), so it gets you around just about every dietary – veganism excepted, because it relies on eggs.

The other magic trick to this recipe is that it can be made with things we have in abundance. It means I can always be sure that, even at the last minute, I can create it without the need for a dash to the shops.

It looks great and it never fails to generate a high degree of 'oohs' and 'ahhs'.

Serves 10

BASE
200 g (7 oz/2 cups) ground almonds
65 g (2¼ oz/½ cup) buckwheat flour
175 g (6 oz/1 cup) brown rice flour
80 g (2¾ oz/½ cup) chia seeds
grated zest and juice of 2 lemons
110 g (4 oz/½ cup) solid coconut oil
95 g (3¼ oz/½ cup) soft brown sugar

FILLING
12 egg yolks (see Tips)
1 teaspoon natural vanilla extract
4 tablespoons rapadura sugar (or soft brown sugar)
grated zest and juice of 3 lemons
250 ml (8½ fl oz/1 cup) coconut cream
75 g (2¾ oz/½ cup) fresh or frozen mixed berries,
  plus 150 g (5½ oz/1 cup) extra
double (heavy) cream or plain yoghurt, to serve
  (see Tips)

Preheat the oven to 180°C (360°F).

To make the base, blitz all the base ingredients in a food processor until the mixture resembles fine crumbs. (Alternatively, combine in a large bowl, rubbing the oil into the mixture with your fingertips.) Transfer to a 20 cm (8 in) tart tin, pressing into the base and up the side, making sure to cover evenly and fill in any gaps or cracks. Bake for 5 minutes then set aside to cool a little.

Meanwhile, blend all the filling ingredients, except the berries and cream or yoghurt, in a blender until just combined.

Pour the filling over the pastry case. Sprinkle the berries evenly over the top. Bake for 50 minutes until the top is set and golden.

Serve with the extra berries and cream or yoghurt.

TIPS
• Freeze the egg whites and use them for egg white omelettes or meringues. Defrost overnight in the fridge.
• The base may be a little dry, so a topping is ideal.

DEHYDRATION DAYS

When the fruit is on, it's ON! And once it's off the tree, the rotting process begins so, as the saying goes, many hands make light work. In the height of the harvest season, gather your huddle and get prepping. Arm your folks with chopping boards and knives, and cut like your life depends on it.

You don't need a commercial dehydrator, but if you have more fruit than space in your domestic dehydrator and you have plenty of sunshine, another option is to simply create some drying racks by stretching fine mesh or chicken wire between timber boards. They are easy to make, can be fit to size and will last years.

TIPS for dehydrating outside
- The thinner the slices, the faster they will dry out.
- Be sure to bring racks inside before the sun fully dips away at night as the evenings can carry moisture.
- Seek a sun-trapped spot with heat bouncing off walls.
- Cover your food with a fine breathable net.

244

The turning

Palettes of burnt orange, magenta red, rusty ochre and sunshine yellow set the landscape ablaze and herald the last hurrah of warm days. It's time for the pace to slow a little as your huddle shrinks back to your closer crew for the cold nights. Head into the pines or paddocks for mushroom hunts that are muffled, quiet mirroring the peacefulness of the place where these little fungi morsels are found. Light a match on early fireside dinners of just-picked-corn before squirrelling inside for new-season apple pies with your people.

246

NOURISHMENT

Rabbit stew

BY MUM AND GRAN

While not a commonly served meat these days, I literally owe my existence to the fact that my mum was raised on rabbit.

She was her father's rabbit-trapping apprentice from the age of four. Living in the Gippsland hills, Victoria, they used to go off together in the afternoon to lay the traps. Then with lanterns for light, they'd return well after dark to release the unfortunates, bag them up, take them home and skin them. Trapping is extremely cruel and has long been banned, but Granddad justified his approach on account of keeping the wolf of hunger from the door for his eight-person family. He transitioned to ferreting when my mother was still in single digits, but the next two generations continued to recall stories of rabbits being caught and skinned right up until Grandad died – ferreting on his very last day.

Mum's recollections are of the old rabbits being tough and undesirable, whereas the young ones were more tender. Once the rabbits were ready for cooking, Gran made up the meat and could use it as stew or, if things called for something more fancy, the mixture was used for rabbit pie.

This recipe is a little more flash than the basic rendition shared with me by my elders. It's been garnished to suit our family's higher expectations of flavour.

Mum and Gran's advice: 'Tell those who don't fancy rabbit that it's chicken. They won't know the difference!'

Serves 4–6

2 prepared rabbits (a good rule of thumb is 1 rabbit will be enough for 2–3 people)
plain (all-purpose) flour, for dusting
olive oil, for frying
2 bacon rashers (slices) per person
1 large onion, finely diced
2 garlic cloves, finely diced

3 fresh thyme sprigs
3 bay leaves
5 whole pitted prunes
1 carrot per person, peeled and sliced
1 large potato per person, peeled and sliced
155 g (5½ oz/1 cup) fresh shelled peas
grated zest and juice of 1 lemon
250 ml (8½ fl oz/1 cup) red wine
500 ml (17 fl oz/2 cups) chicken stock (page 273)
dash of brandy
2 tablespoons fresh flat-leaf (Italian) parsley leaves, finely chopped
salt and freshly ground black pepper, to taste
mashed potato, to serve

Preheat the oven (see Tip) to 180°C (360°F).

Cut the legs and backstrap off the rabbit. Reserve the ribs for another use (such as making stock, page 273). Roll the meat in the flour. Heat the oil in a flameproof casserole dish over a medium heat then brown the meat.

Add the bacon, onion, garlic, thyme and bay leaves and cook, stirring, for 10 minutes until well cooked. Add the prunes, carrot, potato, peas, lemon zest and juice, wine, stock and brandy. Top up with water if the meat and vegetables are not all submerged. Bake, covered, for 1 hour until the vegetables are soft and the meat is tender, adding the parsley 10 minutes before taking out of the oven.

Season with salt and pepper then serve with mashed potato.

TIP
Instead of using the oven, you can also cook this entirely on the stovetop. After topping up with water, cover and simmer over a low–medium heat for 1½ hours.

248

Whole chicken and root veg roast

BY PAUL WEST, OF RIVER COTTAGE FAME

Paul West is a talk-under-wet-cement kind of human, with extremely high levels of enthusiasm. He can tell a whip-fast yarn better than most.

Most would know him from his time on the ABC's *River Cottage Australia*, but our paths crossed because he is the face of grassroots movement Grow It Local and I chatted with him on the *Futuresteading* podcast. Also, we have both been slated to spend a week with my brother on an island filming a documentary called *Eater Versus Foodie* – Paul and I being the foodies, and my brother Beau being the eater. The premise is if we were to spend the rest of our days on an island with just three foods, what would they be?

As the filming dates keep moving, Paul is yet to reveal his but for the record – at this moment anyway – my three foods are coconut, potato and avocado.

Paul tells me that while this meal is definitely not possible with just three foods and despite it feeling quite a decadent meal, this must be one of the simplest dishes to whip up. Even midweek it's doable and it can be made larger at the last minute to feed an unexpected drop-in from friends. It's a great option for a potluck too.

Serves 4–6

1 whole chicken (or 3 chicken breasts or 6 chicken thighs, cut into bite-sized pieces)
750 g (1 lb 11 oz) root veg (such as sweet potato, pumpkin/winter squash, potato, carrot and parsnip), cut into bite-sized pieces
250 ml (8½ fl oz/1 cup) apple-cider vinegar
2 tablespoons olive oil
1 tablespoon seeded mustard
240 g (8½ oz/1 cup) ricotta
4 garlic cloves, thickly sliced
green salad and couscous or rice, to serve

Preheat the oven to 180°C (360°F).

Put the chicken and veg in a roasting tin. Combine the remaining ingredients in a bowl then pour over the chicken and veg. Roast for 40 minutes until cooked through and golden.

Serve with a green salad and couscous or rice.

FORAGING A MUSHROOM FEAST

As the days turn in and the months of hibernation are seen on the horizon, mushroom season kicks in. It lasts about four weeks and is a great time to make a point of heading often into the pine forest with your baskets and foraging knives to harvest the magnificent flowers of the mycelium network beneath your feet. The pine forests hold you in a blanket of muffled quiet. A few years ago we made the family rule that if we take visitors for the experience, we don't run or yell when collecting, as being rushed and noisy takes away the magic from the experience. Forage in silence and enjoy the beauty of just sitting on the soft needle-filled floor and looking up through the sentinels reaching for the sunlight.

Do your best to eat them fresh, and the easiest way is to simply pop them in a pan with plenty of butter and salt and serve them on toast.

250

Mushroom soup

BY BLACK BARN FARM

Serves as many as possible depending on the size of your harvest

This is an easy win post-harvest. It requires little more than finely slicing and cooking mushrooms in a frying pan with butter, salt, spring onion (scallion), bacon and freshly ground black pepper. Once cooked I add them to my soup pot on the Rayburn slow combustion wood stove along with coconut milk, stock and finely diced potato. Let it simmer for an hour before serving (either as a broth or blended) with thickly buttered sourdough.

Dehydrated mushrooms for stock, soup and stew

BY BLACK BARN FARM

If we simply can't get through all the fresh mushrooms, we slice and dehydrate them so we have plenty in the pantry for winter stew, soup and stock.

They dehydrate fast so keep an eye on them to be sure they don't turn to dust. They are exceptionally earthy-smelling during dehydration, so keep the windows open. Store in an airtight jar away from direct sunlight for up to a year.

Thyme, mushroom and onion galette

BY BLACK BARN FARM

Fruit galettes are one of our family's fave dishes during summer, but when the days are cool and the summer fruit finishes, I miss them so I created this savoury galette to keep us running the galette gauntlet.

If we've taken visitors harvesting, it's a well-worn treat to transfer the goodies straight into a quick lunchtime tart.

Serves 4

2 onions, thinly sliced
60 g (2 oz) salted butter, plus extra for frying
2 tablespoons balsamic vinegar
270 g (9½ oz/3 cups) sliced mushrooms
1 × quantity shortcrust pastry (page 222, replacing
   the sugar with 3 teaspoons finely chopped fresh
   thyme leaves)
3 tablespoons fresh thyme leaves
75 g (2¾ oz/½ cup) crumbled feta or Herby chevre
   (page 196, before or after being rolled in garlic
   and herbs)
green salad, to serve

Preheat the oven to 180°C (360°F). Line a baking tray with baking paper.

Cook the onion, butter and balsamic in a heavy-based frying pan over a medium heat until the onion is caramelised. Transfer to a bowl and wipe the pan clean.

Cook the mushroom with a little extra butter in the pan over a medium heat until soft.

Meanwhile, roll out the pastry into a rough circle about 2 mm (⅛ in) thin then transfer to the prepared tray.

Spread the caramelised onion evenly over the centre of the pastry. Sprinkle with half the thyme then top with the mushrooms. Top with the remaining thyme then the feta or chevre. Fold over the edge of the dough so the cooking juices won't escape. Bake for 25 minutes until golden.

Serve with a green salad for a perfect lunch.

252

253

Barley and roast beet salad with yoghurt dressing

BY BLACK BARN FARM

When we first began at Black Barn Farm we ran an event with a friend called 'Smokin' hot Stanley'. It was a five-course meal of locally sourced food, all cooked over open flame in various fire pits. It was a picnic on pallet tables right up the length of our packing shed. Everyone made head garlands with flowers, and we marched to the top of the hill with full bellies and mugs of warm apple cider to the grand finale: the lighting of the bonfire. This hearty dish was served that day.

It can be eaten as a side or on its own.

Serves up to 8

3 whole beetroot (beets), peeled and cut into wedges
2 red onions, cut into wedges
olive oil, for drizzling
440 g (15½ oz/2 cups) pearl barley
500 ml (17 fl oz/2 cups) chicken stock (page 273)
2 cups finely chopped fresh mixed herb leaves (such as basil, dill, fennel, flat-leaf/Italian parsley)
140 g (5 oz/1 cup) toasted mixed nuts (such as almonds, walnuts and hazelnuts)
250 g (9 oz) Herby chevre (page 196)
salt and freshly ground black pepper, to taste

YOGHURT DRESSING
250 g (9 oz/1 cup) plain Greek-style yoghurt
2 tablespoons olive oil
1–2 tablespoons fresh lemon juice, to taste
1 garlic clove, minced (optional)
1 tablespoon chopped fresh herb leaves (such as dill, flat-leaf/Italian parsley or coriander/cilantro)
salt and freshly ground black pepper, to taste

Preheat the oven to 180°C (360°F).

Put the beetroot and red onion on a baking tray. Drizzle over olive oil and massage until well coated. Season and roast for 30 minutes until soft, with a little crispiness.

Meanwhile, put the barley and stock in a saucepan and bring to a simmer over a medium heat. Cook for 30–45 minutes until tender.

To make the dressing, combine the yoghurt and olive oil in a bowl. Stir in 1 tablespoon of the lemon juice. Add more, if you prefer a tangier flavour (see Tip). Add the garlic to taste, if using. Stir in the herbs. Taste the dressing and adjust with more lemon juice, salt or pepper, if needed.

Combine the beetroot, onion, barley, herbs and nuts in a large serving bowl. Crumble most of the chevre through the salad, reserving a little to go on top. Drizzle over the dressing and toss until well combined. Crumble the last bit of chevre over the salad to serve.

TIP
The Greek-style yoghurt's thicker consistency works well for the dressing. The lemon juice adds brightness, and the herbs give a burst of freshness to complement the tanginess of the yoghurt.

254

255

C-soup (carrot, cashew, cumin, coconut and coriander)

BY BLACK BARN FARM

In autumn, when the days are warm but the nights are still chilly once the sun goes down, you want to warm your bellies and your bones. This soup has become a mainstay for us at this time of year, because we are still in the farm gate on weekends. We can make the soup while we're open and by the afternoon, we light the outside fire. Friends have learned that if they come towards the end of the day, we will stoke the coals and enjoy a mug of soup with a beer or a warm apple cider in the twilight.

Serves 6–10

2 tablespoons olive oil
1 onion, chopped
2 garlic cloves, minced
6–8 large carrots (450 g/1 lb in total), peeled
   and chopped
75 g (2¾ oz/½ cup) dry-roasted cashews,
   plus 30 g (1 oz/¼ cup) extra (optional), to serve
1 teaspoon ground coriander
½ teaspoon ground cumin
1 litre (34 fl oz/4 cups) chicken stock, plus extra
   if needed (page 273)
1 × 400 ml (13½ fl oz) tin coconut milk
salt and freshly ground black pepper, to taste
¼ cup fresh coriander (cilantro) leaves, chopped
Greek-style yoghurt or coconut cream, to serve
   (optional)

Heat the oil in a large saucepan over a medium heat. Add the onion and cook for about 5 minutes until soft.

Add the garlic and cook for 1 minute until fragrant. Stir in the carrot, cashews and spices. Cook, stirring occasionally, for 5 minutes.

Pour in the stock and coconut milk and bring to the boil. Reduce the heat to low, cover with a lid and simmer for 20–25 minutes until the carrots are tender.

Use a handheld blender to puree the mixture until smooth. Season, then adjust the consistency by adding a little extra stock, if needed.

Serve the soup garnished with fresh coriander, extra cashews and a dollop of yoghurt or a drizzle of coconut cream, if using.

257

Spiced slow-cooked quince (with extra syrup for bottling)

BY BLACK BARN FARM

This sweet, spicy, slightly tannin-rich fruit sits at the top of our favourites list in this house because we grow it ourselves and have loads of bottled quince for the winter months.

From time to time, I'll do a batch of slow-baked quinces overnight for a steaming warm breakfast treat. On one such occasion we discovered a bonus outcome of the slow poach. A quince syrup came about simply because we never throw anything out – the leftover poaching liquid was no exception. Instead, we bottled it up and gave it a quick water bath so it would be shelf stable. Now it's a pantry staple to use as sauce on ice cream, mid-winter porridge, as a cordial during high heat, on pancakes or even on roasted meats like pork.

Serves 6

10 quinces, peeled and cored
8 star anise
5 cumin seeds
8 cloves
1 vanilla bean, split lengthways
juice of 2 oranges, plus juice of 1 orange extra
1 cinnamon stick
95 g (3¼ oz/½ cup lightly packed) rapadura sugar
  (or soft brown sugar), plus extra to taste

Put all the ingredients except the extra orange juice in a slow cooker, along with 3 litres (101 fl oz/12 cups) water. Cover and cook for 8 hours until deep red.

Use tongs to transfer the quince to a bowl (see Tips).

To make the syrup, strain the mixture in the slow cooker into a measuring jug. Pour the mixture into a saucepan and add the same amount of water, the extra orange juice and some extra sugar to taste.

Bring to a simmer over a low heat until thickened into a syrup consistency. Pour the syrup into sterilised bottles (page 178) and water bath the bottles to make the syrup shelf stable for years (page 178). Once opened, store in the fridge for up to 2 weeks.

TIPS
• Serve the slow-cooked quinces with double (heavy) cream. Any leftovers will keep in the fridge for up to a week.
• The syrup has a strong flavour, so you don't need to use a lot at once, so store in smaller bottles so you don't waste any.

Apple cake

BY DANIA RICHARDSON, A FRIEND FROM
THE INSTA GRID

'A version of this recipe was passed onto me by a childhood friend who would make it while camping over an open fire and serve it with yoghurt,' said Dania Richardson. 'My desire to reduce waste and make something from nothing has led me to my own version.

'This recipe is requested at many family gatherings and there is never enough to go around as everyone wants seconds. The kids lather it with cream and delight in any pieces I can save for their lunch boxes the next day.

'I have three children, including a toddler, so I also have many half-eaten apples accumulating in my fridge. I love to use them for this recipe. Our little lemon tree hasn't fruited yet, so I collect bags of lemons from our friends. I zest then juice them – freezing the zest in a container and the lemon juice in ice cube trays in half and full cubes. This is so efficient and allows me to always have what I need for this recipe, even if our food stores are running low.'

Serves 8–10

110 g (4 oz) unsalted butter (see Tips), plus extra
  for greasing
5–6 apples, peeled, cored and diced
grated zest of 1 lemon
2 large pinches of ground cinnamon
220 g (8 oz/1 cup) white granulated sugar
150 g (5½ oz/1 cup) self-raising flour
dash of natural vanilla extract or 1 vanilla bean,
  split lengthways and seeds scraped
1 egg
cream or yoghurt, to serve

Preheat the oven to 180°C (360°F). Grease a 20 cm (8 in) cake tin with extra butter and line with baking paper (see Tips).

Melt the butter in a saucepan over a low heat then add the apple, lemon zest and cinnamon. Cook until the apple just starts to release a little juice. Remove from the heat and set aside for 10 minutes to cool.

Add the sugar, flour, vanilla and egg to the pan and mix until combined. Pour the mixture into the prepared tin. Bake for 25–35 minutes until a skewer inserted into the centre comes out clean.

Serve warm with cream or yoghurt.

TIPS
• Sub in salted butter for a delicious salted caramel twist.
• When lining the cake tin, just scrunch some baking paper and press it into the base and up the side of the tin so the cake has a rustic look when you serve it.

Clementine's currant butter cookies

BY BLACK BARN FARM

Clementine (Minnie), our youngest, often comments that she is the only one in our household who doesn't have a buddy. Her older brothers are identical twins and Charlie and I are often on a mission in the paddock with our latest project. So, she bakes and, like her mother, she doesn't like to use recipes. Over the years this has made for some very interesting results – equal parts failure and success. This is without doubt one of her successes and has become so loved that we've actually written up the recipe AND we both follow it.

As we grow currants, we have them in abundance and often dehydrate them for the pantry year-round. If we have them fresh, this is our preference. Make these cookies just with the currants or if you wish to make them a tad fancy, cocoa and chocolate can be added for a really rich treat.

These little delights are about as close to heaven as you can imagine, especially when delivered to us on a tray at the farm gate mid afternoon with a fresh pot of tea. They are simple to make and the tart currant tang balances perfectly with the buttery-ness of the cookie.

Makes 28

250 g (9 oz) unsalted butter, chopped and softened
220 g (8 oz/1 cup) white granulated sugar
230 g (8 oz/1 cup firmly packed) soft brown sugar
2 large eggs
1 teaspoon natural vanilla extract
300 g (10½ oz/2 cups) plain (all-purpose) flour
1 teaspoon bicarbonate of soda (baking soda)
½ teaspoon salt
150 g (5½ oz/1 cup) fresh or dehydrated currants

IF ADDING CHOCOLATE
265 g (9½ oz/1½ cups) milk chocolate chips, plus extra 175 g (6 oz/1 cup), melted (optional)
90 g (3 oz/½ cup) dark chocolate chunks or chunks of your favourite chocolate bar

Preheat the oven to 175°C (350°F). Line two baking trays with baking paper.

Use an electric mixer to beat the softened butter, granulated sugar and brown sugar until light and fluffy. Beat in the eggs, one at a time, beating well after each addition until combined. Mix in the vanilla.

Combine the flour, bicarb and salt then gradually add to the sugar mixture, mixing until just combined (do not overmix). Gently fold in the currants and if adding chocolate, add the chocolate chips and chunks now. Mix until evenly distributed through the dough.

Use a cookie scoop or a tablespoon to drop rounded balls of dough onto the prepared baking trays, leaving space between each one.

Bake for 10–12 minutes until the edges are set but the centres are still soft. (The cookies will continue to firm up as they cool.) Set aside on the trays to cool for a few minutes before transferring to wire racks to cool completely. Drizzle over the melted extra chocolate, if using.

262

Deep chill

The days are short and the nights are long. It's a time for deep rest, bottomless pots of tea and a hungry fire that sets the rhythm of your days. Frivolity is tucked away and replaced with quiet days of words in books, slow bubbling soup and planning for the season ahead. Activities are devoid of urgency, and the chance to go gently is here. Snuggle in with your closest huddle and make the most of this nourishing time of year. Winter root vegetable stores keep your bellies full of slow-cooked comfort food. Aside from a midwinter bonfire or salami-making get-together, you can lay low and go slow.

264

Buttermilk-braised pork shoulder with polenta

BY NAOMI INGLETON, FARMACY CO

Naomi is a dairy darling in Australia. As the founder of King Valley Dairy and subsequent behind-the-scenes knowledge holder and mentor for various other cultured butter producers, it made sense that any recipe she shared with us would include dairy of some kind.

As North-East Victorian women moving in agricultural circles, Naomi and I have been circling each other for decades, but it's her more recent infatuation and headlong commitment to herbalism and apothecary creations that has allowed us to connect.

She says this dish is a mainstay for the sheer fact that it can be a meal in its own right or it can be pulled apart and used for lunches, in salads or soups. It's a good one to cook on a slow Sunday afternoon and have in the fridge to be used throughout the week.

Serves 6–10

neutral-flavoured cooking oil, for frying
1.5–2.5 kg (3 lb 5 oz–5½ lb) pork shoulder (see Tip)
1 large or 2 small onions, finely chopped
1 medium carrot, finely chopped
3 bay leaves
3–4 fresh herb sprigs (such as thyme, rosemary, oregano or tarragon)
250 ml (8½ fl oz/1 cup) white wine
500 ml (17 fl oz/2 cups) buttermilk
750 ml (25½ fl oz/3 cups) chicken stock (page 273)
½ teaspoon freshly grated nutmeg
½ teaspoon freshly ground black pepper
2 garlic bulbs, papery outside layer removed
150 g (5½ oz/1 cup) instant polenta
30 g (1 oz/⅓ cup firmly packed) pecorino
180 g (6½ oz/⅔ cup) ricotta
1 tablespoon butter
salt and freshly ground black pepper, to taste
chopped fresh herb leaves (such as flat-leaf/Italian parsley, oregano or chives), to garnish

Preheat the oven to 150°C (300°F).

Pour a thin layer of cooking oil into a cast iron saucepan to coat the bottom and place over a high heat. Pat dry the pork with paper towel then generously season all over with salt and pepper.

Put the pork in the pan, fat-side down, and cook until well browned on all sides. Remove and set aside on a plate.

Reduce the heat to very low. Add the onion and carrot to the pan with a big pinch of salt and some more oil if the pan looks a bit too dry. Cook, stirring occasionally, until the vegetables are golden. Add the bay leaves and herb sprigs and cook for another minute until fragrant. Pour in the wine, then stir in the buttermilk, stock, nutmeg and pepper. Bring to a simmer, then turn off the heat.

Return the pork to the pan, along with any meat juices on the plate. Use a serrated knife to cut a thin piece off the top of each garlic bulb then arrange the bulbs, cut side up, around the pork. Cover with a lid or foil then roast for 3 hours.

Remove the lid, carefully flip over the pork and return to the oven, uncovered, for about another hour until the pork easily falls apart when you poke at it with a fork. Slice or shred with a fork.

Return the pan to the stove (do not turn it on), carefully transfer the pork and garlic bulbs to a plate and remove the herb sprigs (compost them). Add the polenta to the cooking liquid in the pan, stir, then cover and set aside undisturbed for 10 minutes.

Stir in the cheese and butter, then taste for seasoning. Divide the polenta among serving bowls and top with the pork and chopped herbs. Serve with the braised garlic bulbs on the side.

TIP
You can substitute a whole chicken for the pork. Reduce the braising time to 1 hour.

Spicy potato pastries

BY PIP LINCOLNE, AUTHOR OF MEET ME
AT MIKE'S

Pip is the whiz kid behind the crafting community Meet Me at Mike's. She is also a many times author. I met her when I interviewed her for the *Futuresteading* podcast about her book *Days Like These*.

As an open book on her reality of living with chronic fatigue syndrome, Pip is a blessing for so many of us who are managing an invisible illness, which is hard to explain and even harder to exist with. Finding ways to manage what you eat when your energy is up and down is HARD. This recipe came from what Pip terms 'stress baking'.

Makes 10

1 onion, diced
1 garlic clove, minced
500 g (1 lb 2 oz) potatoes, peeled and boiled
ground spices (such as coriander, cumin, paprika, turmeric), to taste
finely chopped fresh mint leaves, to taste
125 ml (4 fl oz/½ cup) passata (page 234)
salt and freshly ground black pepper, to taste
20 sheets filo pastry
2 tablespoons melted butter
1 egg, whisked
pinch each of nigella seeds and sesame seeds

Sauté the onion and garlic in a frying pan over a low heat for 5 minutes until translucent.

Transfer the mixture to a large bowl. Add the potato, ground spices, mint and passata to a bowl. Season, then mash until combined.

Preheat the oven to 200°C (390°F). Line a baking tray with baking paper.

Brush a filo sheet with some of the butter then put another sheet on top. Dollop the potato mixture along one long side of the filo stack and roll up into a long log to enclose the filling. Curl into a spiral. Repeat with the remaining filo, butter and potato mixture. Brush the filo spirals with the egg and sprinkle with the seeds. Transfer to the prepared tray and bake for 20 minutes until golden.

TIP
You can make the filling the day before and store it in the fridge. Roll and bake on the day you plan to feast.

Mexican-style beans

BY SADIE CHRESTMAN, FAT PIG FARM

I met Sadie and her husband Matthew in Tasmania at a Deep Winter Agrarian Gathering years ago. We then shared our stories during a Dan Palmer holistic decision-making day. I have long recalled her warm, straight-shooting vibrancy, so when we were deciding who to interview for our *Futuresteading* podcast, she was the first person to go to air, with great success. To this day, she sits in the top two most downloaded episodes.

When writing this book, I decided to chat with her again and it was bloomin' delightful. To wrap the chat, she shared this recipe as her bomb-proof go-to when feeding her closest huddle. She did say it doesn't photograph very well, but it's such a good one to have up your sleeve as it can be zhooshed up or served just as it is.

Serves up to 10

1 tablespoon olive oil
1 onion, finely chopped
2 garlic cloves, minced
1 jalapeño pepper, deseeded and finely chopped,
  to taste
1 teaspoon ground cumin
1 teaspoon chilli powder
½ teaspoon sweet paprika
½ teaspoon dried oregano
2 cups cooked black beans or red kidney beans
  (or 2 × 400 g/14 oz tins, drained and rinsed)
125 ml (4 fl oz/½ cup) tomato sauce (ketchup)
salt and freshly ground black pepper, to taste
¼ cup chopped fresh coriander (cilantro) leaves
lime wedges, to serve

Heat the oil in a large frying pan over a low heat. Add the onion and sauté for 5 minutes until translucent. Stir in the garlic and jalapeño to taste and cook for 1–2 minutes until fragrant.

Stir in the spices and oregano until the onion is coated and cook for another minute. Add the beans then the tomato sauce. Stir until combined. Reduce the heat to low and simmer for 10–15 minutes to allow the flavours to meld. (If the mixture becomes too dry, add a splash of water.) Season.

Just before serving, stir in the coriander. Serve with lime wedges to squeeze over for a burst of citrus flavour.

TIP
Serve the Mexican beans hot, either as a side dish or as a filling for tacos, burritos or as part of a Mexican-inspired bowl.

269

NOURISHMENT

SALAMI-MAKING WEEKEND

In the depths of winter when you can see your breath hanging in the air, this is the perfect time to gather your huddle, don the layers of wool and get your hands in the soon-to-be salami meat.

An annual two-day gathering where kids run, the barbecue is hot, wine and beer is shared. All the while pork is minced, seasoned and stuffed, before being hung to cure in someone's shed. The costs are split, the jobs are shared and everyone takes enough sausage home to get them through a year's worth of platters.

Our favourite flavourings to add to the pork mince are dried fennel, coriander and chilli, but get experimenting and see where it takes you.

Once all the salami is cured there's a bit of competition in our region to see which group has made the best tasting sausage.

At an annual Chrissy do, the sticks are sliced, blind-tasted and voted on. The stakes are high, but all in joviality.

271

Midweek local lentils

BY HANNAH MALONEY, GOOD LIFE
PERMACULTURE

When I asked Hannah if she had a go-to recipe for her most loved peeps, she didn't hesitate, not even for a second, before responding with this hyper-local and super-tasty meal. Perfect for a midweek feast, she uses lentils from her friends at The Grain Family in Tasmania, and adds as many fresh veggies as she can pick from her garden. Its flavour and nutrition ranking are guaranteed. She says she has to limit herself to making it only once a week in case she turns her daughter, Freida, off lentils.

Serves 6–10

*250 ml (8½ fl oz/1 cup) stock per ½ cup lentils
  (page 273)*
½ cup per person of your favourite dried lentils
½ cup per person of finely chopped seasonal veggies
minced garlic, to taste
salt and freshly ground black pepper, to taste
crumbled feta, to serve (optional)
green salad, to serve

Bring the stock to the boil in a saucepan over a medium heat. Add the lentils, bring back to the boil and cook until cooked through, about 20 minutes.

Meanwhile, sauté the veggies and garlic in a frying pan over a medium heat until browned. Remove from the heat.

Transfer the lentils to the frying pan and toss until well combined. Serve with feta, if using, and a big green salad.

TIP
This can be a meal on its own or served as a side.

272

Stock and bone broth

Cooking up bones is more than just a trick for the frugal household to minimise food waste. It's a nutritional masterstroke that bolsters our health with a nutrient-dense, collagen-rich liquid. It's made simply by slowly simmering marrow-filled animal bones. Any bones can be used (beef, chicken, pork or even rabbit or turkey). Accumulate your bones over time by keeping them in the freezer after each meat meal until you have enough to justify filling the pot. Cover with water and simmer for hours. A 10 litre (340 fl oz) pot of broth will be ready to strain and use after 5–6 hours of simmering. This liquid can be stored in the fridge for up to a week or frozen for up to 6 months.

If you'd like to make a broth that resembles more of a stock, simply add some vegetables, such as onion, garlic, carrot, celery and herbs – flat-leaf (Italian) parsley, thyme, rosemary and tarragon work well. You can add salt and pepper to taste when you use it as the base for soups, stews and slow-cooked meals.

Smoky blackberry barbecue sauce

BY YASMIN PATEL, OUR FARM VOLUNTEER

Sometimes things of magic are created totally by accident. It might even be that their accidental creation makes them even more endearing to those of us who know and love them.

During berry-picking season, we are open for you-pick on the weekends and in preparation for our Friday twilight picks, we spend the day making jam. On one of these days we were also making beeswax wraps and goat soap, and we burnt the bum out of the jam pan, leaving an unmistakable flavour of charcoal in the bubbling blackberries. Having spent hours picking the fruit and stirring the sugary delight, none of us could bear the idea of throwing it out. Yas, our farm volunteer, has a particular penchant for spending her time in the kitchen and said, 'Leave it with me and I'll transform this into something salvageable.'

With a deft sense of flavour combinations, she turned a disaster into a year's worth of smoky blackberry barbecue sauce. It is now a fave recipe kept up our sleeve should the inevitable occur again. If you don't burn your jam first, this won't be as smoky but it will still be delicious.

Makes 6–10 jars

1 onion, finely diced
2 kg (4 lb 6 oz) fresh blackberries
250 ml (8½ fl oz/1 cup) tomato sauce (ketchup)
  or passata (page 234)
250 ml (8½ fl oz/1 cup) apple-cider vinegar
1 fresh chilli, thinly sliced
1 teaspoon freshly ground black pepper
1 teaspoon sea salt
2 tablespoons Worcestershire sauce
1.5 kg (3 lb 5 oz) soft brown sugar

Sauté the onion in a frying pan over a low heat for 5 minutes until translucent.

Meanwhile, cook the blackberries in a large saucepan over a low heat until broken down, about 40 minutes, stirring regularly.

Add the onion to the blackberries, along with the remaining ingredients, except the sugar. Simmer for 20 minutes until soft.

Add the sugar and gently stir continuously until combined. Increase the heat slightly and stir constantly until it's at a rolling boil then cook for 5 minutes.

Pour the sauce into sterilised jars (page 178). Seal and water bath the bottles to make the sauce shelf stable for years (page 178). Once opened, store in the fridge for up to 6 weeks.

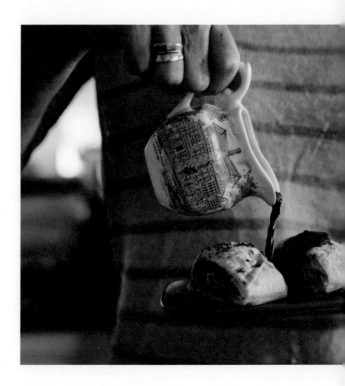

Savoury porridge

BY MARCELLA LARSON-BANKS,
PHOTOGRAPHER FROM SUNDAY MUSE STUDIO

Marcella visits our farm gate often and has taken some beautiful photos of our gardens and orchards. She quietly asked if this version of porridge might be something worthy of being in the book and with just one mouthful, I can guarantee it's definitely book worthy!

Serves 2

½ small onion, diced
100 g (3½ oz/1 cup) sliced brown or button mushrooms
3 large fresh thyme sprigs
100 g (3½ oz/1 cup) rolled oats
250 ml (8½ fl oz/1 cup) gelatinous beef bone broth (page 273)
salt and freshly ground black pepper, to taste

2 teaspoons goat's cheese
2 teaspoons dry roasted and roughly chopped hazelnuts

Sauté the onion in a frying pan over a low heat for 2 minutes until it starts to soften.

Add the mushroom and thyme and cook until the mushroom is soft and the thyme is fragrant. Transfer the mixture to a saucepan then add the oats, broth and 250 ml (8½ fl oz/1 cup) water. Season lightly. Bring to the boil over a medium heat and simmer, stirring occasionally, for about 5 minutes until soft.

Add the cheese and cook for another 1–2 minutes until the oats are cooked through. Sprinkle with the hazelnuts to serve.

276

Bunya nut and buttermilk pancakes

BY EVA ANGOPHORA AND WILL BETTISON,
WILD BEINGS

The beautiful humans from Wild Beings, Eva and Will, came into my ether when we all took a stall at the Off-Grid Living festival. With their bare feet, wild harvested and handmade deer skin clothing and deeply calm manner, they were a salve in an otherwise chaotic world. We invited them to host a Rewilding Workshop at the farm. They've now run a few of these and their knowledge of the landscape and its healing properties never ceases to make my mind tingle.

Feasting with them is always grounding as they use ingredients from the earth, free from packaging and cooked over flames, with names rarely known and herbs freshly picked. This recipe is a twist on the much-loved pancake using bunya nut flour instead.

Makes about 5 pancakes

15 bunya nuts (see Tip)
4 eggs
1 banana, mashed
125 ml (4 fl oz/½ cup) buttermilk
ground cinnamon and ground nutmeg, to taste
butter, for greasing
maple syrup, to serve

Boil the bunya nuts in a saucepan of water for 20 minutes. Drain and remove the shells.

Crush the nuts into a paste using a mortar and pestle then blend with the eggs, banana and buttermilk until smooth and lump free. Add a sprinkle each of cinnamon and nutmeg to taste.

Melt a little butter in a cast iron frying pan over a medium heat. Pour about one-fifth of the batter into the pan and cook for about 3 minutes until bubbles appear on the surface. Flip and cook for another 3 minutes until cooked through. Transfer the pancake to a plate and cover to keep warm. Repeat with the remaining batter, regreasing the pan when necessary.

Serve with maple syrup.

TIP
Bunya nuts must be foraged. Chestnut flour is a close substitute.

Other ways to feast with your huddle

Progressive feast: Nothing says huddle more than this day-long activity that can be as flash or as freewheeling as you like. It's a great activity with kids. It can happen at any time of year and with as few as two courses and as many as five, each one at a different house. Ideally, all the guests live within close proximity, and you can walk from one house to the next. You'll need to allow about 1.5 hours per location so it doesn't feel rushed.

Meal train: This is for those in need of a little help. There are plenty of online apps to help with coordinating this kind of meal support. Involve as many or as few as you like.

Double up: Make more whenever you cook and take it to a friend who needs it.

Surprise progressive bush picnic: These began because I was eager to gift an experience rather than a 'thing' when we were in the guts of wedding season during our thirties. Their success meant they've become a mainstay in our gifting regime as wedding presents, followed with anniversary hampers as annual follow-ups.

Potluck dinner: Yours, mine or somewhere neutral. Weekly, monthly or just a few times a year. You'll never eat as well as you do at a potluck meal.

Abundance swap: It can be with your neighbour, at the school gate, on the office lunch table or on a Saturday at your community garden. Big or small, formal or informal, it's the perfect place to kickstart the language of food to connect you to your people.

278

Make seed bombs with the kids:
Give purpose to making mud pies – not that one needs a reason to get grubby! It's as simple as throwing a mixture of seeds into a bucket with some freshly wet soil (not too much clay or it will set rock hard and never break down, and not too much potting mix or it will never set). Place the bombs with erratic abandon in locations that could benefit from a flurry of burgeoning seeds.

Seed swapping: Practical when done alone, this is so much fun when done together. Seeds are only viable for so long, so sharing them with others, especially those who live in similar climates, is a great way to spread food-growing capability, resilience and love to mates.

Curry night: Swap houses, swap themes, all take a pot and all help with the dishes. Simple enough to do it midweek!

House rules: Everyone eats, so everyone contributes to cooking and everyone cleans. In our house the cook never cleans, but that can be fraught!

Community cookie swap: Just as the name suggests, this is the single most fun way to put one hundred cookies of all shapes and sizes in your pantry in one joyful swoop. Gather your bakers and work out how many cookies you'd each like to end up with before sending everyone off to their kitchens for a mass cook-up. One hundred cookies is a good goal and usually means quadrupling the normal recipe. The cookie swap host invites you all to morning tea to do the swap. With a great big central table, everyone lays out their baked delicacies with a little sign naming the cookie and its ingredients. You move from batch to batch, taking your share of each of them. Not only is the range of cookies good enough to rival a swanky patisserie, but the conviviality and sense of community is heady. Pop them in the freezer and dole out into the kids' lunch boxes each day to extend the delight for weeks.

Gift a casserole in a 'keep dish':
Ever been into an op shop and seen piles of good old-fashioned casserole dishes that remind you of your childhood? Well, snaffle those little gems for the few gold coins they're asking – they make the perfect container when you drop off that pre-cooked meal to a mate in need. Let them know they can keep the dish or pass it on. Share the love!

It's a wrap

Huddlers, gather and galvanise!

You made it! Hopefully you're now razzed to the gunnels and you've got hair standing tall like a dog's bristled neck. You're alert, alive and ready to go. Go be a change maker!

As we embark on an era where division is galloping fast, embrace your role as a disruptive huddler. The time is now for gluing the change makers – of all shapes and sizes – together. It's calling all radical homemakers, system disruptors and those with an eye for the long game together in our efforts to move away from the old and towards the dawning of the new. It's where we seek agency over our lives and do so with joy – together!

This is you, so raise your hand and proudly own the title of being a huddler.

People just like you and me are finding empowerment through our united actions, so let's all stand together and play our part as we shun division. Together we are building locally-owned social enterprises; supporting local farmers; growing our own food; homeschooling; choosing creative over career; returning to our homes to raise kids; choosing voluntary simplicity over endless growth; seeking slow over fast; and rediscovering the cycles of the year through connection to the natural world.

Some of our actions are very small and simple. Some are groundbreaking and revolutionary.

I salute every single one of you for showing up to bring them to life!

Together we've got this!

X

280

Thanks

Charlie: Everyone needs a Charlie! As brilliant as you are humble and hardworking, you fill all the gaps that appear when I over-stack our plates. You are indeed the level-headed, deep-thinking, system-challenging, self-assured soulmate who needs little from others but puts everyone first. Beginning your day at 5 am with, 'Are you awake? I've got something to chat with you about,' has formed the concepts for this book. While I put the words to paper, in truth they are spurred on by your ability to think, seek, learn and share. I couldn't imagine a better huddling half than you. You hold us even when it's hard and for that my gratitude cup is always full.

Harry, Bertie and Minnie: My closest huddling crew, it's really all for you! An uncertain future drives my commitment to build a tight-knit crew who can hold us and fill our cups. You're an incredible trio of spirited and curious individuals, who teach me more than you can know. I'm proud to be walking you into adulthood through our small-town life filled with ritual, homegrown food and just a little nagging.

Mum/Cherry: Selfless, stoic and family focused to the end, Mum you're a fierce advocate for your huddle. While tough when needed, you are the soft-landing place for everything that gets hard. We all run back to you – multiple generations, in-laws and friends. Your gift to the world has been an endless capacity to be in service of others. I'm not that – not many I know truly are, but I aspire to be. We all should.

Karen Webb: A magician with a camera, creating beauty while in casual conversation. Talented beyond words and a beautiful human to boot. Book two is gorgeous thanks to you.

Catie Payne: The best first editor a girl with too many ideas and words could ever wish for. A genius with words, capable of whittling and whipping with cleverness and wit while holding a sensitive ego with kid gloves. Separated by geography, I dearly wish we could huddle in the same place with more regularity. You inspire me like few others, and watching you land this game of life, beautiful woman, has been an absolute gift.

Team Hardie Grant: Legends who leaned into the idea of huddling in an instant and backed it all the way with creativity, amplification and gentle guidance to make it sing. It's been a really beautiful process with you on my side.

Knowledge library

When in doubt, read more! The sanctity of culture and knowledge are indebted to the thinkers who've scribed their thoughts and offered them to the tumultuous scrutiny of conjecture, conversation and celebration. They've been the storytellers of their time, creating written witness to history and inspiration for imagination.

Local libraries are now our keepers of knowledge. The spines sit side-by-side on the shelf for anyone to read. Make use of this!

With the books I know we'll thumb until dog ears appear, we've slowly built our own home library. We make a point of preferencing these pages over the screen equivalent, and our visitors, friends and WWOOFers all put them to very good use.

Books to read

If you want to rewild and connect more to the natural world:
- *The Overstory* Richard Powers (W. W. Norton & Company, 2018)
- *Women Who Run with the Wolves: Contacting the Power of the Wild Woman* Clarissa Pinkola Estés (Ballantine Books, 1992)
- *Nature and the Human Soul: Cultivating Wholeness and Community in a Fragmented World* Bill Plotkin (New World Library, 2008)
- *The Web of Meaning: Integrating Science and Traditional Wisdom to Find our Place in the Universe* Jeremy Lent (Profile Books, 2021)
- *The Memory Code: The traditional Aboriginal memory technique that unlocks the secrets of Stonehenge, Easter Island and ancient monuments the world over* Lynne Kelly (Allen & Unwin, 2016)
- *Wilder: A Journey Back to Life* Meg Berryman (Regenerating Ways, 2022)
- *Rewilding the Urban Soul: Searching for the Wild in the City* Claire Dunn (Scribe Publications, 2021)

- *Earth Grief: The Journey into and Through Ecological Loss* Stephen Harrod Buhner (Raven Press, 2022)
- *The Secret Network of Nature: The Delicate Balance of All Living Things* Peter Wohlleben (Vintage, 2019)
- *Coming Back to Life: The Updated Guide to the Work That Reconnects* Joanna Macy and Molly Brown (New Society Publishers, 2014)

If you want to upskill for resilience:
- *Good Life Growing: How to Grow Fruit and Veg Anywhere in Australia* Hannah Moloney (Affirm Press, 2023)
- *RetroSuburbia: The Downshifter's Guide to a Resilient Future* David Holmgren (Melliodora Publishing, 2018)
- *A Year of Practiculture: Recipes for Living, Growing, Hunting and Cooking with the Seasons* Rohan Anderson (Hardie Grant Books, 2015)
- *The Milkwood Permaculture Living Handbook: Habits for Hope in a Changing World* Kirsten Bradley (Murdoch Books, 2023)
- *Grown & Gathered: Traditional Living Made Modern* Matt and Lentil Purbrick (Gingko Press, 2019)
- *The Village* Matt and Lentil Purbrick (Plum, 2018)
- *The Art of Fermentation: An In-depth Exploration of Essential Concepts and Processes from Around the World* Sandor Ellix Katz (Chelsea Green Publishing, 2012)
- *The Complete Book of Self-Sufficiency* John Seymour (Corgi, 1978)
- *The Art of Frugal Hedonism: A Guide to Spending Less While Enjoying Everything More* Adam Grubb and Annie Raser-Rowland (Melliodora Publishing, 2017)

If you want to build your foundational systems knowledge:
- *The Biggest Estate on Earth: How Aborigines Made Australia* Bill Gammage (Allen & Unwin, 2012)
- *Dark Emu* Bruce Pascoe (Magabala Books, 2014)

- *Permaculture: Principles & Pathways Beyond Sustainability* David Holmgren (Melliodora Publishing, 2002)
- *Surviving the Future: Culture, Carnival and Capital in the Aftermath of the Market Economy* Shaun Chamberlin and David Fleming (Chelsea Green Publishing, 2016)

- *The One-straw Revolution: An Introduction to Natural Farming* Masanobu Fukuoka (New York Review Books, 1978)
- *The More Beautiful World Our Hearts Know is Possible* Charles Eisenstein (North Atlantic Books, 2013)
- *Radical Homemakers: Reclaiming Domesticity from a Consumer Culture* Shannon Hayes (Left to Write Press, 2010)

If you are eager to know more about the power of a regenerative food system:
- *The Omnivore's Dilemma: A Natural History of Four Meals* Michael Pollan (The Penguin Press, 2006)
- *Farming Democracy: Radically Transforming the Food System from the Ground Up* Paula Fernandez Arias, Tammi Jonas and Katarina Munksgaard (Australian Food Sovereignty Alliance, 2019)
- *The Local Food Revolution: How Humanity Will Feed Itself in Uncertain Times* Michael Brownlee (North Atlantic Books, 2016)
- *The Resilient Farm and Homestead: 20 Years of Permaculture and Whole Systems Design* Ben Falk (Chelsea Green Publishing, 2013)
- *Restoration Agriculture: Real World Permaculture for Farmers* Mark Shepard (AcresUSA, 2013)
- *Call of the Reed Warbler: A New Agriculture, A New Earth* Charles Massy (University of Queensland Press, 2020)

To create more ritual in your life:
- *For Small Creatures Such as We: Rituals and Reflections for Finding Wonder* Sasha Sagan (Murdoch Books, 2019)

- *The Power of Ritual: Turning Everyday Activities into Soulful Practices* Casper ter Kuile (HarperOne, 2021)
- *The Wild Edge of Sorrow: Rituals of Renewal and the Sacred Work of Grief* Francis Weller (North Atlantic Books, 2015)

Pods to plug in
- *Futuresteading* – of course!
- *The Great Simplification with Nate Hagens*
- *Unlocking Us with Brené Brown*
- *Peak Prosperity*
- *Reskillience*
- *Emergence Magazine*
- *A New and Ancient Story*
- *The RegenNarration*
- *Accidental Gods*
- *Team Human*
- *On Being with Krista Tippett*

Mags to devour
- *Pip Magazine*
- *Breathe*
- *Resurgence & Ecologist*
- *Orion*

FUTURESTEADING PODCAST
If this book has piqued your interest and stirred some deep rumblings, plug in your earbuds and get a regular dose of thought provocation with the *Futuresteading* podcast. With more than 170 episodes, all manner of topics have been covered. From season nine the episodes are dedicated to topics of huddling.

Index

284

287

Published in 2025 by Hardie Grant Books, an imprint of Hardie Grant Publishing

Hardie Grant Books (Melbourne)
Wurundjeri Country
Level 11, 36 Wellington Street
Collingwood, Victoria 3066

Hardie Grant Books (North America)
2912 Telegraph Ave
Berkeley, California 94705

hardiegrant.com/books

Hardie Grant acknowledges the Traditional Owners of the Country on which we work, the Wurundjeri People of the Kulin Nation and the Gadigal People of the Eora Nation, and recognises their continuing connection to the land, waters and culture. We pay our respects to their Elders past and present.

Mum's Sweet and Sour Bean Soup recipe on page 236 from *Kindred: Recipes, spices and rituals to nourish your kin* by Maria and Eva Konecsny, published by Plum, copyright © 2023. Reprinted with permission of Plum.

A catalogue record for this book is available from the National Library of Australia

Huddle
ISBN 978 1 76145 058 7
ISBN 978 1 76144 176 9 (ebook)
10 9 8 7 6 5 4 3 2 1

Publisher: Simon Davis
Head of Editorial: Jasmin Chua
Project Editor: Ana Jacobsen
Editor: Alex McDivitt
Creative Director: Kristin Thomas
Designer: Claire Rochford
Head of Production: Todd Rechner
Production Controller: Jessica Harvie

Colour reproduction by Splitting Image Colour Studio
Printed in China by Leo Paper Products LTD.

The paper this book is printed on is from FSC®-certified forests and other sources. FSC® promotes environmentally responsible, socially beneficial and economically viable management of the world's forests.